BERLIN COMMAND

BRIGADIER GENERAL FRANK HOWLEY

BERLIN COMMAND

BY BRIGADIER GENERAL

FRANK HOWLEY

U. S. ARMY

G. P. PUTNAM'S SONS · NEW YORK

AN UNCOMMON VALOR REPRINT EDITION
Complete and Unabridged

Printed in the United States of America

ISBN: 9798869078049

MANUFACTURED IN THE UNITED STATES OF AMERICA
BY THE CORNWALL PRESS, INC., CORNWALL, N. Y.

FOREWORD

HERE'S to the Yanks who, working day and night with our British and French allies and with democratic Germans, made the Berlin victory possible—to men like John Digges, who purified the water; to Ben Scheinman, who brought justice to German courts; to Ray Ashworth, who created a strong, democratic police force; and, above all, to Bill Babcock who, as my deputy, carried a terrific load; to the five hundred officers and civilians, men and women, not mentioned by name, who turned Berlin into a Communist repulse; to the woefully thin line of fighting troops, under direct orders of Colonels Bob Willard and Jimmy Duke, who, threatened with annihilation, created an American Army epic with their calm, unflinching courage.

Here's to my wife, Edith, and our four small children, who took the daily insults, threats, and privations of the Communist rats who walked like bears, and to all the wives who stood by their men, as American women have always done, stanch in the conviction that where the Stars and Stripes wave, there is the indestructibility of decency and there is the inspired might of a free people.

FRANK HOWLEY

BERLIN COMMAND

CHAPTER 1

THE cold, inhuman minds in the Kremlin had reached a wicked decision, the most barbarous in history since Ghengis Khan reduced conquered cities to pyramids of skulls. In order to retain their tottering control of Berlin, undermined by the development of democratic processes, they decided to starve the Germans into revolt against the Western powers and thus drive us out. When this atrocious crime was to be committed against two and a quarter million people in the American, British, and French sectors was merely a matter of timing. The crime had not gone unrehearsed and the Russians had shown only callous disregard for the consequences.

One Saturday before they imposed the blockade, my medical officer came to me, sad faced and perplexed. "I'm sorry, Colonel," he said, "but the Russians have cut off our milk supply. Unless we get that fresh milk, six thousand German babies in our sector will be dead by Monday."

This news appalled me. I am a family man and I could share the anguish of the German mothers and fathers who were faced with this dreadful calamity. As commandant of the American sector of Berlin, I could not let this happen.

Here is the background of the situation. The Russians possessed the only milk herds in Berlin. When they captured the city, they seized seven thousand cows and drove them over into their sector. The German babies in our sector were fed with fresh milk from these cows, according to an agreement whereby we exchanged American flour for Russian milk. The Russians collected the milk from their farms, and every morning I sent trucks, loaded with flour, to the Russian border to bring back the milk.

The Russians, obviously laying the foundation for the general blockade, kicked at this agreement. They demanded that my trucks collect the milk direct from the farms, saving them labor and, what is more important, precious gasoline. I objected; they were getting our good flour and it was up to them to furnish the milk. An agreement is an agreement. The result was that our fresh-milk supply failed.

"Can't you give these children anything else?" I asked my medical officer desperately.

"We've got skimmed milk," he replied, "but that's useless for their formula."

I had to admit I was licked. There was nothing to do but eat crow and submit, for the time being, at least. The milk shortage was a lesson to me; perhaps I should be grateful to the Russians for providing it so early.

When the blockade was clamped down, I was ready for them. No longer were the German babies in my sector in danger. I had brought in 200 tons of condensed milk and 150 tons of powdered milk. When the Russians screamed to German mothers over the radio that the Americans couldn't feed their babies, I fought back over the air and in the newspapers with a special formula, using prepared milk as a substitute for fresh milk. Not one of my babies died!

I left Berlin on September 6, 1949. On the parade ground outside Truman House, stood a guard of honor. Since I was a cavalry man, a horse platoon lined up with the infantry. Many fellow American officers and representative Allied officers were there to see me off. In the reserved enclosure sat Dr. Ernst Reuter, lord mayor of Western Berlin, and members of the City Assembly. Most impressive was the German crowd of fifteen thousand, almost bursting through the MP ropes.

John J. McCloy, the new American high commissioner for Germany, acting in behalf of President Truman, pinned the Distinguished Service Medal on my blouse and spoke a few complimentary words. It was a unique ceremony, because McCloy was our first civil chief administrator for Germany.

As I stepped back with my wife, Edith, to enter the waiting car, the crowd did break through, and mobbed me. It was as much as I could do to shake a few of the many outstretched hands.

Pushing her way through the crowd came a determined, hatless woman, her hair strained back from her face, her features pinched and wan, for Berlin rations were still very low. But the sparkle in her eyes transformed that face and hid the marks of suffering and privation.

In her arms she carried a blue-eyed baby—as healthy a child as I've ever seen pictured in a baby contest. "This is my baby you saved when the Russians would not give us milk," she told me, tears filling her eyes. "We will never forget you, sir. Goodby and good luck!"

As the car drove away my wife, understandably overjoyed as she was to be returning to the United States with our children, was wiping her eyes. So was I. The German mother's tribute was as high a reward as I will ever merit. I treasure it.

During my four years in Berlin, I earned a variety of sobriquets from the Russians, mostly uncomplimentary. As first, I was an American "brute colonel," and later was promoted to "brute general." After being an "enemy of democracy," I achieved the ultimate in perverse recognition when I was dubbed the "Beast of Berlin." But when I was leaving the city, the British press softened the opprobrium by saying that "a legend leaves Berlin."

I was returning to the United States after four years' service in Germany. On July 2, 1949, McCloy, a lawyer from my home town of Philadelphia and former president of the United Nations' International Bank for Reconstruction and Development, had replaced General Lucius D. Clay, who had been United States military governor in Germany since shortly after the fall of Berlin. Military rule was out; civil rule was in.

For four years I had fought the Russians on the tensest, most delicate, and most explosive postwar frontier in the world. Yet I didn't want to fight them. I didn't go to Berlin with a chip on my shoulder. I went there with every intention in the world of trying to get along with the Russians, trying to understand them, trying to co-operate with them.

During those four years I was deputy, and later commandant,

of the American sector of Berlin and head of the Office of Military Government, Berlin Sector, abbreviated to OMGBS. In this capacity, I was the American member of the four-man Kommandatura established to administer the four areas—American, British, French, and Russian. The Russian sector was the largest, ours came next, and was followed in size by the British and the French.

The Moscow Conference of 1943, of the United States, Britain, and Russia, set up a European Advisory Commission in London to study the postwar occupation of Germany. One of its acts was the creation of an Allied Control Authority for Germany, consisting of a four-power Allied Control Council of the four military commanders, with a co-ordinating committee and a number of groups of military and civilian specialists. The Control Council originally included General Eisenhower, Field Marshal Sir Bernard L. Montgomery, Marshal Grigori K. Zhukov, and General Pierre Joseph Koenig. General Clay later replaced Eisenhower, General Sir Brian Robertson succeeded Montgomery, and Marshal Vassily D. Sokolovsky became the Russian delegate.

Joint occupation of Berlin was decided by the European Advisory Commission in September, 1944, and was confirmed in London in April, 1945, and again in Potsdam in July, 1945. The agreement provided for the creation of a special Berlin area under joint inter-Allied control, the area to form no part of Russian or any other zone of occupation but to be divided into sectors, each of which would be occupied by one of the Allied powers. To administer this area, an Allied Kommandatura, subordinate to the Control Council, was established, a small but vital cog in the Allied control machinery.

Occupation originally was to have been tripartite: the United States, Britain, and Russia only. France, our oldest ally, was out of the picture. Subsequently, the agreement was modified to permit a French zone. After all, General Le Clerc's army had fought gallantly in North Africa and spearheaded the attack on Paris. France was entitled to a place in Berlin.

Berlin, however, was a quadripartite city in theory only. In reality, the former German capital was divided into two areas

by the most significant ideological cleavage in modern times—
Russian communism versus Western democracy.

When I closed our house on Gelferstrasse and said good-by to
Berlin, I am sure the Russians were happy to see me go. Although we drank hollow toasts to each other at formal parties,
the only genuine pleasure I ever detected among them was
on the occasion of my farewell.

Despite incessant verbal blackguarding by the Russians, I
had maintained American prestige in the former German
capital. My actions may offend the naïve and outrage the ap-
peasers, but I spent four years in Berlin lying awake at night,
trying to think up ways to keep the Russians from stealing the
city from under us.

That was one aspect of the situation. On the constructive
side, I quote from my official report on the result of the impact
of Western Military Government policies on Berlin:

> We have succeeded in giving Berlin a complete school reform,
> which is the basis for the end of class distinction in the city. We
> have created a city constitution and held city-wide elections
> under four-power supervision. Nazis were removed from all
> levels of public influence.
>
> The number of agreements at the Allied Kommandatura ex-
> ceeds 1,200 and even includes agreed loans to Catholic, Protes-
> tant and Jewish churches.
>
> We have succeeded in reviving the social and political life of
> the city. We have guided Berlin Germans to a concept of de-
> mocracy similar to our own.

What we did not succeed in reaching was any agreement in
the fundamental conflicts between Russian communism and
Western democracy. Politics was always a touchy subject with
the Russians. We couldn't even agree on the control of potato
bugs, because the boys from Moscow insisted on making potato
bugs a political issue—which was the first time I ever knew
that a slug comprehended the dialectics of materialism according to Marx.

Berlin has the largest area of any city in the world. It is
half again as big as New York, with a postwar population of a

little less than Chicago. At the end of the war, the German capital was the world's biggest heap of rubble, with a starving population of 3,200,000 dazed people scrabbling among the ruins, but still a city, rising once again from the desolation.

If I were asked today what we were doing in Berlin, I might be tempted to give the question a second thought, but my overriding opinion would be: We had to be there. Berlin is the symbol of the new Germany. The Russians realized quite early that the city would be the focal point for their postwar Communist plans. If we had any hope of implanting the ideas of American democracy in the minds of a deluded and Nazified people, of re-educating them to resume their place in the family of nations, it was essential that we should be in Berlin, too. And if we lose Berlin by default, we may as well kiss Germany and Western Europe good-by.

We could have been there earlier, and with more justification. By the time the Russians had completed the conquest of the city on May 2, 1945, American troops were strung along the Elbe River west of Berlin, across the river at certain points, and were streaming deep into Czechoslavakia. Indeed, the Russians were astonished how far our drive had carried us. If it had been so decided, we and not the Russians could have captured Berlin, and we would have inflicted less physical damage in the process. There was nothing to stop the Ninth Army.

But higher up—General Eisenhower admits he was responsible—it was decided for military purposes not to take Berlin, but to allow the Russians to come across the Oder River, east of Berlin, and take the city, placing us at an enormous disadvantage we have never overcome.

On this decision was based the Russian premise, developed *ad nauseum* later, that they captured Berlin and won the war while their timid allies lagged. Every time I attempted to voice rightful claim to an American share in the common victory, I met this propagandist reply: "We won the war! We captured Berlin!" To the Germans, the Russians bellowed: "We are your saviors, not the Western imperialists!"

In refutation of these claims I always quoted the remark of

General James Gavin, who commanded the 82nd Airborne Division: "When I look over my shoulder, I see a long trail of American crosses, all the way from North Africa, through Europe, to Berlin. Don't tell me the Russians alone took Berlin!"

What did we do to get our Berlin sector? We started by losing the first round to the Russians. While they were looting and raping, stealing everything in sight—from rings and Mickey Mouse watches to the American Singer Sewing Machine plant—we had checked our advance and halted. We controlled the two prosperous states of Thuringia and Saxony, within whose boundaries lay some of the richest and most fertile land in all Germany.

We could have stayed right there and developed Western Germany, abandoning Berlin, but we traded this territory to the Russians for a small corner of the Berlin rubble heap.

This arrangement had its inception during the Russophile enthusiasm of the war, at a period when we knew very little about our Eastern Allies and were promising them everything they wanted. The European Advisory Commission, on which John G. Winant, our ambassador to London, sat as American member, agreed on postwar occupation zones in Germany, establishing the boundary of the American and British zones on an approximately north-and-south line, west of Berlin. The understanding, which Marshal Stalin confirmed with President Truman and Prime Minister Churchill, was that after the American and British forces withdrew to these zonal boundaries, access by rail, road, and air to Berlin would be assured.

If American forces advanced nearer the city (which they did, and reached the Elbe River, only one hundred miles from the German capital), the intervening territory would be evacuated and we would fall back to the agreed line. No American suspicion of Russia's subsequent "keep out" attitude over Berlin tempered those early, statesmanlike promises. Thuringia and Saxony were within this zone and therefore we surrendered the provinces. Instead of marching on Berlin, we acquiesced in placing the city entirely within the Russian zone of occupation. And then Russia broke her word.

Two months after the Russians arrived, we entered the city and established ourselves in the southwest, the British and French being our northern neighbors, the Russians occupying the eastern sector. We had made one of the war's costliest bargains to get there, but from the very beginning we found ourselves unwelcome. What's more, we were expected to pay through the nose to stay.

While we waited across the Elbe, the Russians brought in Moscow-trained stooges and formed their own puppet city government. When Berliners repudiated the Communists in the elections of October 20, 1946, showing definitely that they wanted no part of the Soviet regime, the Russians put the squeeze on the three Western powers to drive us out and tried to starve the city into submission by imposing the blockade.

What was our predicament after the blockade? There we were, in a land-locked city, trapped in the Bear's paws with no way in or out except by air. A Danzig without a corridor. There, in the three Western sectors, two and a quarter million Germans faced starvation because they refused to submit to Russian dictatorship. Militarily, we didn't stand a chance. The Russians could have moved into the areas and liquidated us before you could say, "Politburo!" We had only two battalions of troops, which would have been powerless against the Soviet panzer divisions, but our men had orders to shoot if the Russians came over. So plenty of Russians would have passed over the Golden Volga. Also, such an encounter would have meant war with the United States, an eventuality that the Communists wished to avoid. So the Kremlin took the more ruthless way—conquest by starvation.

The plan didn't work. We started the airlift—Operation Vittles. In eleven months, 277,204 flights of American and British planes brought in 2,343,315 tons of supplies. If the Russians had not lifted the blockade, we planned to step up the airlift. Berlin was saved from starvation and the Russians began to appreciate the strength of our determination.

The military lessons of the airlift cannot be overlooked. Although it was conceived primarily as a humanitarian project to defeat a political purpose, it taught us the practical importance of supplying an army by air. Amphibious operations were the key strategy of World War II. Air-phibious operations, if I may coin a term, will be the key strategy of future wars. The Army and the Air Force have stepped up training of airborne troops, now confined to the 82nd and the 11th Divisions, and are heavily committed to the movement of men, material, and supplies by air. A considerable part of the supplies flown into Berlin were for civilian needs only. In wartime, we could carry the same load of essential military supplies, omitting things that could be described as luxuries, that is, useless to an army.

During the airlift days, we knew we had the Russians licked. They didn't want war. They weren't ready for it. They feared American military, economic, and industrial might. But by the time the last C-54 sat down at Tempelhof airfield late last September, the world picture had altered dramatically. President Truman had announced the news of the atomic explosion in Russia. It was an atomic bomb. Of this I am convinced. Whether the Russians have the plane to deliver the A-bomb, I do not know, but now that they possess the ultimate means of destroying us, the balance has changed. They no longer fear war with the United States, and I consider it imperative for the American people to know the lessons we learned in Berlin. These are the same people we dealt with there, and they will not hesitate to attack us one year, two years, or five years from now, when they have accumulated a stockpile of bombs and when it suits their purpose. Beyond doubt, world domination is the Soviet aim.

We went to Berlin in 1945, thinking only of the Russians as big, jolly, balalaika-playing fellows, who drank prodigious quantities of vodka and liked to wrestle in the drawing room. We know now—or should know—that we were hopelessly naïve. You can't do business with the Russians except on their own terms, which means complete surrender of all the ideals Americans have lived by since our country was founded. They can't be trusted. They will promise anything, sign anything, provided it benefits them, and will scrap the pledge the moment it doesn't. American business life is carried on largely by checks, which imply trust. The Russians are ideologically incapable of such a system, because they would dishonor their signatures the next day—if it happened to be expedient.

Let's forget evasive parliamentary rhetoric. We must not get lost in sonorous phrases like Winston Churchill's "terminological inexactitudes." The Russians are the world's most colossal liars, swindlers, and cutthroats, and there is no reason to think they will change. They will smother you with pleasant words and steal your shoes. It is all very well poking our heads in the clouds and saying the Russians are misunderstood, or airily contending they live by another code. Such rationalizations fail to alter the fact that by our standards, or by any standards of common decency, they are liars, swindlers, and cutthroats.

Our wedding with them in Berlin never even produced a honeymoon, much less a happy life together. General Eisenhower and General Clay enjoyed fleeting moments of what appeared to be understanding with Marshal Zhukov and Marshal Sokolovsky, the top Russian commanders, and their subordinates, but after the vodka fumes were dissipated and the caviar savor vanished, our leaders discovered their pockets had been picked.

For example, at the outset Sokolovsky assured Clay that the Red Army would not be used as an instrument for promoting communism in Germany. I had a funny feeling at the time that "Wise Guy" Sokolovsky was lying and I said so.

"But I know Sokolovsky," Clay protested. "He wouldn't lie to me."

General Clay is a scrupulously honest soldier, who finds it impossible to understand an unprincipled man. Later on, of course, he discovered that Sokolovsky *had* lied. The Red Army *was* an instrument used in efforts to communize Germany.

At the Allied Kommandatura, housed in a modest administration building in the American sector, we made the most crucial effort at international co-operation on a down-to-earth level attempted since the end of World War II.

We tried every means to do business with the Russians. At first, we acquiesced in order to get a working basis. Then we accepted unfavorable terms. We tried appeasement; we tried to buy them out. But, like blackmailers, once you give them a check and think everything is settled, they always come back for more. There is only one way to deal with gangsters, Russian-uniformed or otherwise, and that is to treat them like gangsters.

The Russians are utterly ruthless in achieving their ends. Everything the decent American stands for in his home and family, his principles and his humanitarianisms, is lacking in Russian character. When starvation and probable mass murder were considered the best weapon to employ to drive out the Western powers, they didn't flinch. That a Berlin "horror story" did not take place was not due to any change in the Russian heart. It was because we anticipated some such devilish scheme and were able to circumvent it.

While they were prating about the "rights of man"—as propaganda window dressing for the Germans—the Russians were kidnaping German judges and sending them to new Siberias because they were faithful to their judicial oath and training.

The Russian interpretation of justice is as wicked as their political ideas. While we were discussing the creation of people's courts in Berlin, I asked a Russian officer if the Soviets ever tried an accused person. "No," he said in amazement. "We never do. If a man is brought before the court, he's guilty; otherwise he wouldn't be there. All the court has to do is determine the punishment."

How alien this is to our Anglo-Saxon judicial creed, holding that a man is innocent until he is found guilty by a jury of his peers.

Our high domes and hands-across-the-Iron-Curtain cranks say that we must try to understand the Russians. Understand them? That's beyond the power of any Westerner. But the Russians understand us perfectly.

Unwittingly, I once almost wrote a man's death sentence—by paying him a compliment. I am not so certain, looking back, that I didn't send him to his death or to some severe punishment. He was a man whose services I really appreciated, and I said as much to his superior. "So-and-so," I remarked sincerely, "is a real friend of America."

"He is, is he?" replied the superior, his eyes narrow with suspicion. "Then why don't you take him to America, where he can continue to work for you?"

The damage was done; I realized that too late. The man was removed and I never saw him again. I learned from that experience that you can't compliment a Russian for his co-operation, which is regarded as a sign of weakness and an offense against the Soviet state. Russians can be friends of only one country—the USSR—and keep their health.

In my efforts to understand them, I was in closer contact with the Russians than any other American in Europe. I met thousands, from Marshal Zhukov down to field privates. At Kommandatura sessions, I spent two thousand hours in discussions with them, wrangling chiefly with my Russian corresponding number, Major General A. G. Kotikov, commandant of the Russian sector.

Outside the Kommandatura, I met them on all planes and on all sorts of occasions—official, social and *en famille*. I tried every form of approach a human mind could devise to get near them, and employed every convention of civilized society to crack their shell, but without result. I have wined and dined them, wined and dined with them, swapped Bourbon for vodka and chicken à la Maryland for chicken à la Kiev, but the politeness of the gala night always disappeared in the bitterness around the Kommandatura table the next morning.

My four children used to play with the five youngsters of a high Russian officer. They romped around the house with his kids, ate Russian cakes, and amused themselves with the model electric train he had installed on the drawing-room table—an excellent example of Russo-American toy railroading. The Russian practiced his burgeoning English on me and I tried my Bourbon on him. But this interchange brought us no closer to understanding. He was still the inscrutable Russian.

My corresponding number at the Kommandatura, Kotikov, was my number-one antagonist. He was the epitome and the quintessence of the evil doctrines Moscow preaches. A big, bulky man, with flowing white hair, icy blue eyes, and a mouth like a petulant rosebud, his mind turned on and off automatically with switches operated in the Kremlin.

My four years in Berlin gave me gray hair, but I have the satisfaction that I gave him stomach ulcers. That, at least, makes us even.

CHAPTER II

MY INTRODUCTION to the Russians came on a gray April afternoon in 1945. I'd had very little contact with them previously. To me, the defenders of Stalingrad were a brave people, stanch allies who were doing a great job in the war. I was looking forward to meeting and working with the Russians, and was prepared to co-operate to the fullest extent.

At that time, I was commander of the American Military Government detachment scheduled to begin joint occupation of Berlin with the Russians. My orders were of a very sketchy nature, but I assumed that the American Ninth Army would continue its smashing advance and capture the German capital. I proposed, if humanly possible, to be with our army when it marched in.

I was on my way to Ninth Army Headquarters at Guetersloh, north of the Ruhr pocket fight, when my command car slowed down to cross a pontoon bridge spanning a small, turgid stream. The shooting was some distance away and I suppose I must have been daydreaming when I looked up to see a husky man rush toward the car. Running at full speed, he leaped onto the running board and vaulted almost into my lap. More in surprise than in anger, I swung a left hook to his jaw and knocked him back into the road. His uniform was strange and I assumed he was a German.

I couldn't have been more surprised when he jumped to his feet and shouted, "Russky! Russky!" Colonel R. N. D. Nunn, my British deputy, who was riding with me, also was speechless. Then, with an air of amused chagrin, he blurted out, "My God, Colonel, you've just bashed the first Russian we've met!"

And so I had. One of many Soviet soldiers captured by the Germans, the man apparently was escaping in the confusion of the final days of the war and was at liberty, seeking his unit somewhere in the distant east. We dusted him off, gave him the customary cigarettes, and put him back aboard. He asked our ranks and we both said, "Colonel." He was not impressed, though the Russians are tremendously rank conscious. Several kilometers later he dropped off the car and, without so much as "Thanks," disappeared into a small German town, perhaps forever.

This was my first encounter with the Russians on the road to Berlin from Paris, but I think that it would be more accurate to say the road actually started for me, not in the French capital, but way down in Georgia, in the summer of 1943, when I, a reserve, was executive officer of the Third Cavalry Mechanized. Riding down a hard dirt road in the back country, I discovered that I wasn't as good a motorcyclist as I had thought. My machine bucked and I broke my back and pelvis. For five months I lay in the hospital; it looked as though I never would get overseas. Then the choice was put to me: Go back to civil life, discharged from the Army as physically unfit for combat, or go overseas as a Military Government man. I chose the latter.

I was assigned to schools in the United States and then in England; only my insistence on taking part in the Normandy invasion prevented me from being stuck in Shrivenham, England, as director of the Military Government Officers' Division. Finally, for the invasion, I was designated commander of the Civil Affairs Detachment—an outfit with the mystifying code name of A1A1. I landed on Omaha Beach on D plus 4—June 10 —with a mixed American-British unit, with French liaison officers. On the LST, I opened my secret orders and learned that my unit was earmarked for Cherbourg. It took three weeks for the fast-fighting Ninth Division to smash its way into "the most important port in the world," as it has been called, and I went in as soon as most of the street fighting was over.

After completing the basic job at the French invasion port in six weeks, I received orders—two conflicting sets, in fact. In one, I was ordered back to England, to fly south for the second invasion of France—to head Civil Affairs at Marseilles, I imagined. Later, in a second order, I was designated to go to Paris instead. I'm very glad that I never went south; the man who took my place in the invasion was shot down and broke both legs.

Paris was a big job—far bigger than Cherbourg—and we amassed an enormous team for it. I took the first food into besieged Paris through the breaking German lines. We found the disorganized population down to nine hundred calories a day, and we helped the French to help themselves. Berlin seemed a long way off in the fall of 1944, when Brigadier General Julius Holmes, Deputy G-5 (Military Government) at Supreme Headquarters, walked into my Paris office at 7 Place Vendôme.

"Frank," he asked, "how would you like to go to Berlin?"

"Fine," I answered rather quickly. "The job is done here and I'd like to stay on the main line east. Berlin sounds good to me." I was anxious to get to our supreme goal. I was also anxious to learn what our allies from the East looked like.

"Well, get ready," Holmes ordered.

I was told that I had been selected by General Eisenhower's British Military Government chief, Lieutenant General A. E. Grasett, to lead a Military Government detachment to Berlin. In addition to the enlisted men we needed, I was asked to recommend twenty-five American officers and twenty-five British officers for the detachment. After I had done so, the British and Americans were ordered to separate training areas. On November 14, 1944, the British exchanged salutes with us at Place Vendôme and immediately took off for England to complete preliminary preparations, while we moved up the Seine to Troyes, a little town about 180 kilometers southeast of Paris. I started with only thirteen American officers and thirty enlisted men, but they were the pick of the crop in the Military Government and Civil Affairs divisions. Colonel Harry Pendleton, who had been one of my horse-cavalry instructors when I was a reserve officer, was in charge of the European Civil Affairs division for France and Germany. Although Aachen was the only German city of any importance we had yet taken, he knew

Berlin was going to be a tough job and started sending me his best men.

Of course, we knew little of Berlin. All our briefing and training had been for Cherbourg and Paris. Moreover, although feelers had been put out, the Russians expressed no interest in working with us, implying that they would worry about the end of the war when they came to it. Nor had any provision been made for the French to participate in the occupation of the city. However, I invited French officers to attend our staff studies as observers. It didn't take a genius to figure that the demand of General de Gaulle for a share of Germany would be honored. French troops, fighting valiantly, were earning that right.

Shortly before Christmas, 1944, it became imperative to find a headquarters where the British and American staffs could work out final plans together. My group subsequently marched to Barbizon, a quiet village in the Fontainebleau forest, and a spot of my own choosing. I had been in no hurry to reveal the name, because I knew that if I did, all kinds of cat-and-dog units would rush in and take up buildings and billets. Around SHAEF, Barbizon was called "Howley's mystery town."

I picked the place because it had pleasant memories for me from prewar days, and was ideal for training purposes. As a student in Paris, at the Sorbonne and Parson's School of Fine and Applied Arts in the late twenties and early thirties, I used to travel out to Barbizon and cycle through the forest. It was a serene place, off the beaten track, and as yet undiscovered by any other Army units on the prowl for comfortable headquarters. As soon as the name was published in orders, one agency, UNRRA, did race down to French military headquarters in Paris and tried to beat us to Barbizon, but UNRRA was too late.

The place was ours. I posted armed guards on all buildings, following a principle that always is good policy: If there's an argument, possession is not nine tenths of the law, in wartime it's ten tenths.

At Barbizon, we girded ourselves for virtually all eventualities, except, of course, the curious behavior of our Russian "allies." I knew that Berlin would be a tough job, because I had been following the rising cost of victory. I knew what hunger was and what thousands of orphans on your hands could mean. I was familiar with the scabby look of scabies. I knew what destruction after bombardment and attack would be and I knew pretty well that Berlin was getting the real treatment and was going to be a mess.

In addition, military government by only one nation is a difficult task. We were going to have to run Berlin on a unanimous four-power basis. Americans, British, French, and Russians would have to agree on every single point, from education to food distribution. That was really an assignment. The United States hadn't recognized the Soviet government until 1932. Even then, in 1944, the Russians wouldn't tell us their attack plans.

However, on the theory that any trouble we might have would come from the Germans, we set up a physical-training program parallel to our Military Government studies. I had three or four judo experts and every officer and enlisted man learned all the dirty tricks of close-in fighting.

The average age of my unit was forty-two, which happened to be my own age. The over-forties weren't given the rough tumbling acts, but we learned how to disarm a man and how to protect ourselves in hand-to-hand combat. Every member of the team qualified as a pistol and rifle shot. We stacked boxes of hand grenades alongside that other deadly weapon, the mimeograph machine, all because of anticipated trouble with the Germans.

We did a thorough job of study on Berlin. We sent to London for air-bomb-damage pictures, learned from maps and charts exactly how the sewers were laid out, how much coal was needed to pump them, where the water lay in the 1,300 deep wells throughout the city. From aerial pictures, we knew how many of the fourteen pumping plants were still working. We studied Berlin's schools, hospitals, language, people. We even tried to locate, also from air pictures, a building where we could set up joint headquarters with the Russians, still believing in the myth of a joint and harmonious city government, wherein serious dissension would never arise.

Military officers fresh from Aachen briefed us on the trials of German occupation. At that point American troops had not penetrated very far into Germany. Unaware that the storming of Berlin was to be a strictly Russian show, we worked out complete plans for twenty officers and twenty enlisted men either to drop into the city by parachute or land in gliders, with the First Airborne Army.

All our airborne troops were itching to get into another airborne fight, but the trouble was that General Patton's army was running so fast across Europe that, every time the air boys got plans made to jump, the place was swarming with ground troops. However, Berlin did seem to offer prospects for an air operation and so we Military Government men had a plan, too.

There were endless unknowns and variables, but we laid down a very thorough plan for the type of government we would establish. So massive and comprehensive was this plan that not a detail was lacking, not even methods of feeding starving Berliners. One of the few criticisims I ever received from SHAEF involved food. Part of our plan was a project for bringing in emergency food supplies for the civil population. SHAEF came back with a mild reprimand. "Feeding Berlin is a Russian responsibility," I was informed.

Someone in the rarified atmosphere of Supreme Headquarters had assumed, in his innocence, that all food would be brought in by the Russians from the captured provinces of Brandenburg and northeast Pomerania, the traditional suppliers of the city. The SHAEF reprimand added specifically, "Food will come into Berlin from the places it has always come in—that is, 93 percent of the basic foods, potatoes, rye flour and such, which, in modern times, always has come from Brandenburg and northeast Pomerania."

My plan for bringing in food for the civil population was based on the rather obvious assumption that the Russian Army itself would be living off these two rich provinces and would not enjoy going hungry while Berliners ate. As events proved,

I wasn't far off in my first calculations, but our food plan was thrown out.

Although I was frustrated occasionally by higher headquarters, I could find solace in the forest near Barbizon. Deer were plentiful and we had several excellent wild-pig hunts, with as many as forty hunters, until one winter afternoon a wild sow ran through the drive and we discovered that it was the season for little pigs. Someone shot the sow. Her two little ones, striped like watermelons, came tumbling through the woods after her.

Softhearted G.I.'s picked up the twins and brought them to me. I called off the hunting season and decided we would keep the two as mascots. We named them the Smith Brothers—a little prematurely in view of the fact that one turned out to be a female. They were fed with milk, from bottles with nipples, and proved a good morale factor. After all, the Air Force had gremlins: why shouldn't Military Government, AlAl detachment, have the Smith Brothers?

We carried the little pigs all the way to Berlin, where they lived for two years, assigned to quarters in a converted garage. The Sergeant who, in addition to other duties, was in charge of pigs, would open the garage door and shout, "All right, Smitties. Come along!" And they would follow him like dogs. But there was a difference between the Smiths and the average dog: you couldn't lay your hands on them. We maintained this was symbolic of France. The French can be very friendly, but they refuse to be pushed around; keep your hands to yourself is their motto.

In Berlin, we allowed the Smith Brothers to run around at our banquets, to the consternation of our guests. They finally grew three feet high, rather large for pets. One day, the Sergeant let them out and they wandered down the streeet alone, as they often had done before. But this time he heard a frightful squealing. Running toward the commotion, he jumped over a fence into a back yard, where the pigs did their rooting, and found a husky German giving the female a final blow with a club. The German muttered something about *"essen"* (eat) and the Sergeant snarled something about "murder" and let him have it, with a hard right and left. The German went to the hospital. The enlisted man recovered the pig and gave her smelling salts to no avail. The female of the Smith Brothers was buried with military honors.

After the tragedy, the other Smith Brother, a boar, became uncontrollable. Finally, my executive officer, Lieutenant Colonel Wilbur Maring, came to me and announced, "Colonel, I think we ought to butcher the pig."

I hadn't been following the boar's activities for some time, owing to other business, but, remembering the circumstances under which we had acquired him, I replied, somewhat shocked, "What? Butcher our friend? Kill our mascot? No, a thousand times no." Putting on the drama, I thundered, "The men wouldn't stand for it."

"Stand for it?" my exec repeated. "Why, there isn't a man in the outfit who will stand up for the pig. The darn animal has caused all kinds of trouble. He's a nuisance. We all hate him. He bites us. He kicks us. He knocks us down."

Assuming my best judicial attitude, I ruled, "Very well. We will put it to the vote."

At the next Saturday conference, attended by about two hundred men, I put the pig to the vote. "Colonel Maring wants to kill the pig and I'm sure you won't agree with him," I began confidently. "Let's vote on it. All those in favor of murdering the pig and eating our mascot, raise your right hands."

Every man in that room raised his right hand—except me. Of course, I could have used the Veto—anticipating another Russian weapon—but I did not consider such an action within the limits of free and unfettered democratic expression of opinion. The pig was barbecued that night. I ate two eggs for dinner.

But I'm running ahead of the story. By the time we had finished our staff work for Berlin, in the early spring of 1945, the Western armies were driving deep into Germany. We still had no contact with the Russians, but when we bade farewell to Barbizon I optimistically raised my glass and expressed complete confidence that we were going to be firm and fast friends with our allies. It never occurred to me that it could be otherwise.

As the war in Europe rushed to its climax, I began to agitate to get farther up front, closer to Berlin. Our Berlin group pulled out of Barbizon early in April and stopped briefly at Namur, Belgium, which I remember chiefly for its church bells and trains in the streets.

From Namur, I took a small detachment and worked my way over the Rhine to Lieutenant General William H. Simpson's Ninth Army Headquarters at Guetersloh. There I was greeted cordially by Colonel Craigy, the G-5, who exclaimed, "Thank God, you're here. I've been trying for weeks to get SHAEF to release you and your unit to me. We've had three bridgeheads across the Elbe. One was knocked out yesterday, but we've got two other good ones. There's nothing between us and Berlin but an SS regiment at Potsdam."

He spoke with emphasis and assurance on the American capture of Berlin. That was on Tuesday. "If we get our orders tomorrow, we can be in Berlin before Saturday. Can you join us?" he asked.

"We can join you and we will," I promised. That night I shared a bathroom with two captured German generals. The next day I left two of my officers and a couple of motorcyclists with Craigy, so that if communications with Namur failed and the Ninth Army did move on, I still would get word by the cyclists.

My precautions weren't necessary. American troops did not advance and capture Berlin. Neither did the British, although one of Prime Minister Churchill's fondest hopes was to see Montgomery beat the Russians into the city. General Eisenhower, as Supreme Allied Commander in the field, decided against capturing Berlin from the west. He preferred to join forces with the Russians in a final effort to divide and destroy the remnants of the German Army in a series of thrusts that would prevent them from acting as a unit, and allow the Russians to enter Berlin first.

The German capital, he said, was no longer a particularly important objective. Its usefulness to the Germans had been largely destroyed. More important was to gather together Allied forces for a single drive to bring about the fall of Berlin, the relief of Norway, and the liberation of two million tons of Norwegian and Swedish shipping. His decision was made on a purely military, not a political, basis. Eisenhower's plan was also approved by the United States Chiefs of Staff. It probably was the last great decision in history to be made on such a limited basis, ignoring political consequences, for the Russians moved into the German capital and stayed. Meanwhile, the German Army surrendered and American forces halted their advance at the line of the River Elbe, one hundred miles from the city.

For our entry into Berlin, tremendous organizational changes were started and I obtained permission to move my Military Government unit forward. Hanover was suggested to me officially as a temporary base, but I found the city unsuitable, although it was supposed to have been reconnoitered by an American colonel. I sent out my own reconnaissance detachments and they came back with the report that Bielefeld was the spot for us. There we moved, waiting for a chance to get to the German capital.

By this time, the unit I commanded consisted of 150 American officers and 200 enlisted men, all of them hand picked, well educated, and well trained. It was a wonderful team. We had men like Ben Scheinman, of the California Supreme Court, as head of the Legal Section. John Digges, head of Public Sanitation and Water, was an engineering graduate of Purdue University and had been a water-sanitation engineer in Indiana for twenty-two years. Most of them were reserve officers, drawn from civil life. I had engineers, professional policemen, municipal experts, public accountants—terrific men and good soldiers. They were the type needed to revive a city, not by cracking the whip and shouting, but by a few quiet, firm words of expert advice. This probably was the greatest Military Government unit that ever existed. This type of unit, unfortunately, never lasts long.

After the capture, General Eisenhower and members of his staff flew into Berlin to discuss with Marshal Zhukov, the Russian commander, the future of beaten Germany. They were among the first Americans to enter the city, but as yet no one had driven across the Russian zone. The Iron Curtain already had been lowered.

Eisenhower was still supreme Allied commander when he met the Russians in Berlin but later, when SHAEF was dissolved, he became American military governor of Germany. His deputy was General Clay, who succeeded Eisenhower as military governor when he returned to the United States to become Chief of Staff.

Field Marshal Montgomery and General Koenig also flew into the capital, and the first formal meeting of the Allied commanders was held on June 5, 1945. At that meeting the formation of the Allied Control Council, which assumed joint responsibility for the administration of Germany, was announced. But many questions remained unsettled.

Major General Floyd Parks, commander of the First Airborne Army, was designated the first American commandant of Berlin, under General Clay, and my Military Government unit was attached to his headquarters.

From Berlin, where Parks had flown, he sent a message to Bielefeld to inform me that I would lead the preliminary reconnaissance into Berlin. We were to move up to Halle and be ready to leave for the capital in twenty-four hours. It was generally understood, I was informed, that the Russians would occupy the eastern, the British the northwestern, and the Americans the southwestern sectors of Berlin.

My unit was all keyed up and ready to go. We had requisitioned a fleet of German cars, which we had repainted and housed in special garages. Captain Bob Foley, my aide, who was a former bond salesman, made two attractive discoveries. One, near Madgeburg, was a whole village of two thousand college-educated German girls, who could take dictation and type in both English and German. They had fled from the Russians in Berlin and could have made up our secretarial staff. It was a temptation to load up the best qualified of these girls and take them along—but I resisted.

Foley's second discovery was a car, which was destined not only to serve my subsequent transport needs, but to be my passport and safe conduct during the dangerous Berlin days. It was a Horsch roadster, the biggest and best car in Germany. Foley found it hidden under a haystack on a burning farm. He hitched his jeep to the bumper and brought the roadster back to me. The car had belonged to a Nazi leader and the odd thing was that the chauffeur, who lived nearby, appeared and cheerfully offered us all his tools and spares as long as we were going to keep the car. He pointed out that he doubted if the Nazi owner would ever come back.

This car led the first American road convoy into Berlin. We moved up to Halle, near the bridge over the Elbe at Dessau, and occupied some old Wehrmacht barracks while waiting for word to start for Berlin.

The preliminary party was not Military Government; it was purely reconnaissance, of about five hundred officers and men, comprising elements of staff, intelligence, logistics, and headquarters command, supported by half tracks and machine-gun teams. I was picked, not because I was Military Government, but because I knew from my cavalry training how to get a motorized outfit from one place to another. The job, as I understood it, was to make a reconnaissance of our sector, hire workmen to repair buildings, and make ready for the arrival of the First Airborne headquarters and the main body of the Second Armored Division troops several weeks later.

At daybreak on June 17, we started for the German capital. I lead the column in my Horsch, which was the only piece of non-American equipment. The Stars and Stripes flapped from the right fender of my car, as from the other command cars, and every windshield bore identifying American stickers. In the column were perhaps 500 officers and men and 120 vehicles. It was quite a parade, with a company of the Second ("Hell on Wheels") Armored Division bringing up the rear, formal-looking machine guns bristling from the half tracks. This security company was to protect us against the Germans. We had nothing but good wishes for our friends, the Russians, whom we would meet at the Elbe River.

Months before, my Military Government unit had established a certain weird contact with the Russians at Dessau bridge, over which we planned to cross the Elbe. Moving thousands of captured Russian soldiers and displaced civilians across the river had been quite a problem at that time and I had sent one of my units, under the command of Captain Joe Walsh, another Philadelphian, to help out on our side of the river.

Joe was able to move as many as twenty-two thousand soldiers and civilians in a single day. He reported that the Russians at the bridge appeared friendly enough but, without warning, they would throw a monkey wrench into the repatriation machinery and refuse to handle any more people. This meant that trains dumped DP's on our side of the river and we had to feed and house them until the Russians changed their minds again. Eventually, again without warning, they would decide to take another ten thousand, and traffic would start to move. The unpredictable Muscovites certainly had got on Joe's nerves, and he wasn't a jittery man.

Our column reached Dessau and crossed the small pontoon bridge, built by American engineers. Above the bridge rose a great arch, erected by the Russians, with huge pictures of Lenin and Stalin gazing down upon us, and a banner with the curious inscription, "Welcome to the Fatherland," as though this were no longer Germany but already had been annexed by the USSR. The Commies' advance propaganda worked; it inspired the returning Russian soldiers to form singing columns as they marched across the bridge into the "Fatherland."

We dipped under the great welcoming arch, crossed the river, down which had floated uncounted bodies of German soldiers, women, and children, and made our Russian contact on the far side of the pontoon bridge, where a Russian WAC directed traffic. She carried two small flags, red and yellow. As we crossed the bridge, she pointed the red flag at us, whipped it past her body, and then stuck out the yellow flag, whipped them both under her left arm, and came to a snappy salute. I never knew what her flag-waving formula signified. It must have meant something, but not to me. There was absolutely no traffic except ours.

A waiting Russian officer, in a battered German car, took over the column and guided us forward. We moved for perhaps a mile toward the main span of the Elbe bridge, then suddenly

we were confronted by a road block, a red and white pole leaning across the road. a pole whose significance we appreciated
much later. We could have pushed beyond it, but we didn't
want to break the pole or force the guard.

Our Russian escort jumped from his old rattletrap, hurried
back to me, and announced brusquely, "You must stop here.
You are expected at headquarters." That suited me; I wanted
to pay my respects.

My G.I. driver, not the man to get jumpy normally, promptly
backed our car into the one behind us in his excitement. During the war he got blown into the air by a shell, while carrying
a box of ammunition, and came down on the box with nothing
more serious the matter with him than a back injury. But he
did get the jitters on the road to Berlin.

We finally halted and parked on the right side of the road.
Units closed in, so that my car stood at the head of the column
at the bridge and at the tail were the half tracks and other
vehicles of the Armored Division company.

With Brigadier General Stewart Cutler, who had come along,
and an interpreter, I went back to a rickety German house,
which served as Russian headquarters. Although the place had
been occupied for weeks, it hadn't been fixed up at all. Climbing the creaky stairs, we met the Russian commander of the
bridge, Colonel Gorelik. and shook hands with him.

The Colonel was a typical Slav, heavy set, round faced, and—
reserved. He didn't say much, as though he wasn't too sure of
himself. His interpreter was a lieutenant or captain, who spoke
fairly good English, with a sprinkling of slightly obsolete slang.

"Won't you sit down and have a drink with us?" the Colonel
invited. We were pressed for time, with one hundred miles
more to go before reaching Berlin, but we said we would be
pleased to join him. German champagne was served and toasts
drunk. We thanked our host and prepared to depart.

"Ah, you cannot go just yet," the Russian demurred. "There
is a formality."

He didn't elaborate. While we sat there wondering what on
earth the formality was, a Russian sergeant came in, walked
over to the piano in the corner of the room and, without any

preamble, began banging away. In the States, he would have been at home in a dime-a-dance hall, with a limp cigarette hanging out of the side of his mouth. The Sergeant tore through all the tunes he knew, repeating some of them, while the Colonel paced nervously up and down, pausing frequently to stare out of the window. After forty-five minutes of this formality agony, with the music growing progressively more horrible and the champagne gone, we still didn't have permission to proceed to Berlin.

I was starting to clear my throat politely to inquire when we could move on, when the Colonel sidled over to the window again, took another look, and asked, "How many vehicles, officers, and men do you have?"

"Roughly, 500 officers and men and 120 vehicles," I replied promptly.

"The agreement," he said coldly, "says 37 officers, 50 vehicles, and 175 men."

"What agreement?" I asked blankly.

"The Berlin agreement," he told me.

I thought that one over for a while. I hadn't heard of any such agreement. "Perhaps you are confusing some offhand estimate made by one of our officers as to what we would need with an actual agreement," I suggested.

"There is actual agreement," he said flatly.

At that, I felt the hairs rising on the back of my neck. I also began to suspect that someone at the top had casually mentioned to the Russians that my spearhead *probably* would consist of about 37 officers, 50 vehicles, and 175 men.

"Well," I told him, "I haven't heard of any agreement. We have our orders, and they are in proper shape. All I know is that I have to go to Berlin to make a reconnaissance. Besides, within a couple of days, there will be hundreds of Americans coming in, according to plan."

"Oh?" he replied doubtfully. "Then I must check headquarters."

That seemed reasonable. But we didn't know that Russian communications were so bad that the Colonel had to send a car to a village, twenty miles away, where the Berlin telephone lines ended, every time he wanted to ask his superiors a question. Consequently, we waited two hours longer, while he checked headquarters. Fortunately, the piano-playing sergeant had worn out his arm. Unfortunately, we were down to warm beer and white wine.

More Russians drifted in and out of the room. Some took only one look at us and went away again. Others stayed to talk. One young officer demanded, "Why are you Americans going to fight us? You know it's German propaganda that causes this trouble."

His question came as a surprise to me. I never had heard anyone even suggest that we were going to fight the Russians. Consequently, I laughed and pooh-poohed the remark. But the Russians kept coming back with the same accusation. General Cutler fidgeted as the hours wore on. Finally, I got mad.

"Look," I said to the Colonel, "we have orders to go to Berlin. These orders cover every unit and they don't say, 'If the Russians are willing.' Let's be frank. You are keeping us from going to Berlin and I want to know who is responsible."

The Russian glared at me. "My superior ordered this."

"Then let us speak to your superior," I demanded.

In something like forty-five minutes his superior, a one-star general, arrived. We went through the same dreary routine and he said firmly, "The agreement is for 37 officers, 50 vehicles, and 175 men. We must make sure that you don't take in more than General Parks wants you to take in."

The one-star general was not friendly; he was firm and he was not scared, though General Cutler had begun to test him with, "This incident could have serious repercussions. Our entry into Berlin is based upon high-level international agreements." We both tried to bluff the one-star general; we tried to scare him; we tried to kid him; we even tried to reason with him. But we might just as well have saved our breath.

Defeated, we asked for his superior and a two-star general joined the one-star general and the Colonel. The two-star Russian was definite and abrupt. "My orders are that you stay," he said.

More delay. More telephoning. Finally, a three-star colonel

general, a corps commander, joined the other two. He differed only in rank and in the fact that his right eye kept twitching. He went straight to the point.

"My colleagues have explained to you that you are to take into Berlin only 37 officers, 50 vehicles, and 175 men," he said. "You have more than that. What is your decision? You can do one of two things. You can wait here and conform to the agreement, or you can go back to Halle."

General Cutler and I looked at each other. We said that, under the circumstances, we would have to wait for further orders. There was nothing else we could do. We were trapped. Six hours later, orders came from Parks in Berlin, through the Russians. Cutler was to take the excess men and vehicles back to Halle and I was to shift the baggage and come on to Berlin with—37 officers, 50 vehicles, and 175 men.

At long last, we were ready. We had changed our baggage and moved things around. The Russians refused to permit us to bring in any half tracks and machine guns. These went back to Halle. So we had only the jeeps and command cars I had thought necessary for the mission. The Russian colonel came out and saluted.

"I won't count," he promised, dead pan.

"I can assure you," I replied coldly, "that we have exactly 37 officers, 50 vehicles, and 175 men."

The Russian in the ramshackle car resumed his place at the head of our column and we moved off down the road to Berlin. As I had expected, the Russian colonel was there counting, not too obviously.

The original orders said we would follow the four-lane *Autobahn,* but instead we were guided down a parallel secondary road, cobblestoned. From the Elbe to Berlin was a bizarre trip for me. Eerie silence drenched the countryside. The land was empty and desolate, the crops unattended. Stark sentinels in the fields, Russian soldiers stood guard over the cattle.

Where are the Germans? we asked ourselves. We saw only a few in the villages, where white flags fluttered in token of surrender, and women scurried through the streets or peeked furtively from behind curtained windows. Strangely enough, some raised their fingers in the Allied V-sign for Victory!

Along the road, at what first seemed strategic spots, stood tall Cossack soldiers, with big, blond, handlebar mustaches. Apparently they all grew these imposing mustaches and it soon appeared that they had been stationed there solely for effect; some stood at points where there were no crossroads. They waved at us the same combination of red and yellow flags as the Russian WAC on the bridge, with the same quick duck under the arm and the same smart salute as we passed.

Nearer Berlin, we encountered masses of troops, thousands of horses and horse-drawn convoys of Asiatic wagons looking like boats on wheels, holding a ton or more. They were the poorest troops I have ever seen. The men wore shabby cotton, a strong contrast to the smart uniforms of my convoy. And were they dirty! A third had distinctly Mongolian features. Unlike the Cossack show troops, they didn't salute, they didn't answer our salutes, and they didn't respond to our questions. They just plodded along the road. I began to realize the power of Communist propaganda: these men had been briefed that we were their enemies, merely enjoying an armistice, and they regarded us as such.

On the road to Berlin, I became curious as to the fate of the DP's we had shunted across Dessau bridge by the thousand daily—provided, of course, that the Russians were in a co-operative mood. Nothing of the elaborate organization that the Ninth Army had established on our side of the bridge for handling them was visible in the Russian zone. Except for a few DP's who were lucky enough to get rides in thirteen Studebaker shuttle trucks, they simply took off down the road. Under Lend-Lease, we had supplied Studebaker trucks to Russia and the Russians consequently called all cars Studebakers. Except for the top officers, our Muscovite allies thought that they were Soviet cars, manufactured in Soviet plants.

The DP's grubbed in the fields for potatoes, or whatever food they could salvage, and slept on the bare ground under sheets of corrugated iron or made shelters of wood, mud, and leaves. The Russians provided no conveniently spaced rest centers and food stops, as we did west of the Elbe. The DP's were reduced to conditions of the simplest denomination. Most of them had been told, "Thatta way is Russia. Get going." And they kept going.

Everything was primitive—as it was with the entire Russian Commissary. For example, there was no refrigeration, which the American troops took for granted. The Russians solved the problem of fresh meat by driving up some cows to a regiment and saying, "Boys, here's your meat for the week." The regiment then slaughtered the animals, which had to be eaten immediately, before the meat spoiled.

As for the DP's, I learned later that no effective telephone communications existed at the Berlin railhead. When a train arrived to transport the unhappy people eastward, the Soviet train commanders fired military rockets into the air and thousands of DP's rushed to the depot from all over the countryside. Those who could climbed aboard, the others crawled back into their holes to wait for the next flight of rockets.

But to get back to my convoy; it was after dark, and we should have been approaching Berlin, when we learned that we weren't going there. The Russian lead car turned off the road and guided us into a town we later learned was Babelsburg, a suburb of Potsdam, about ten miles from Berlin. To my surprise, we were taken directly to a compound of better-than-average houses that used to be a movie center—a sort of Berlin Hollywood—before the war. The idea, I discovered subsequently, was that we were supposed to refurbish this compound and provide quarters for the American, British, and Russian delegations to the forthcoming conference of President Truman, Prime Minister Attlee, and Marshal Stalin to be held at the nearby Cecilienhof Palace in Potsdam. A number of American officers, who had been flown into Berlin, were already in the compound, and we all found ourselves virtual prisoners.

Scores of German women were working under Russian guards in the courtyard, cleaning it up, throwing things out of windows, hauling rubbish away. I could find no place to sleep; it was worse than a May housecleaning at home.

In every street leading out of the compound rose the familiar red and white barricade, manned by Russian soldiers, beyond which we could not pass. Scarcely believing that the Russians actually were treating us as enemies, I walked to one of the barricades with my interpreter, Pat Artzeruni, an Armenian-born engineer, who spoke perfect English, French, and Russian.

"Is this the boundary of the American section?" I asked the guard.

"I don't know," he said.

"Is this the limit of the compound, which is being set up for the conference?"

"I don't know."

"Can we get past?"

"*Nyet!*"

The guard didn't know a great deal, but he did know that none of us was to get past him. This also was true of all the guards at the other barricades I tried. And no amount of attempted fraternizing could induce them, or any other Russians, to loosen up about themselves, their names, their homes, their families. No babies' pictures! They would answer no questions, except strict line-of-duty queries, even off duty.

The next morning, I began agitating to get out of the compound and go to Berlin, but I couldn't seem to get in touch with the senior Russian officer. The Russians were like mercury: I would think I had one trapped, but when I looked around, he would be gone. General Malinin, the local Soviet NKVD general, could never be reached. And when we did contact a fairly senior Russian officer, we never could obtain a clearance from the compound because Malinin alone possessed the authority to issue it.

Occasionally, we did sneak into Berlin on the pretext that we had to meet a plane bringing in important American officers. These were the only circumstances under which any of us ever were given permission to visit the city.

I made my first visit to Tempelhof airfield in this way. Off to "meet a plane," I took a car driven by an American chauffeur, who had a Russian guard sitting beside him so that the Americans wouldn't go where they were not supposed to go. Accompanying me on this jaunt was Colonel John Maginnis, one of my aides.

Very soon, I discovered that the guard didn't know much about the city. Mac, unfortunately, turned up for the trip with an armful of maps. Now, to a Russian a map is like a camera: it scares him out of his wits. I finally allayed the guard's suspicions by explaining that Maginnis was a connoisseur of maps and carried them around just for the fun of it.

While this explanation didn't exactly convince the Russian, it confused him sufficiently to let us get into the city with the maps. In view of the fact that the Russian didn't know the city as well as we did, we were able to get a glimpse of what was to be the American sector. We guided the command car through the district, both going and coming, and returned by way of devastated Unter den Linden. Also, the guard proved a trifle more communicative than the others, and threw out the titbit that the Russians were feeding the German population from captured *Wehrmacht* stocks, which were running low. This, I learned later, was true. At the first conference we had with Zhukov, the first demand he made was for American food.

We were still "prisoners" in the compound, however, and finally there was nothing to do but send most of our officers and men back to Halle, on the understanding that we could replace them with more useful personnel. If we were to clean up that compound, working with the British and Russians, and prepare it for the forthcoming conference, it was perfectly stupid to have reconnaissance personnel for a housekeeping job. What we needed was not jeeps and observers, but housekeeping troops, to work and organize the compound. Since we were not allowed to contact Germans in Babelsburg, the Russians had promised to supply the labor, which they did in such an unsatisfactory manner that they created a frightful mess. Therefore, there was no alternative but to go back across the Elbe and get our own men and equipment.

Subsequently, permission was obtained from the Russians to return, and it was understood that we could make any exchanges we desired, provided we never had more than the magic number: 37 officers, 50 vehicles, 175 men.

In my Horsch car, I took off early in the morning for Dessau, followed by jeeps and trucks. At the bridge, I paid another visit to Colonel Gorelik, and explained to him carefully what I was doing, reinforcing my remarks with a social gesture—a bottle of schnapps.

"My orders are to let you fellows out who come in," he said.

"How about coming back?" I asked warily.

The Colonel shrugged his shoulders.

"That isn't the agreement at all," I said. "This is the way I understand it and this is the way it's going to be." I knew that it would mean another long delay getting to that telephone twenty miles away, and I knew how cumbersome Soviet staff work could be, if I argued. To make things clearer, I drew a chart for him, with columns representing the interchange of vehicles and men from one side to the other.

"This is the column that shows you how many go out," I explained, "and this is the column that shows you how many we bring back in. Each day my liaison officer, Lieutenant Bacon, will come down here, just the same way I have. He will step out of his car and come to your office and check with you that we never exceed 37–50–175."

After two hours, aided by the schnapps and, perhaps, my charts, the Colonel understood and I sent the convoy back to Halle. On our side of the river, we established a rendezvous and exchange point, where the Babelsburg convoy could be checked, and I cautioned the officers in charge never to send in more than came out, although they could send in fewer.

Grabbing some food from the nearby Military Government office, I led my new convoy back across the Elbe. In place of the jeeps, which were too small for our purposes, I brought ten-ton trucks to carry the heavy equipment and supplies we needed for the compound job.

Back at the bridge, the Russian colonel looked out of his window again. His eyes stuck to those trucks.

"No," he said loudly, "you cannot do that. You took out little trucks (meaning jeeps) and now you bring back big trucks. That's not in the agreement. Why do you bring back big trucks?"

"Because that's what we need to carry food, tentage, and supplies," I explained patiently.

The Colonel thought a minute. "You do not have to bring the same trucks back, but if you take a small truck out you must bring a small truck back."

That's where I blew my top. "To hell with that idea," I yelled at him. "It won't go with me. It isn't the agreement, and it isn't going to be that way. It can't work and it won't work. It's a truck for a truck, whether it's a big truck or a little truck!"

The Colonel quieted down immediately. He asked, quite meekly, to have a look inside to see if we carried any guns or ammunition—which we didn't—and forty-five minutes later I was off through the twilight to Babelsburg and Berlin.

CHAPTER III

THE journey back to Babelsburg with my new 37–50–175 convoy, as twilight deepened into black night, was one of my wildest rides in Germany. Having successfully unsnarled Soviet red tape at the Elbe bridge, I ran smack into a Russia flushed with victory and stripped of inhibitions.

All along the crowded road reeled Russian soldiers, who had been swilling anything they could lay their mouths on. They were noisily demanding and taking rides—but not from us. One of the first things I observed about a Russian soldier is that he never asks for anything. He demands. Even if it's only a ride in a car, he demands with the attitude of a conqueror.

The American G.I. gives you the old moving thumb; a good-looking girl ostentatiously puts her best foot forward; but the Russian simply steps out in front of your car and demands a ride. When he gets it, he doesn't bother to thank you at the end of the trip. Getting that convoy to Babelsburg taught me a lot about Russian character. Russians frequently pointed tommy guns at me, but I replied by blowing my horn to give them fair warning that I wasn't having any, and then moved right down on them. They stepped aside and they never fired.

That's one difference between a Russian and an American. He will pull a gun on you and threaten you, but he doesn't necessarily mean to fire. Russians have pulled guns on me many times and threatened to shoot, but I can't recall a single case where they fired first. From our Wild West days, we have a tradition that when you pull a gun you fire: the man who fires first lives. That is not true of the Russians. Perhaps it is integrated with higher policy. The Kremlin uses the threat of war just as the lower-level soldier uses the threat of a gun, without intending to employ it.

Babelsburg was a weird place when my convoy arrived. It was indeed well named. At first, the suburb had been occupied by Mongolian soldiers; then the ugly, ragged undisciplined men from the Tartar steppes and the Mongolian wastes disappeared and smart young Russian NKVD troops replaced them. The new arrivals marched and drilled like parade-ground troops. At dawn and dusk, they burst into moving Russian songs, terrific masculine airs, tuneful and vigorous. Even my interpreters of Russian ancestry began to be proud of their musical heritage. The Soviets obviously were rehearsing for a big show. The NKVD troops actually sang at all the Big Three conferences, very effectively.

However, they were still Russians with Russian minds. A dump near Babelsburg contained some old, burned-out German Tiger tanks. Several American officers obtained permission to examine them, accompanied by the usual Russian guide. When the Americans arrived at the dump, they were astonished to see the Russian officer change the guard at the entrance. When they left, he restored the original guard.

"Why did you bother to change the guard just to let us go in and out?" an American visitor asked.

"The first guard had orders to let no one through," the Russian explained. "Therefore, I put on another guard, who had orders to let just you through."

That was simple and logical, from a Russian point of view. It is easier, and better policy, to change the guard than to change the orders. Soviet officers are allowed neither freedom nor discretion. They simply obey the order and change the circumstances if necessary.

I spent the next three days commuting between Babelsburg and the Elbe, switching men and vehicles for the conference compound job. The brief glimpse of Berlin I got on the sneak trip to Templehof, giving me some conception of the utter destruction of the capital; the "liberation" propaganda of the Russians, aimed at turning the Germans against us; and finally the Russian treatment of the Americans as enemies created in my mind a serious doubt regarding the future.

Since the housekeeping was organized at Babelsburg, I finally asked and was given permission to rejoin my unit at Halle. Once again, I crossed the Elbe bridge at Dessau.

Back in Halle, I assembled my officers and told them with absolute confidence, "Gentlemen, we are never going to Berlin. The Russians are hostile, and they've merely granted us an armistice. They are impossible to deal with, and I think it's deliberate. Berlin is a shambles. It's not worth an acre of good land with cattle on it. I think the smart thing is to keep what we've got and let the Russians keep what they've got.

"I can't imagine a nation of good businessmen like us turning over to the Russians the fertile land of Saxony and Thuringia, with thousands of cattle in the fields, crops standing waist high and houses undestroyed, in exchange for our share of the rubble pile in Berlin. The diplomats will start talking soon, and if they know anything at all, they will start changing that original agreement with the Russians."

I was so convinced that we would never get to Berlin that I added, "Let's look around the country and find ourselves a place to sit down and relax. It's been a tough war and we can get into a little hill town somewhere and wait. We've got just the right-size detachment to take over Military Government in Saxony and Thuringia, and my guess is that's what we will do."

We found the right spot, a little hill village in Thuringia, twenty miles from Halle, with a lake and sailboats. Overlooking the village rose a huge *schloss,* a castle atop a wooded hill, large enough to accommodate all my officers, and also the enlisted men when we had fixed up places for them.

Thuringia wasn't like my native Pennsylvania, with its undulating country and rambling white farmhouses, but it had fresh verdure and repose. At the *schloss,* my bathroom had marble steps leading down to the water. Looking out of my window, I could see, through a Versailles-like clearing in the woods, a pond with wild ducks. The woods were full of deer and in the barn were 136 milk cows.

Life was going to be beautiful for a couple of weeks, or perhaps a couple of months, until the situation clarified. I got clearance to move out to my *schloss*, although I didn't tell my superiors what I thought was going to happen. I simply told them that I was getting out of Halle because it was so crowded —which it was.

I issued orders to move to our hilltop paradise by July 1, and arrangements were made for the transfer. Then came a most surprising development. As one who already had learned not to trust the Russians any farther than he could throw them, I assumed that they would try to cross us up at the last moment by suddenly refusing to let us occupy our sector in Berlin. As a matter of fact, all indications pointed to the soundness of my opinion. We were being barred from Berlin and it appeared that the Russians were doing everything within their power to keep us out indefinitely. I must admit, however, that I underestimated Russian acquisitiveness.

On June 30, I was ordered to abandon all my plans and move to Berlin. Instead of keeping us out, the Russians suddenly reversed their field and delivered an ultimatum demanding that we go to Berlin. We were given three days to clear out of the area we occupied. The Russians were taking over our territory of Saxony and Thuringia, crops, cattle, castle, marble bath, wild ducks, and all.

There was nothing subtle about the three days' grace in the ultimatum. Russian haste was understandable. They had a covetous eye on those two rich provinces, which we had captured and then docilely agreed to turn over in return for an interest in the battered German capital. The Russians had been looting Berlin for two months, while we held back at the Elbe, and they obviously assumed that we would follow their established procedure of conquest. It was plain that the ultimatum was designed to get us out of the two provinces before we had time to strip them clean.

To beat the ultimatum, we acted at once. Instead of taking time for an orderly move, we grabbed our hats and went piling down the road as though the Cossacks were after us.

On July 1, 1945, the road to Berlin was the highroad to Bedlam. It was jam packed with tanks, trucks, and other vehicles, Military Government people and troops, all hurrying toward the previously forbidden city. Russian officers, in captured ramshackle cars and trucks, raced up and down our columns to see that we weren't escaping with plunder from the territory we had surrendered. They couldn't get it through their thick heads that anyone would evacuate provinces as rich as Saxony and Thuringia without looting them first.

Other Russians attempted to control the movement of our columns for the simple pleasure of indulging themselves. The road to Berlin was paved with Russian drunks. Some wanted only to exchange toasts in vodka; others behaved like little commissars. One unit was stopped by a welcoming committee, including colonels, who had been there all day and got thoroughly drunk waiting for us. When our convoy did arrive at this point along the road, the committee stopped us and would not let us through until everybody had drunk bottoms up in vodka. After this ritual, the committee was so petrified and had developed such alcoholic stubbornness that the American unit had to force its way through the group.

When one particularly obstreperous Red Army officer tried, for no apparent reason, to halt a column at a bridge, an American general, whose name I have forgotten but whose deed I will cherish always, jumped from his car and personally deposited the struggling Russian in the ditch to allow our column to pass.

A disagreeable summer rain was pelting down when we finally straggled into Berlin late in the afternoon. The Russians had not allowed us to look over our sector before coming in, although that had been the agreement, and none of us knew exactly where to go once we arrived. Had we been able to follow our original plan, my preliminary reconnaissance party would have been there, followed by the housekeepers, and our army—as always—would have moved in quietly on an organized basis. As it was, hundreds of officers and men milled around, looking for places to stay in the ruins, and most of them, in Class A uniforms, wound up sleeping on the muddy ground in the rain.

My Military Government detachment, always realistic and ready for emergencies, entered Berlin better prepared than the others. We came in with field equipment—steel helmets and packs on our backs, as we had done through France—because that's your bed and that's your tent, and moved into Grünewald, a forestlike park. Under the dripping trees, I pulled up my vehicles in a protective circle, as in the old covered-wagon days on the prairie, and posted guards. Not a Russian, not a German could have interfered with us. By ten o'clock, we had eaten a hot meal and were set for the night.

I conferred with General Parks at Babelsburg until midnight, discussing the murky future. What we wanted to discover was how quickly the Russians would evacuate the sector assigned to us, and how soon we could move in. No answers to these questions were available immediately, but we did not mind spending a few days in Grünewald, where we were comfortably set up.

Word spread around that we were not permitted to leave our quarters. But this was one occasion when the Russians were too late with their restrictions, or too cocksure of their power. We had been ordered around quite enough and weren't having any more. During the next few days, my detachment commanders took off blithely all over town, looking around and reporting conditions. Sometimes they got in dutch with the Russians. Sometimes they were turned back. On the whole, they managed to pick up an amazing amount of information.

For example, take looting, or what the Russians euphemistically called "reparations," on the grounds that they were doing to the German capital only what the Nazis had done to their cities. My commanders discovered that the Russians were winding up two months' looting of the Western area, including the American sector. They had picked it pretty clean. All the horses they could find and 7,000 cows had been driven away. They had dismantled the refrigeration plant at the abattoir, torn stoves and pipes out of restaurant kitchens, stripped machinery from mills and factories, and were completing the theft of the American Singer Sewing Machine plant when we arrived.

Over in the British sector, they had taken out generator equipment from the only modern power plant in the city. Much of the looted equipment either was of dubious use or had been wrecked through ignorance. Since Russian unskilled combat troops, instead of trained engineers, were employed, crowbars were often used to tear out machinery, which could have been removed simply by unbolting it. Valuable lathes and precision tools were stacked in open railroad cars to rust in the rain. If the Russian intention was to expand home and satellite country industry with confiscated German machinery, even this cursory survey showed that they must have failed.

The morning after our arrival, bursting with high resolve, I accompanied General Parks to see Colonel General Gorbatov, the local Russian commander, to discuss our sector. Parks was there as commander of American troops and I as his G-5, commanding the Military Government detachment. Later, I was his deputy.

Gorbatov was a beefy, red-faced combat general with three stars, who had filled his new job only a few weeks. The former Russian commander of Berlin, whom Gorbatov succeeded, was the general whose troops actually captured the city, but he liquidated himself one night by riding his motorcycle into the rear end of a Russian truck.

For the first time, we learned from Gorbatov the extent of the American sector. I had understood that we were getting only five boroughs, out of Berlin's twenty. Gorbatov produced a map that showed the United States got six boroughs, not five, the British six, and the Russians eight. Since Parks and I were not disposed to argue, we took six. We thought at the time we were profiting by a Russian mistake, but we were laboring under a delusion. We didn't get away with anything at all; the agreement had been for six boroughs all along, only higher headquarters had not bothered to tell us. The boundary question settled, Gorbatov asked when we would be ready to take over our sector.

Parks turned to me and asked, "What do you think, Frank?"

"Right now," I said.

Parks thought a little and said, "Well, the Fourth of July would be a good time, and we ought to have a little ceremony." Our national holiday was two days away.

Gorbatov nodded. "Agreed," he said simply. British officers

were present at the conference, but could set no date for occupying their sector. They said they were not even there yet, and did not expect to enter until July 6. The Americans had more trucks and material and always moved faster than the British. That is why we were ready to take over our sector sooner.

The next two days were spent recruiting German labor to fix up billets. By the second day, we had a gang of twelve hundred working for us. Other than that, we scattered all over the city, sometimes getting pushed out, but having a good look at our future home. All the Russians we encountered were not hostile. Some were unusually convivial. Perhaps the most unusual episode involved Major Kasparazycki, an American combat engineer, who, on the eve of Independence Day, accepted the invitation of one of the local Russian commanders to supper in the restaurant that was later to be my mess. The Major took two fellow officers along with him.

Rudolph, the German who ran the place and still does, said that all afternoon, in preparation for the party, the Russians were busy boiling some noxious liquid, which smelled like gasoline. He had to open all the doors and windows to get rid of the stench. When the Americans arrived, they sat down with their hosts and ate the cold cuts on the table and drank this liquor, which was diluted with fruit juice—probably Lend-Lease.

As the night grew wilder, one of the Russians asked through an interpreter, "Where are all the other Americans?"

Kasparazycki looked around the room, counted the three Americans and turned to the dozen Russian officers. "Oh, we didn't all bother coming over," he said. "Anyhow, three Americans are equal to twelve Russians."

"That remains to be seen," observed the senior Russian colonel. "Come forward," he said, beckoning to one of his officers.

The Russian stepped forward confidently. The American exchanged lefts and rights with him and floored him. The Colonel then produced another officer and Kasparazycki disposed of him, too. According to the Major's story, he knocked out six of them, proving the soundness of his claim. That was the kind of boisterous, rough-and-tumble party the Russians loved in the early days. They acquired considerable respect for American stamina.

During this period, parties came so thick and fast that it seemed likely Berlin would be pickled in vodka. There was a difference, however, in the parties. Ours were just parties. Russian parties were sounding boards.

For all the ostensible gaiety of the Russian affairs, it was obvious they were using their vodka as a truth serum to extract information from us. Marshal Zhukov himself apparently fancied this method of spying on his allies. On one occasion my interpreter was standing directly behind the Russian when he turned away from a woozy French diplomat and said, disgustedly, "Come on. We've got everything from this fellow we're going to get."

Undoubtedly, the Russians did loosen some tongues enough to get some information, but it is questionable whether they got very much or very useful information. On the other hand, they assumed rather ingenuously that we had no idea what they were trying to do when they fed us their vodka.

At one party in Berlin, I recall the reaction of a Russian political adviser who had just proposed a bottoms-up toast. We raised our glasses and touched them. Both of us put the glasses to our lips. After a sip, I stopped abruptly. The Russian noticed and also stopped short. Peering at me over the rim of his glass, he grinned broadly.

"Oh," he said, "a diplomat, eh?"

On July 4, we got down to serious business. Outside onetime Adolf Hitler SS barracks, now called McNair Barracks, the Russians lined up two companies of troops. Facing them, we lined up two companies, with a number of Sherman tanks. General Omar Bradley had flown into Berlin especially to represent the United States on what we considered a rather historic occasion.

Gorbatov, however, did not deign to appear at the handing-over ceremony. Instead, he sent Baranov, his deputy, a one-star general, to represent him. General Bradley gave no hint that he had been snubbed. In a nicely phrased speech, he warmly complimented the Red Army's performance during the war and expressed the hope for lasting peace and friendship.

Baranov thanked Bradley and replied by practically claiming for Russia credit for winning the war singlehanded. The Russians broke the back of the German Army at Stalingrad, he said, and implied that they would have gone on to victory, with or without American aid. His speech gave only slight credit to us for supplying equipment. Having delivered this speech, he sat down, leaving us all with our mouths open, wondering if we had heard his incredible insults correctly. However, there were no overt acts of resentment; we were all so polite in those days.

Russian artillery fired salutes; our artillery replied; the troops passed in review. For the first time, we saw the peculiar, stiff-legged rolling gait the Russians affect for parades, and the mass formation they have developed to excess in Red Square parades in Moscow, which is part of their theme song, "Mass of Infantry." The men march with the rifle at the carry and the bayonet thrust under the arm of the man ahead.

Flags were exchanged and I received orders to occupy the American sector, with its boroughs and city halls, by midnight. I returned to Grünewald, and had issued the necessary orders to my Military Government detachment, when I received an urgent message from General Parks telling me to come to his headquarters at Babelsburg immediately.

When I walked into the room, he silently handed me a note signed by Marshal Zhukov, the Russian supreme commander in Germany, which said, "In view of the fact that Berlin is to be ruled by an Allied Kommandatura and that Kommandatura is not yet set up, your sector will not be turned over to you until the Kommandatura is set up."

"What do you think of that?" Parks asked.

"I think it's a lot of nonsense," I said, boiling. "I think they're throwing sand in our eyes again. It's just another excuse for the Russians to gain time to finish looting our sector before we move in. Unless you change your orders, I'll carry them out and occupy our sector according to the agreement."

We both thought a minute. Then Parks said, "Yes, I think

you're right. That was the agreement, so go ahead as planned, but don't get into too much trouble. After all, the occupation is just beginning."

Back at Grünewald, I called together the officers earmarked to take over the six boroughs. They were the toughest and most competent of my detachment commanders.

"We move in at daybreak and set up Military Government. The Russians don't get up until noon," I told them. "Don't get into a fight, but protect yourselves if you have to. Don't back out and don't make any concessions. If the Russians challenge you, tell them you are just obeying orders."

At daybreak, my men moved in, while the Russians were still slumbering. Each detachment contacted the local mayor, took over his house as headquarters, hung out the American flag, and posted SHAEF ordinances numbers 1 and 2. The first announced the formation of a Military Government and the second established courts, with the penalties for crimes committed against us.

The Russians awakened around eleven o'clock and found the awful fact accomplished. They reacted swiftly, however, and each of my commanders was visited by a Russian officer, who strode into the Military Government Headquarters, saluted stiffly, and told my fellows to get out, saying that Zhukov had ordered that we could not take over. None of these borough headquarters had any American combat troops. Each had three or four Military Government officers and half a dozen enlisted men.

In each instance, my commander was equally formal. "Your General Gorbatov gave a clearance to our general," was the explanation. "Our general ordered us to come here, and here we shall remain. We are soldiers, as you are. Therefore, we obey our orders." Another stiff exchange of salutes, and the Russians backed off, temporarily balked.

By the next day, more friction had developed. It was nip and tuck between us. American soldiers were beginning to look Russian soldiers right in the eye. Then came the explosion. Shortly before noon, I got a telephone call from an American major at Tempelhof, saying the local Russians were swarming over his headquarters and had announced they were going to tear down our posters and put him out of the building.

"Don't budge an inch," I ordered him, "but don't shoot. If they want to rip down the posters, all right. I'll try to handle this another way."

A second call, from another detachment commander in another borough, said the Russians already had started to tear down our posters. The officer told me he had refused to obey the Russian order, and a colonel was doing the ripping job— somewhat reluctantly, he thought.

I jumped into my car and raced across to General Baranov's headquarters. It was Sunday morning and I went through the guard without any difficulty, although normally you would need a Charge of the Light Brigade to get through. The secret was my Horsch car. Everybody recognized it on sight and knew I represented a commanding officer. So they never bothered me.

Baranov was sitting at his desk, working alone, when I walked into his office.

"Your men are tearing down American posters," I announced, not wasting time on pleasantries. "We are not going to shoot. We are not going to have a street fight over it. But it's bad business. You are letting the Germans see we are having differences right at the start. They must be getting a big laugh over the way the victorious allies are behaving."

"You shouldn't have moved in and put the posters up in the first place," Baranov said.

"Maybe we shouldn't, but whether we should have or not, they're up now," I answered. "In a few days the whole thing will be settled, so why fight about it now?"

Baranov grumbled a bit, muttering again that we were wrong and shouldn't have put them up, but it was obvious his heart wasn't in it. He was faced with a *fait accompli*, the favorite Russian technique, and there was nothing he could do but acquiesce. Picking up the telephone, he called the Soviet colonel at Tempelhof, who had been tearing down the posters. There was rapid-fire conversation in Russian, during which Baranov did considerable shouting before he dropped the phone back into its cradle.

"All right," he said. "You can leave your posters up. I hope the matter will be settled in the near future."

On the way out, my interpreter turned to me wonderingly. "When that Baranov talks to you he is real polite, and looks like a gentleman, but when he talks to a soldier—Wow! Isn't he tough!"

"What was he saying?" I asked curiously.

"I would be embarrassed to tell you," my interpreter replied.

Although the ceremony was held on July 4, we didn't take over our sector officially until July 12, when the Russians finally moved out, in some cases under compulsion. In the interim, there were two Military Governments in the sector—American and Russian. The local mayors were in the middle and perplexedly tried to obey both governments. We had little to do in the way of Military Government, and simply stuck it out while the Russians hung on.

During that cooling-off period, I think the Russians developed a lot of respect for us, at the comprehensible level that we would stand up for our rights. There were plenty of hot brushes, and in one case I had to be unusually firm. Hearing that they were going to be moved out, a Russian colonel went down and tried to empty the bank at Steglitz. All German banks had been closed for some time, but in some way he got a key and tried to force his way into the building. An American MP stopped him.

"I'm coming back at two o'clock," the furious Russian warned the MP, "and I will shoot my way in if necessary!"

I notified the Second Armored Division and at two o'clock, when the angry Russian was due, we had two tanks and an American general from the Second Armored there to meet him. The would-be bank robber didn't show up on time. Nor did the company of troops he might well have brought with him. Much later, he rather sheepishly contacted the local Military Government commander and explained, "All I want is to get some stuff from my safe-deposit box."

German bank officials confirmed that the Russian did have some property in one of the bank's lockers and he was allowed to take it out—with the guns of those two tanks bearing down on him in case he had more ambitious ideas than to empty the deposit box. His property consisted of watches, rings, and jewelry, obviously stolen, but stored in the bank. Legally, he was entitled to take his possessions out, but the truth of the matter was that he showed plain relief that we did not seize them. That would have been the appropriate Russian action in such a case.

The poster incident and these cases of Russian acquisitiveness occasioned excitement but quickly paled into insignificance. The next few days in Berlin completely overshadowed previous events.

It was still the first week in July when General Clay, deputizing for General Eisenhower, Robert Murphy, Eisenhower's political adviser, and others flew into Berlin for a high-level conference with the Russians, the first real business meeting of Allied military governors who composed the Allied Control Council. By this time, the French had obtained a sector. They were awarded the boroughs of Reinickendorff and Wedding, sliced out of the British sector, as their share of the city, but were excluded from the conference for fear of offending the Russians, who had neglected to invite them to attend.

If the fate of Berlin was in doubt, it was sealed at that meeting on July 7. General Parks had me prepare a general plan for the basis of an Allied Kommandatura, proposed by the Russians, outlining the conditions under which we felt Berlin should be governed by the four powers. It is needless to dwell upon the ill-fated plan now, except to say it anticipated correctly what finally happened to the city.

We had based our calculations on the supposition that there would be questions on which we never would be able to agree with the Russians. The plan also listed demands we would make upon the Russians. In the event of irreconcilable differences, we proposed that each individual commandant should handle the situation in his own way in his own sector. We definitely were opposed to letting the Russians hamstring us with the veto.

Our plan was a good plan, carefully worked out, anticipating all contingencies, and an amazingly accurate forecast of the future. Behind it was the accumulated knowledge of my four chief legal advisers: Colonels Wesley F. Pape, Clarence Richmond, Sigmund W. Fischer, and Benjamin J. Scheinman. Parks used to call them "Howley's Four Wise Men." This was no jocular description; they deserved the name, and I kept them standing by at the conference.

General Clay and Mr. Murphy flew into Gatow airfield, in the British sector, and went immediately to British headquarters to join the British delegation before going on to the meeting with the Russians at Karlshorst. With Clay was General Oliver P. Echols, his deputy. General Sir Ronald Weeks and Sir William Stang were the principal British representatives. No one had much to talk about, but a few questions were discussed in a general way over a snack and a drink before the main meeting with the Russians.

As a colonel, I was wandering aimlessly around headquarters, waiting for the generals to break up their meeting, when I was summoned to the conference room.

The discussion revolved around the plan I had submitted. General Clay was letting General Parks know, in fairly blunt terms, that he didn't like it and had no idea we proposed handling the city on a divided basis. Although it eventually worked out that commandants had to solve their individual problems when agreement could not be reached, Clay insisted that all questions arising in Berlin must be settled unanimously by all the powers.

Being a humble colonel among the highest brass, I timidly put in, "If I may say something, General Parks—" but nobody even heard me. I then put my head in the lion's mouth by making a strong protest.

"I know the plan very well, having worked on it in accordance with general instructions," I said, taking the initiative boldly. "General Parks has no idea of setting up a little empire in the American sector. After all, we don't know the Communists; we didn't even have diplomatic relations with them until 1932. There are going to be many questions that can't be solved on a unanimous basis. They might be questions of religion, or education. The British, French, and Americans may agree on a million things: there will be many on which the Russians won't agree."

Clay glared at me. I felt like a brash, uninformed junior in that Olympian company of omniscient generals.

"You are entirely wrong," he said coldly. "I have just come from Washington, and it certainly is the intention of our government to administer Berlin on a unanimous basis."

He said much more, but I suddenly realized I had become his whipping boy. Had I not also realized that Clay, a great soldier, was obeying orders from Washington and describing our policies to me for the benefit of the others, I would have been angry. So I shut up. As the meeting wore on, the sinking feeling in my stomach got worse and worse after it dawned on me that, while Clay and the others opposed Parks's and my plan, they had no alternate plan of their own. They were bound for the most momentous conference yet held regarding Berlin and they thought it was to meet the Russians socially.

So much time was consumed by this preliminary meeting that we had to tear like mad across the city to get to Russian headquarters. When we arrived, a few minutes late, Zhukov, Sokolovsky, and the others were waiting. Zhukov at the head of the table and "Wise Guy" Sokolovsky on his left. Behind them stood a group of experts on everything from coal to food and transportation.

The atmosphere was social. Sure enough, the Russian version of tea had been set out, but there was too much shuffling of papers by the experts in the background to make it a real tea. Glancing absently about the room, I noticed that the SHAEF flag, on the wall behind Zhukov, with the SHAEF symbol and the letters SHAEF, was so far to one side that it hung practically upside down—symbolic, perhaps, if I had realized it at the time.

The Americans sat on the right side of the table and the British on the left. Neither of the two delegations had brought along any experts.

Zhukov called the meeting to order immediately. "Well, gentlemen," he said, "shall we start business?"

The two delegations seemed a little stunned. If they thought it was going to be a social call, that fantasy went out of the window immediately. It was obvious both were unprepared. We had no plan. Neither had the British, who had taken over their sector much later than we had. And the first business of the day was the creation of a Kommandatura.

The British and American representatives were even more stunned when Zhukov, cynically enjoying the silence around the table, whipped out a one-page statement describing how the Kommandatura would be set up, naturally providing for the veto: "The resolutions . . . are to be passed unanimously."

One or two generalizations were put forth hopefully, in a vain effort to cover the fact that we had no concrete proposals to offer, and finally Clay, who had received the single-page statement, turned to Parks and asked, "Do these translations check?"

Parks turned to me. "Frank," he said, "take the interpreters and check this, will you?"

With the interpreters, I started out to an anteroom, when the Russians suddenly noticed I was a full colonel. Their officer was also a colonel, but rank consciousness took charge. The colonel was pulled back and replaced by a one-star general. It was a typical Russian move: they refused to be outranked. In almost any negotiations, they prefer to have their representative the highest ranking officer, on the theory that it gives them the upper hand. Once in Italy, soon after the fall of the country, a Russian colonel attended an international conference and found himself badly outranked. He came back a day later a major general.

In the anteroom, there was trouble at once, and I learned something about the intricacies of the Russian language, its lack of shades of meaning, and its bilateral words. The British had a couple of university professors there that were interpreter-translators. We had a good team, too, and the Russians had their men, but all three in combination could not understand some of the Russian or agree on the exact translations.

One sentence particularly baffled me. It read, "The Chief Military Commandant [by this the Russians meant chairman] will exercise the administration of all Berlin zones, utilizing for this purpose conferences of the Allied Military Commanders to solve questions of principle and problems common to all zones."

We soon discovered that in Russian there seemed to be no difference in meaning between the words "principal" and "principle." In English, of course, the difference in meaning between "principal questions" and "questions of principle" is wide. The Russians agreed it was impossible to say which meaning was intended and, when we went to a great deal of trouble to explain the difference in English, they countered, "Well, it's the same thing in Russian, anyway."

Our translators patiently pointed out that it wasn't the same thing. There is a vast difference between the Kommandatura sending a mass of all-important work to the Allied Control Council or merely sending matters involving principle. We all agreed that wasn't the way it was written and decided to accept the English phrasing, meaning "questions of principle."

Back in the conference room, I handed my copy to General Clay, who half-turned and asked, "Is it okay?"

"Well," I said, "as a legal document it stinks, but as a rough note on what you've been talking about, it's all right."

Clay took his pen out and wrote his name across the bottom of the page, thereby indicating that he had no intention of quibbling about commas, periods, or—anything else. We were going to get along with the Russians and we were quite willing to start off on their terms. I think it was a good indication of the policy we were to follow in Berlin for many months, doing almost anything to win over the Russians, allay their suspicions, and convince them we were their friends. Even Henry Wallace couldn't have asked for more appeasement.

CHAPTER IV

ONCE the Kommandatura agreement put the Russians in the saddle, our Moscow allies squared their shoulders and got down to real business. Any feeling that may have lingered among representatives of the Western powers that this was a social occasion vanished completely when Zhukov announced brusquely, "Now, gentlemen, we will discuss the question of the food and coal you will supply for the maintenance of Berlin."

An icy blast from the steppes swept the room. The American and British commanders glanced at each other in quick consternation, but retained their composure. This was the first intimation by the Russians that we were expected to feed and fuel Berlin. SHAEF had instructed us that the job of feeding Berlin was solely a Russian responsibility, since the Russians controlled the traditional food sources of the German capital, Brandenburg and Pomerania. In addition, we had contributed Thuringia and Saxony, two equally rich agricultural provinces, which should help fill the Berlin larder.

General Clay, backed into a corner by the Russian bear, was the first to speak.

"It is not our plan to bring food into Berlin," he said. "For one thing, we don't have food to bring in. Everything Berlin needs should come either from the territory we've just turned over to you, or from the surrounding areas of Brandenburg and northeast Pomerania, where it always has come from."

Zhukov brushed aside the American expostulation, and put the issue point-blank to the meeting. "Let's be realistic, gentlemen," he said. "What have you come for, anyway? Let me tell you frankly, we are not going to supply food to Berlin. Our warehouses are almost exhausted. We must have food, and we must have it quickly."

I could see that the peremptory tone of Zhukov's remarks was getting under Clay's skin. General Weeks, the British commander, was also setting his chin.

"There are difficulties of transportation and organization," Clay was compelled to say defensively against this outrageous Russian demand. "Even if we were willing to bring in food and coal, it would be difficult, because there is no big bridge across the Elbe."

"Wise Guy" Sokolovsky, who sat on the right of Zhukov, was not impressed. Smiling cynically, he asked from the side of his mouth: "What have you been doing since the Yalta Conference? Why don't you clean up the bridges and use them? That's what we do."

"We didn't realize the situation until a few days ago," Clay replied helplessly.

"It is unfortunate that these matters were not decided previously," Sokolovsky observed icily, with obvious relish.

I was very annoyed at the general treatment we were getting from the Russians and the "Wise Guy's" attitude infuriated me. We were being pushed around again, but Sokolovsky's remarks were taken in good part by our commanders.

Clay, who was supported by Weeks, said that the question of food and coal would have to be referred to Washington and London. He added that he assumed Zhukov meant supplies coming into Berlin from the zones in Germany that the United States and Great Britain occupied.

"As you know, neither the American nor the British zone has a surplus of food," he told the Russians, and added facetiously, in an effort to relieve the tension, "I can give you mountains, but no coal. That's General Weeks's problem."

Zhukov smiled, but promptly ended the persiflage. "What I want to know, gentlemen, is when you will start bringing in supplies. I think there should be no ambiguity about this arrangement."

Eventually, the food question was referred to Washington, and we agreed to provide our share of food for Berlin. The

British, since they occupied the Ruhr, would bring in our share of coal, in addition to their own—approximately 6,000 tons being the daily requirement for power purposes. At the conference, the British raised transport problems and mentioned the unsettled condition of the Ruhr.

Sokolovsky was impatient. "There is a saying in Russia," he announced, "that coal which has fallen off the wagon is lost forever."

Listening to the Russian food demands and realizing the indecent haste in which we were expected to meet them, I sadly recalled the plan I had drawn up months before to supply Berlin civilians. SHAEF had reprimanded me for being presumptuous when I had questioned what Supreme Headquarters assumed were Russia's intentions. But, according to Russia's actual terms, we were to provide sufficient food to take care of the people in our sector, which was downright unreasonable in view of the territorial adjustments we had made to Russian advantage.

The American zone was Bavaria, Wurttemberg, Baden, and Hesse, provinces that never had supplied Berlin. Why should the American people ship food to the U.S. zone for further shipment to Berlin? The Soviet zone of Germany is the only zone producing a food surplus. By turning over Thuringia and Saxony, we had bought our way into Berlin, and now the Russians were asking us to buy another entrance ticket.

They had scored both a political and an economic victory. Since the British and French sectors also were dependent upon us for food, 80 per cent of the cost being on the American taxpayer, that initial transaction had cost us hundreds of millions of dollars and, conversely, had saved the Russians the same staggering amount. The economic game of Take has always been one of their favorites.

Having wrung from us everything but our gold teeth, Zhukov announced, "Well, gentlemen, the meeting is now ended." It was the general understanding that we would report back in a few days on the conditions the Russians had imposed upon us.

"Now I would like to invite you to have a tea," he said, almost graciously.

Everybody stood up, prey to mixed feelings, but faced with the obvious fact that the Russians had got the best of us on every count at our first meeting. Of course, it wasn't tea at all that Zhukov provided, just mountains of caviar and rivers of vodka, beer, and other drinks the Russians call tea because they flow around four or five o'clock.

As we were leaving, General Clay stepped up to Zhukov and presented him with a small, engraved pistol—the type general officers carry. The Russian merely glanced at the gift, produced one of his frigid smiles, passed the pistol over his shoulder to an aide, and strode into the next room.

To me at least, a friend of France, one disheartening recollection of the conference is the shabby treatment of the French. I know that President Roosevelt didn't like General de Gaulle; they never got on well together. Whether this was due to De Gaulle's policy or to F.D.R.'s underestimating the strength of our first ally, I do not know. A small party of Frenchmen, under General de Beauchesne, turned up in Berlin without any sector and stayed with me. By an arrangement with the British, they obtained two boroughs, Wedding and Rheinckendorff, and moved in without any occupying troops. The Russians raised no objections. They argued: If the British want to surrender any of their sector, that's their business, but we certainly will not.

The French were the real orphans of the storm in Berlin. We first offended them and then tried to make amends by inviting them to the conference. Three times in a single day our invitations went out and were canceled, because we didn't know whether the Russians wanted the French to come—and we couldn't offend the Russians! One of the first questions Zhukov asked at the conference was, "Where are the French?"

Then I realized we all had pulled a boner. After the session, I called in Lieutenant Helen Woods, a French girl married to a British naval officer, and one of my best translators. She sat down and typed the minutes of the conference in French. I got into a car with Parks and rushed the translation over to General

de Beauchesne in time for him to send it by courier to Paris
that night. He was depressed, but I explained what had happened, and I think I helped restore our traditional friendship
with France by this little act.

Our next meeting with the Russians was on July 11 and, although we did not realize it at the time, it was the first meeting
of the Allied Kommandatura, the four-power Council of Commandants governing the city. Two weeks later, the Kommandatura was formally established in its permanent headquarters
in the American sector.

Once again, we surrendered to the Russians. When we arrived in Berlin, control of the city was in the hands of the Soviet military administration and its appointed city government
—a puppet Communist body, headed by Moscow-trained Germans, who had been kept in cold storage like many other Red
stooges, waiting for a job. They belonged to the same tribe as
Georgi Dimitrov of Bulgaria.

The Berlin city government had been set up with certain
nonparty front men, but the real power was in the hands of
Soviet tools like Deputy Lord Mayor Maron and the almost
illiterate Mittag, a former locksmith, who headed the legal
branch of the *Magistrat,* the municipal governing body.

On July 11, we signed another document, which became the
first of nearly 1,300 quadripartite orders to the *Magistrat.* It
read:

> The Inter-Allied Kommandatura has today assumed control
> over the City of Berlin. Until specific notice, all existing regula-
> tions and ordinances issued by the Commander of the Soviet
> Army Garrison and Military Commandant of the City of Berlin,
> and by the German administration under Allied control, regu-
> lating the order and the conduct of the population of Berlin,
> and also the liability of the population for the violation of such
> regulations and ordinances, or for unlawful acts against Allied
> occupation troops, shall remain in force.

In other words, when we signed that document we acquiesced
to Russian control of Berlin. Later, every time we protested
against a Russian action, the Russians countered by saying

blandly that they were acting according to a regulation that was in effect before our arrival in Berlin. But when we asked to see that particular regulation, they refused to produce it. Even today, the Russians won't give us a copy of their Berlin telephone book, let alone a copy of the mysterious preoccupation regulations they always quoted in answer to our protests.

On July 12, when we finally took over the sector officially, the Military Government detachments were already set up, certain German clerical help hired, headquarters was a going concern, and the summary courts were in session.

The Kommandatura was established on three levels: the commandants (Major General Parks), the deputy commandants (my level, until I succeeded as commandant), and the committees. These were made up of experts in various phases of city government, and at one time numbered twenty. On the whole, however, the Kommandatura was rather like an army division with four generals, all of whom had to agree on the most insignificant move.

At first, Kommandatura meetings were strictly at the highest level. Then, of necessity, deputy meetings grew up. I often could visit General Baranov, the Russian deputy, or Brigadier W.R.N. Hinde, the British deputy, and obtain agreements at our level on behalf of our commanders. Eventually, at commanders' meetings, we began to be referred to as "deputies," a title we took from the Russians—as we did Kommandatura— and soon, from deputies expressing the views and decisions of their commanders, we started holding out-and-out deputy meetings, deciding a vast majority of questions and passing on to our commanders only questions of vital importance or those upon which we were unable to reach a decision.

One of the first decisions of the deputies was on Kommandatura headquarters in the battered city. The Russians could offer only one place, far out in a Berlin suburb. The British had only two badly damaged buildings and a hotel in their sector. I suggested a building in the American sector, on beautiful Wannsee Lake. "It's a wonderful place for a holiday," Baranov admitted, "but we never would get any work done." Perhaps he was right. Finally, when I suggested another building in our sector, in Zehlendorf, the Russians agreed on condition that we put it in shape.

Having decided where we would meet, we now had to decide when we would meet. Here the established habits of three different nations clashed violently, with no Emily Post to act as social arbiter.

We wanted to meet early in the morning, say nine o'clock. The British thought eleven would be better. The Russians favored noon. We said Americans got up early, ate lunch at noon, and avoided night work as much as possible. The Russians said they didn't get to the office much before noon and liked to work very late at night. The British said they started their day earlier than the Russians, but later than the Americans, adding they preferred one o'clock for lunch. We said we had dinner at six. The British said that was all right, but they had tea at four and waited until eight for dinner. The Russians said they ate lunch late in the afternoon and dinner about ten. And so on . . .

Finally, in desperation, we agreed to set the time for the next meeting at the end of each meeting. I was not familiar with Russian dietary habits, but I was suspicious of their aversion to having lunch at either noon or one o'clock. My suspicions were confirmed later. With a late breakfast under their belts, the Russians frequently suggested our lunch hour to start a lengthy meeting, which meant we had only our early breakfast to sustain us in our hours of trial.

The boys from Moscow didn't flinch at trying to starve Berlin, and they even stooped to trying to starve the Kommandatura. By four o'clock in the afternoon we would be so ravenous that we were inclined to agree to anything—just to get something to eat.

The first meetings of the Kommandatura were informal, and rules of procedure grew up as we went along, just as common law did. Chairmanship changed every two weeks initially, but later the switch was made monthly. General Parks suggested we flip a coin to fill the chair. The Russians won and provided the first chairman. The Americans and British followed in rotation, with the hope that after three months the French might also occupy the chair. At the first four or five meetings, they were present only as observers. They had no vote, but after the chairmanship was settled and the other three powers had completed the rotation, the French took their rightful place in the deliberations.

While the Kommandatura wrestled with the general problems of Berlin and its 3,200,000 people, we had our own problems in the American sector, establishing and retaining physical control of the six boroughs turned over to us by the Russians. The problems of Berlin ordinarily are not military; they are economic and political, but in the early stages of our occupation the military problem was important to us. If we had had no troops in Berlin, and if we had been unwilling to fight, we never could have kept the Russians out of our sector or given the German police courage to perform their normal duties in face of grave threats.

Our military setup was this. In the American sector, we had the U.S. Control Council for Germany, which also was General Clay's headquarters, and later became the Office of Military Government United States (OMGUS). When Military Government came in, we had Berlin district headquarters, which also was headquarters for the First Airborne Army.

We had a large number of service troops to take care of billets and a squadron of cavalry for patrol duty, who did an effective job. For troops, we had a complete division—the Second Armored Division—who kept their tanks lined up outside town so they would not rip up the streets.

Berlin in late July was still a shambles from the effects of Allied bombing, especially incendiary raids, and of Russian street fighting, but the Russians already had put large squads of German women to work clearing the rubble in various parts of the city. As the women wearily passed the fallen bricks from hand to hand, in a long human chain, they presumably were spurred on to heroic efforts by the great posters the Russians had erected to assure the Germans they had not been conquered but "liberated" by the Communists from their Fascist oppressors.

Emaciated German soldiers, bearing the Berlin trade-mark of a loose collar, also had been rounded up and were slowly being worked to death on a ration of less than one thousand calories a day. They were not SS men, but ordinary soldiers. The Russians had instituted an effective system of eliminating the most celebrated of Hitler's troops, who were the last to resist. When they found an SS man, they simply threw him face down on the sidewalk and described an X on his back with a tommy gun.

This was a little different from the Communist method in Paris, when I headed the Military Government there. Bodies of victims of the Reds were picked up with shots neatly drilled in a pattern around the heart.

The Russians had been all steamed up to capture the German capital. "On to Berlin!" was the magic rallying cry that carried them forward over every obstacle. A newspaperman, liberated from a prison camp in Poland, told me that he saw a Russian soldier fall off a tank and get his leg mangled under the tread. The soldier was picked up by his comrades and tossed back on top of the tank, still yelling, "On to Berlin!" The city was the war's great prize for the Russians, and they had to fight like the devil to get it. But when they did capture Berlin, they just went to hell.

Berlin became another Nanking, with Russians instead of Japanese doing the raping, murdering, and looting. There was no discipline, no control. All ranks, officers and men, took part in the barbarities. This is a grave condemnation to make of a supposedly civilized army, but the charge can be substantiated. Probably the element of vengeance was strong in this Russian savagery. A Russian general admitted to me that the rape cases did the Red Army's reputation no good. "But," he added in extenuation, "they are nothing compared to what the Germans did to us."

The Russians raped and looted at will for two months before we arrived, and made forays into the American sector long afterward, until we stopped them. A former secretary of mine, a girl of seventeen, had to be wheeled in a baby carriage several blocks down her street to a hospital, after seven Russian soldiers had taken turns raping her and her mother in their apartment in Steglitz. Passing by, the soldiers came in through the garden window and attacked the two women, returning time and again during the afternoon, on the same errand. This was only one of many cases. Two hundred and thirty German girls were treated at the same Berlin hospital in a single day—all victims of Russian lust and brutality.

Inevitably, looting and murder went hand in hand with the raping. The wife of a leading German city official was murdered by a Russian, who entered her house and demanded something in Russian, which the woman did not understand. He must have wanted the keys to the kitchen, because later he broke down the kitchen door. The woman thought he had asked to see her papers and, fumbling in her bag, produced her police identity card. Bellowing in fury, the soldier drew his pistol and shot her in the head, yelling, "Capitalist! Capitalist!"

Russian officers and men snatched everything in sight, especially money, jewelry, and silverware. By the time we arrived, looting had been developed on an organized scale. Back salaries of Red Army men were paid in German currency, which the troops couldn't send back to Russia. So they went out buying bicycles, watches, jewelry, anything they could use themselves or send home. What they didn't buy, they stole—which was a lot.

These experiences gave birth to the two most hated expressions in Berlin, even today. One is *"uhre, uhre,"* the Russian way of pronouncing the German word for "watch"; the other is the dreadful cry, "Com Frau." A Russian would catch the first girl he saw on the street, grab her by the wrist and, with the leering invitation, "Com Frau," drag her into the nearest building and rape her. If no building was convenient, he violated her in the street.

If a German father or brother objected to this treatment, he was shot in the head. To avoid attack, the women of Berlin resorted to all sorts of tricks to make themselves as unattractive as possible to the Muscovites. They smeared their faces with mud and kept their usually well-scrubbed persons as filthy as possible. But very few Russians minded the dirt.

Even after our arrival, Russian soldiers invaded the American sector almost every night, returning to haunts they had known before we came. They knew the geography of the city much better than we did and the list of Russian "incidents" was endless—until we called a halt.

During the first week of our occupation, the Germans began to feel more secure and there was a marked improvement in the personal appearance of Berliners. But this happier period was darkened by a tragedy that hurts me still when I recall it. A young German girl, Gertrude Gretz, was cycling through Zehlendorf, in our sector. Where Gertrude had managed to hide her bicycle, I don't know, but she had it. It was a beautiful summer day and she was wearing a pretty white dress. She even had on her wrist watch, since she felt perfectly safe in the American sector.

An ancient car, carrying three or four Russians wearing what appeared to be naval uniforms, drove up. One jumped out, knocked Gertrude off her bicycle, grabbed the girl's arm and tried to tear the little watch from her wrist. She fought and screamed to defend herself. Stepping back, the Russian took out his pistol and shot the girl through the heart. Then he calmly removed the watch from her wrist, climbed back into the car, and drove away.

The tragedy was witnessed by half a dozen horrified Germans, powerless to interfere.

Naturally, we didn't catch the murderer's car. The German police were useless in such an emergency; they didn't carry guns and were forbidden to touch an Allied soldier. All the former police chiefs had been Nazis, who fled, and we were in the process of reorganizing a new force. The utmost we could do was to register a protest with the Russians. We got the usual shrug of the Muscovite shoulders.

"They couldn't have been Russians," the Russian commander had the nerve to say, "because there are no Russian sailors in Berlin. They must have been bad Germans in stolen Russian uniforms."

One night during the first week of our occupation, two hundred Russian officers and men came over in a body from the Russian sector into Kreuzberg, one of our boroughs right in the center of town, near the Soviet border. They started going through a big apartment house, looting and raping. Screaming women and howling children awakened the neighbors, who appealed to the nearest Military Government post. A small jeep patrol of American soldiers rushed over to the apartment house and futilely attempted to scatter the lecherous Comrades, who finally went back across the border.

Again we protested, and again we got the same evasive treatment. But by this time the cup of international friendship was drained dry. We started shooting. The men of the Second Armored Division were fine soldiers. You couldn't expect them to stand by and watch women being raped and kids frightened out of a year's growth. When the tank boys shot, they shot to kill, especially if a Russian pulled a gun on them.

An incident at the Potsdamer *S-bahn* (subway) station brought the issue to a head. Early one evening, I received a report that five Russians, including an officer, had stopped a German refugee train in the station and at gun point were systematically stripping the passengers of their possessions. The train was coming from either Silesia or Czechoslovakia, with refugees who swarmed in the coaches like bees, packing the inside and clinging to the roofs, from which they were often swept to their death, when the train passed through a tunnel.

My Public Safety officer in that borough was Captain Charles Leonetti, a former FBI man, and one of the best pistol shots in my detachment. He and another officer from local Military Government headquarters were already on their way to the station when I received the call.

Running toward the steps leading up to the station platform, the two Americans got separated. Leonetti arrived at the steps first. On the platform he could see hundreds of refugees being frisked by the five Russians, who were piling up the loot in neat heaps for subsequent collection.

As Leonetti started up the steps, he let out a war whoop. The Russians swung around and started firing at him. My man fired one shot into the air as a warning, but when they kept right on shooting, he let them have it. Still running toward them, he fired four shots, killing two Russians and wounding another. The rest ducked along through the crowd and disappeared across the tracks, leaving most of their loot for the unfortunate refugees to recover.

In a precarious situation like this, it is difficult to recommend a man for a citation when he has shot an "ally," whatever the provocation. However, I am convinced that Leonetti deserved definite recognition for his courage. But official action had to take its usual laborious course. A report was made out for General Parks that night, giving the incident in detail. Strangely enough, two American G.I.'s were on that train—what on earth they were doing there, we never did discover—but they saw everything and verified our facts.

The next day, Parks had a conference with the Russians, British, and French. Aware of the twisted pattern of Russian facts, we were ready for any claim they might make.

Colonel General Gorbatov immediately launched into an attack against us, charging us with murdering—they love the word "murdering"—Soviet citizens and Soviet soldiers. At the Potsdamer station the night before, he said, a Soviet captain had been shot in the back. The rest of the story was just as accurate.

Parks spoke up firmly. He is a smooth, quiet man, but hard beneath his smoothness.

"Your facts are entirely wrong," he told Gorbatov and went on to cite the details of the incident outlined in our report. "You must control and discipline your troops. You can't expect us to let them run wild in our sector, looting and shooting, without doing something about it."

"Maybe they had a few drinks and the wine caused them to get out of hand," the Russian conceded reluctantly. "Besides, we don't shoot Americans when they get drunk and come into our sector."

"We don't usually shoot your men, either," Parks retorted. "In fact, I have some reports here to prove it."

From his records, he produced transcripts of 150 cases of Russian soldiers who had misconducted themselves in the American sector in two weeks and showed that, in all but the most extreme cases, we had simply arrested the Russians and turned them back to their own authorities. He also indicated that, in many cases, the Russians had pulled their guns on the M.P.'s, who let them go without shooting.

Gorbatov agreed to drop the matter. His final version of the Potsdamer incident was a masterpiece: No Soviet soldiers were there but, if they were there, they must have been deserters from the Red Army in Poland.

Helpless, in the middle of this international conflict, stood the unarmed German police. To assist them with their difficult job, we provided them with a small card, printed in both English and German, with the words "rape," "theft," and "murder," and a few simple, useful phrases, to which they could point in an emergency. When anything serious happened, the German policeman ran to the nearest American soldier, produced his card and pointed to the word describing the emergency, thus overcoming the language barrier without loss of time.

There was another cry for help some nights later. German police saw two junior Russian officers break into an apartment and start molesting a German girl. The police ran with their cards to an American jeep patrol, told the story by pointing to words on the cards, and the MP's rushed to the building and got the Russians out of the apartment, holding them in the street. After one MP had taken the jeep to find an interpreter, the Russians started swinging on the other two Americans, finally making a break for it. In the melee, shots were fired and when the jeep driver returned, he brought his machine gun into action. One bullet broke the thigh bone of an American, but the two Russians were jailed.

During the next week, the Russians complained that a dozen of their men had been shot by American patrols. One was a Russian officer, caught robbing a German home. He had pulled a gun on the American MP, who had surprised him as he started looting, and the MP promptly poured eight slugs from a tommy gun into the Russian's stomach. The officer was in the hospital a long time but, miraculously, he lived.

Gorbatov protested strongly against this shooting, and I replied by letting him have the facts.

"Your man pulled a gun on our man," I said, "so we treated him just as we treat our own soldiers who pull guns."

"But the officer has eight bullets in the stomach," Gorbatov replied. "Do you Americans call that self-defense?"

"Certainly."

"One bullet, yes," the Russian agreed. "Eight bullets, no. The extra seven were aggression."

The British had a different system of dealing with misbehaving Russians. They didn't shoot; they preferred strong-arm methods. Baranov, the Russian deputy commandant, went out of his way to congratulate the British for not shooting Russian soldiers. Someone pointed out to him that the British simply preferred beating hell out of them.

I recalled the incident in which a British sergeant caught a Russian looter. The Russian pulled a gun, but the old sergeant knocked it out of his hand with the butt of his rifle, then knocked out the looter's front teeth with the same weapon. Picking the soldier up by the seat of his pants and the scruff of his neck, the Sergeant ran him to the border and kicked him over into Soviet territory.

"Ah, yes," Baranov sighed. "That was all right. If you beat them up, they wake up wiser in the morning. But if you shoot them, these Russian heroes who fought their way to Berlin only die at the hands of our allies."

From investigations of shootings of Russians, which occurred only when they were caught ravaging the American sector, the inescapable fact emerged that not a single American soldier had been shot in return.

This was baffling until the truth dawned on us. The Russians obviously were using their guns only as "persuaders," with no intention of shooting, although they flourished their weapons recklessly, whereas the American soldier is inclined to shoot first, and ask questions later, when threatened with a gun.

The shooting finally ceased. So did the raping, looting, and murdering, when word got around among the Russians that a so-called joyride into the American sector was apt to end in an ambulance—or a hearse. But this took time.

Meanwhile, Parks patiently tried to explain to Gorbatov why

an American is inclined to shoot first. He recalled the American tradition, growing out of frontier days, that the man who shot first lived. The Russian was skeptical. Behind his quizzical expression, you could see he considered it an ingenious American tale to bolster up an argument. He was a fighting general and he looked for no explanation in tradition for shooting: Gorbatov simply killed the enemy.

I followed Parks, and went to work elaborating our theory of self-defense. Gorbatov continued to protest vehemently about the shootings but, in the end, he agreed to joint Allied patrols of Berlin's trouble spots. Eventually, these patrols became unnecessary, but we had trouble in getting the Russians to recognize this fact, because they liked to keep their units over in our sector. They always had five or ten times the number of men required, apparently observing what our troops were doing.

For my part, I issued orders to the Military Government detachments that there would be no more shooting, regardless of the provocation or circumstances, and shooting ceased. The 82nd Airborne succeeded the Second Armored as our combat troops. The air boys were quicker on the trigger than the tank boys, but there was no necessity to shoot. The Russians decided it was safer to stay home, and peace was restored.

One of the last raids in our sector occurred one night in Neukoelln. A large number of Russians came over the border and raided a wine distillery, smashing windows and battering down doors to get at the wine stocks. We promptly sent over enough troops to surround the distillery. Had we needed a legitimate excuse to shoot, it would have been easy to find that night, because the Russians were in a belligerent mood when their fun was curtailed. However, following orders not to shoot, our men wore down their resistance and persuaded them to leave. Like uniformed lambs, the whole body marched meekly back into their own fold.

Some days passed before we finally cleared out all the Russians and could regard the sector as completely American. Although we had only a few night carousals to handle, we still were faced with the problem of Russian guards, which the Soviet military maintained at public utilities, gas and electric plants, and other vital points in our sector. We supplied coal for the gas and electric plants, but never could ascertain exactly how much fuel was required, because the Russian guards refused us entrance and, what's more, declined to withdraw from our sector.

Again we had to be firm. The order was passed down to the 82nd Airborne Division to station guards at every point guarded by the Russians. The result was that at many installations a Russian soldier glared across a few feet of Berlin at an American soldier. We feared a serious flare-up at first. Within a week, however, the Soviets had withdrawn their guards. If we had not taken strong measures, the Russians would still have guards in the American sector of Berlin.

An incident of that period served to shed fresh light on Russian character. If it had not been so typical of the rank hypocrisy motivating Soviet thought and action, it might have been funny. But four long years of dealing with the Muscovites in Berlin have robbed me of the capacity of being amused by anything they do.

On August 6, 1945, the United States Army Air Force dropped the first atom bomb on Hiroshima. Two days later, the Russians declared war on the Japanese, already a hopelessly defeated nation. For almost the entire duration of the Pacific War, Russia had been able to keep out under the terms of the Non-Aggression Pact, signed at the historic kissing-bee in Moscow, when Josef Stalin gave Yasui Matsuoka, the frock-coated Japanese envoy, two resounding smacks for the benefit of the newsreels. But the Kremlin voted for war when Stalin saw a chance to snatch territory in the Far East.

The following day, August 9, the Kommandatura met and I somewhat witlessly suggested to Parks that he formally congratulate Gorbatov on the Soviet declaration of war on Japan.

Parks agreed that it would be an appropriate gesture, although the temptation to be sarcastic was almost overpowering. However, Parks is diplomatic, and the remarks he addressed to Gorbatov before the meeting settled down to business were very gracious.

"Soviet Russia always lives up to her agreements," Gorbatov

replied smugly, ignoring the compliment and an impressive string of his own broken promises in Berlin. "Declaring war on Japan was simply one of the agreements we have with our allies." He then turned to the papers in front of him, indicating that he had nothing else to say.

Parks and I glanced at each other and gritted our teeth. Mentally, we both chalked up another error for trying to be nice to a Russian.

However, we could not allow victory over Japan—bringing World War II to a close—to pass unhonored in Berlin. Parks proposed a big international parade along Unter den Linden to celebrate V-J Day. As usual, the Russians immediately suspected political maneuvering on our part, but when they referred the parade suggestion to Zhukov, he fairly leaped at the idea.

In fact, the Russian Supreme Commander felt the parade was so important that General Eisenhower, Field Marshal Montgomery, and General Koenig should be invited to Berlin. Zhukov also suggested that someone should make a speech. It was pretty obvious who was going to do the orating. Not Eisenhower, to be sure. Not Montgomery. Not Koenig. They weren't even invited to speak. Zhukov announced that he would make the speech himself.

A committee was formed and, after petty squabbles and minor delays, the details of the celebration were settled. The parade was to be a spectacle to impress the Allies as well as the Germans. It was set for September and each nation was limited to one thousand soldiers and not more than one hundred vehicles, the type of vehicle not being specified.

That was one of the strangest parades I ever saw on the European continent. Few Berliners turned out, understandably being unable to digest an Allied victory demonstration at that dismal point in German history. Eisenhower, Montgomery, and Koenig were unable to attend, but thousands of Allied soldiers lined Unter den Linden as spectators.

Zhukov was there in all his glory. He wore robin's egg blue trousers, with yellow stripes, topped off with a dark green blouse and a bright red sash. Across his chest, and almost down below his hips, hung so many decorations that a special brass plate had to be worn to house this immense collection, giving the appearance of being riveted to the Russian's chest. The decorations included the highest in the Soviet Union, as well as many from the Allies. Zhukov is a big man, with a big, broad chest, but there was no room left. In an emergency, he had hung one decoration, a gold saucer affair, on his right hip.

One dazzled G.I. blurted out, "That's the God-damnedest Roxy doorman I've ever seen!" when Zhukov appeared.

General Eisenhower sent the spectacular General George S. Patton to represent him at the celebration. Patton, too was a magnificent spectacle—but in another way. He was dressed in a simple battle jacket, with a few ribbons, but his gleaming boots and polished helmet outshone all Zhukov's medals. As far as I can remember, nobody else on the platform attracted the slightest attention.

Zhukov planted himself in the center of the platform, jealously guarding his position, and each time Patton shifted his feet the Russian eyed him nervously, then moved nearer the front of the platform. When he did so, Patton inched up to him. In the end, Zhukov's rather expansive stomach was hanging indelicately over the rail while Patton stood, grim and soldierlike, beside him.

The less said about Zhukov's speech the better. He was never drearier. The only bright spot in the entire monologue was Margaret Bourke-White, the photographer, whose flashing skirts and silk-stockinged legs completely distracted the usually stoic Russian Supreme Commander when she knelt in front of the reviewing stand to take his picture.

The parade was impressive and the Russians had arranged their customary surprise. Each nation paraded its best troops. The 82nd Airborne, with white gloves stuck through their shoulder straps, white parachute silk scarves, and polished guns slung over their backs, looked very dressy, not at all like the sky devils of Normandy. The French scout cars performed the neat trick of turning turrets in salute; the British marched along, taking it all in the day's work.

As for vehicles, the Western powers were content to parade

with light armored cars and other comparatively light equipment. There the Russians had us. With a dreadful clanking of
steel treads against concrete, one hundred giant, new Stalin
tanks rumbled into view and rolled down the historic street
past the reviewing stand. All Unter den Linden was dwarfed.
As they passed in review, the shiny muzzles of their big guns
pointed up to the sky.

Patton watched the Russian tanks narrowly. Finally, turning
to General Nares, the British commandant, who was staring,
fascinated, at this display of Soviet might, he whispered, "They
look good enough tanks, but don't worry. If they start shooting,
I'm on your side."

One more recollection of the parade helped me keep my
sanity in those insane days. When the British light tanks passed,
following the Russian juggernauts, a young, blond major, with
a mustache turned up at the edges and the nonchalance of a
handsome rogue out of Kipling, barked his command, "Eyes
right!"

He snapped his head to the right and looked straight into the
eyes of a pretty little French WAC in the reviewing stand. The
Major gave her a broad wink, then turned up the corner of his
mouth and pulled a poker face as he passed the wondering
Zhukov.

A parade's a parade, I said to myself, Zhukovs come and go—
but a pretty girl is a joy forever.

CHAPTER V

THE first and biggest job of the Kommandatura was feeding Berlin and saving a city of 3,200,000 from starvation. Many of the early sessions were devoted almost exclusively to formulating plans to this end, and joint discussions were augmented by individual studies outside the conference room.

Although we still considered that Russia had got the best of us on the food deal, and that the responsibility was fairly and squarely in the Soviet lap in view of her acquisition of Berlin's traditional food basket, once we had agreed to provide our share, we set to work implementing our promise.

Basically, the agreement worked out this way: we would provide the food and Britain would provide the coal. But neither of the problems was solved without two-fisted boxing and slugging with the Russians. We were normally conciliatory. The British were cautious, and extremely conservative. The Russians were aggressive and blunt, backing their arguments with figures which, at first, we could neither confirm nor refute. They had the upper hand at these first meetings, and refused to give way or compromise on a single question, because they knew more about the situation than we did.

General Draper, economic and supply chief of the United States Forces, European Theater (USFET), and I sat in on the first three-power meeting with Russian and British representatives and discussed and defended every point. In addition to Russian intransigence, there were many difficult problems of supply, transport, and exchange to be settled. For instance: What foods were most needed in Berlin? Would the Russians accept flour instead of potatoes? What would be the exchange rate on commodities when one country could supply, say, flour in place of meats, fats, or cereals? These technical unknowns worked down to specific questions like this: What was the exchange rate between canned fish brought from Bremen and dressed meat in Berlin?

Since none of the Western powers had available stocks, obviously it was Russia's job to continue feeding Berlin until our supplies began to arrive. Our plan was that the Russians would supply the western sectors and, when we were able, we would turn over the equivalent amount of food to them.

The Muscovites didn't even bother to conceal their suspicions of this plan. Probably they thought that after they had supplied our sectors, we would double-cross them and refuse to replace the food, considering our reaction to the highhanded way we had been forced into the food-and-fuel compact.

"I do not have any surplus food to supply to your sectors," Zhukov said flatly. "As I have told you before, my only supplies are in the Wehrmacht warehouses and those are nearing exhaustion."

However, we pressed him, pointing out that the problem was merely one of availability and delivery of supplies, and eventually he agreed to our proposal. Zhukov promised that he would draw the food from the Red Army, replacing it later with our supplies and, incidentally, thereby admitting that the Red Army was well provisioned, which it was. When Berlin was captured, all German herds were driven east; the Red Army had imposed a capital levy on potatoes and was busily collecting all the vegetables and cereals it could find.

In order to get our food into the city, the Russians agreed to accept cattle on the hoof at the Bavarian border and to deliver a corresponding amount of meat in Berlin, the ratio being two pounds on the hoof to one pound of dressed meat in Berlin. There was a lot of argument about these ratios, but in most cases the Russians won.

The fish-and-meat ratio was a case in point. When we protested, they would say, with the finality of a young minister quoting Scripture, "In the Red Army book, the exchange ratio between fish and meat is two to one." And we ended up two to one, with sometimes a trifling reduction like 1.99.

Corresponding caloric values were accepted as the basis for the food-exchange rates, and there again we collided violently with the iron-clad Soviet economic system. Once more, we finally had to accept the exchange rates on the ration cards issued by the Russians in Berlin before we arrived, which were the same rates in effect in the Red Army.

For example, they were making 145 pounds of bread from 100 pounds of German rye flour, a cereal entirely different from Russian rye, which would yield that amount. With the moisture required for such a yield, German rye bread is indigestible and mildews quickly, but it took months to persuade the Russians of this obvious fact and get them to reduce the yield to 135 pounds or less.

When we got to Berlin, we found the Russians had instituted among the civilians a ration system exactly the same—they claimed—as in Moscow. It consisted of five categories, the highest of which allowed 2,485 calories and the lowest 1,248 calories.

Here, of course, American and Russian ideas of rationing differed sharply. While we thought in terms of physical needs—the humanitarian approach to the individual—the Russians used food as an incentive to increased industrial production and for political propaganda. Their philosophy is to help those who work for them and ignore those who don't, or can't. According to our ideas, an old, infirm man, incapable of producing, needs special food, but according to the Marxian dialectics of materialism, he is given barely enough to keep body and soul together. On the other hand, a younger man with a high productive record, a doctor, or a political leader, gets the royal treatment.

When I studied the Russian VIP category, the number of politicians, officials, intellectuals, and teachers enjoying Soviet munificence was staggering, whereas one million people, or more than one third of the population, was on an almost starvation scale.

Naturally, we protested at the meagerness of the lower categories. The average subsistence limit in the United States is three thousand calories. The Russians professed to be surprised by our protest. They claimed that the Berlin ration was as high as Moscow's and double that of Dresden, one of the three cities in the Russian zone placed on a ration basis.

At this point, I had to point out the fallacy of the Russian argument. In Moscow, the ration might be the same as in Berlin, but in Moscow, in addition to basic rations, unrationed food could be bought at free markets and from other sources by those who had sufficient money to pay for surplus commodities. Of the German cities on rations, Berlin was the only one where the quota could not be supplemented by foraging the surrounding countryside for vegetables, fruits, and other food. The Soviet military would not permit this, because they were requisitioning, or buying, quantities of food for their troops.

We argued heatedly on that point and Zhukov agreed to lift the ban and allow Berliners to go outside the city and pick up what they could find. This agreement was never honored; we never got it in writing. Neither the people themselves, nor the city authorities, were allowed outside the city limits on such errands. Finally, weeks later, when we were pushing the Russians to live up to their agreement, the local general admitted that a certain number of Germans were going out into the country for food, and added that he had no objection, provided it was "off the record."

"If you make an issue of it," the General warned, "orders will come down tightening restrictions, and the practice will be stopped altogether."

That was the best we could do for the people. Berliners, either walking or taking trains to the country, were bringing back on their shoulders, or in shopping bags, one hundred tons of fresh vegetables every day. This helped feed the city.

American representatives were able to sit back and relax when coal was discussed at Kommandatura meetings. That was a fight between the British and the Russians. The Russians insisted upon 7,200 tons of coal a day for electric power, sewage, subways, and lighting, including our share of 3,600 tons, because we had no coal resources. The Russians also were supposed to contribute.

No mention was made at the time of 50 per cent of the city's power, which came over our lines from Thuringia, once our bailiwick. Three years later, the Russians came back at us and made us pay for that power. They wrung an agreement from us whereby we paid .85 kilos of hard coal per kilowatt hour of power originating in Chernowitz, the brown-coal region, which originally was captured by our troops and turned over to the Russians.

After demurring that they had heavy commitments in other parts of Germany, and quoting transport troubles and shortage of wooden pit props, the British were silenced and converted to the Russian view by the gruff Sokolovsky.

"We do not care about your obligations or your difficulties," he said. "There is only two days' supply of coal in Berlin and we must have your coal at once."

The British agreed to make the full deliveries, although they complained that the total was too high. Later, they had considerable trouble with their rolling stock and were not keen on running trains into the Soviet zone for fear of losing them. Under their confiscation policy, the Russians tore up railroad tracks and removed equipment to such a degree that they endangered the entire Central German rail-transport system. Orders for these seizures came from a higher authority than the zonal commander.

Labor difficulties in the Ruhr, arising from postwar disorganization, were quoted by the British when they fell sixty thousand tons behind in their deliveries. "There are plenty of people in Berlin," Sokolovsky barked, "why don't you put them in the mines?"

He made no attempt to explain why the Russians had fallen thirty thousand tons behind in furnishing Berlin with brown-coal briquettes.

We did get Berlin's food and fuel on a working basis but, as the months dragged wearily on, we fought over a variety of battlegrounds. It became necessary to reduce Berlin's milk from approximately 250,000 liters to 148,000 liters. Much of this reduction was achieved by eliminating milk from the diet of children between the ages of nine and fourteen. The Russians couldn't increase their contribution, because they had only seven thousand cows—which they had taken from the Berliners —and were using them to provide their own share of liquid milk, approximately 70,000 liters.

The British put up a strong argument to keep milk on the children's diet and we were willing to supply the Russian share, in exchange for other considerations. But the Russians refused to retain the ration for German children because, they said, Russian children of the same age were not getting milk. Gorbatov, who advanced this characteristic explanation, seemed to think it was all our fault, anyway.

A measure of agreement was reached. It was arranged to throw all supplies into a common pool, with powdered milk augmenting liquid milk. At first, we were afraid that powdered milk could not be given to young children, but the doctors proved otherwise. Another hurdle was the Berlin mothers, who did not take kindly to powdered milk, thinking it was another *ersatz* product, a hangover from wartime shortages. However, we started an educational campaign in the newspapers advocating powdered milk, and so bridged the dietetic gap.

Gorbatov was stubborn. His weakness was that, as a combat soldier, he could see a battle plotted before him and know what to do, but at the conference table he was lost. He could not distinguish between important and trivial matters, and was apt to fight bitterly against something he failed to understand, solely on the ground that he was a Russian and should not agree with the Americans.

One dispute illustrating the Gorbatov obtuseness involved the issue of postage stamps.

With the British, we had issued Allied postage stamps to the Reichspost for use in our sectors. We immediately were attacked by Gorbatov, who claimed we were using the stamps to make money, a predictable Russian conclusion. The Russians had used their own stamps before our arrival and he declared that it would be better and more equitable to use these instead of ours. Although we tried to convince him that actually we were donating these stamps to the Berlin city government, not selling them, because of the acute shortage of Berlin stamps, he was so thoroughly committed to his objection that nothing on earth could make him withdraw it. A week later, we did withdraw the stamps, not because of Gorbatov's objection, but because a sufficient supply of regular stamps had become available.

The Russians tried to pirate an excessive number of street cars in Berlin to send to Warsaw, and naturally we had to protest. With customary secretiveness, they never told us when their trains were coming into the city. Six Russian trains arrived almost simultaneously one morning in the Tempelhof yards, with the result that it took us four days and nights to unload them.

Ignoring our protests, they continued to dismantle their own sector for shipment to Russia and refused to return equipment they had stolen from the American sector. So savage was their cannibalizing of power plants and so wholesale their theft of generator equipment that only the strongest representations saved Berlin's remaining power supply. We pointed out, as forcefully as we could, that these depredations had reduced the city's power-plant productivity to such a dangerous low that it was almost impossible to maintain normal functions.

Although we had enough trouble trying to accommodate the Russians on other matters, it took us several weeks to straighten out the details for an international sports meeting. This event grew out of an offer by the British to share the Olympic Stadium in their sector. A committee was appointed to arrange the meeting and ran into almost insurmountable problems. The French wanted all distance races; the Americans preferred sprints; the Russians wanted all weight-lifting events; the British wanted tea served at four, for sure.

We finally ironed out national preferences and set the date for Sunday, September 23, for a real track meet, guaranteed to suit everybody—sprints, long-distance runs, and field events. Consternation took over on the eve of the meet when the Russians, on sudden orders from the unpredictable Zhukov, withdrew without explanation. The other three powers conferred hurriedly and decided to hold the meet without the strong men from Moscow.

The Americans won easily but, despite the lopsided score, every event was closely contested. Officers and men packed the stands and among the delighted spectators were thousands of Russians. No real explanation for the absence of the Soviet athletes was ever given, although we knew the men had been in training for weeks. At the Kommandatura meeting on the following Monday, Gorbatov—rather red and a little flustered— lamely announced that the Russian athletes had been "occupied" on Sunday, but now they had permission to compete and would be glad to take on the Americans. The invitation was not accepted.

Berliners still had their loose collars and their nagging stomachs as winter approached, but no one was dying of starvation. The four powers deepened the autumn gloom by announcing that no coal would be brought into Berlin for domestic heating; the fuel was needed for civic purposes. At the same time, we realized that some form of emergency heating must be provided. Without internal or external heat, thousands would freeze to death when the bitter German winter arrived.

Consequently, the Allied Control Authority approved the increase of the lowest category from 1,248 to 1,500 calories. To help externally, we ordered the Lord Mayor to set up a woodchopping project, which would not destroy the city's parks but would help solve the fuel problem. Nevertheless, there were protests from a few Berliners, who preferred unmarred beauty even if they froze to death. The Lord Mayor's project wasn't worth a tinker's dam, but our own project in the American sector was very successful. We cut 182,000 cubic meters in three months.

The ration increase came about this way. A visiting colonel from USFET Headquarters dropped into Berlin, looked around for a few minutes, and forthwith wrote a long and startling report saying that the people of Berlin were dropping like flies, that they could be seen in thousands in the fields, gathering acorns to satisfy their hunger. Unless something was done, he warned, there would be an international calamity.

His report set off all kinds of explosions. USFET started to scream, and the British papers didn't help the situation any by publishing stories saying that thousands of Germans were being employed in the Tiergarten, digging their own graves and graves for other Berliners, while they still had strength to lift a spade. There was a rumor in the German papers that 65 per cent of the children in Berlin were doomed to die that winter. All of these reports I listed in my personal diary as "bushwah."

General Clay called me immediately. "Are the people of Berlin starving?" he asked point-blank.

"If by starving, you mean that they are losing weight, yes," I replied. "If you mean that they are dying from lack of food, no."

"How about the part of the report that says they are foraging for acorns?" Clay asked.

"Well," I said, "the people of France used acorns to make *ersatz* coffee during the Occupation. As a matter of fact, the Germans also learned to make a fairly decent beverage out of acorns. They use acorns for pudding and horse chestnuts for making bread. That still doesn't mean that anyone is starving. City records don't show a single case of death from starvation."

The next day I was called to the office of General Draper. Various generals were bustling around preparing an answer, for General Clay's signature, to the USFET colonel's report. I was jumped on immediately for advice and repeated what I had told Clay, adding that I was speaking as of that day, not being in a position to gaze into the future.

"You mean people in Berlin are not going to starve to death this winter?" someone demanded.

"I am talking about right now," I repeated. "All I know is that nobody is dying of starvation. As for the future, I will take the word of the doctors, because they alone are able to poke pins into people and determine what eventually will happen to them."

I met with General Clay again the next day, when his attention was called to Category V—1,248 calories.

"If I had known of this low category when the Russians produced the ration scale, I never would have approved it," Clay said, apparently surprised at his discovery of Category V. It appeared that he had agreed to the over-all ration plan proposed by the Russians without examining it thoroughly.

"I understood that the scale here in Berlin was supposed to be the same as it is in Moscow," he went on. "Nobody is starving in Moscow."

"The scale is the same," I told him, "except that in Moscow there are free markets and other sources where unrationed food can be bought to eke out rationed food. That makes all the difference in the world. Berliners aren't officially allowed out of the city even to pick up potatoes in the country."

The upshot was that General Clay instructed me to present a request to the Kommandatura for the elimination of the lowest category because he was convinced that a minimum of 1,500 calories—a figure set by Major General Stayers, his surgeon general—was the minimum for human subsistence. At the Kommandatura, there was the inevitable disagreement. We wanted to get rid of the lowest category entirely and induce the Russians to put everyone in that starvation group into a higher category, with 1,610 calories a day.

The Russians refused to go along with us. For reasons they didn't elaborate, they said they were unable to increase the amount of food they could bring into the city as their share. They apparently wanted all the extra food they could get their hands on to portion out for political purposes, instead of giving it to the people who really needed it. The issue finally got so hopelessly snarled that it was referred to the Allied Control Authority, where it was decided not to eliminate the lowest category but to retain it and boost it to 1,500 calories. This was a face-saving device for the Russians, too, who felt they could not eliminate the category while it continued in force in Moscow.

If they accomplished nothing else, the food discussions at the Kommandatura shed a revealing light on Russian techniques. In talking over the problem with Colonel Dalada—who had become Russian deputy after several changes in that post— I said, apropos of the hungry Berliners, "Well, anyway, you can't kick a lady when she's down."

Dalada smiled indulgently. "Why, my dear Colonel Howley," he replied, "that is the best time to kick them."

"You mean food is political?" I snapped.

"Of course," he said, smiling.

His remark exemplified one of the many inconsistencies of the Russian attitude. Although they never hid their hatred of the German people, they were always pushing us to hurry food into the city and urging us, again and again, to get even more food. The Russians were the first to set up soup kitchens in the streets of Berlin, but there was nothing humanitarian about the enterprise. Food was a channel for Communist propaganda.

I had been operating on a different basis. Where the Russians parceled out extra bits of food in return for services rendered and for general political loyalty, I distributed food to the Germans to keep them from starving on our hands. I was not, however, in favor of giving them American sirloin steaks every night. Perhaps I had been unnecessarily blunt in saying so, but I had come to Berlin with the idea that the Germans were our enemies. Even though it was becoming more evident every day that it was the Russians who really were our enemies, I still was not prepared to embrace the Germans as allies.

Unfortunately, I reiterated that proposition publicly. I already had received a hangman's noose, dipped in red paint, the gift of a German crank.

Now, when I repeated that I was not giving the Germans food because I loved them, someone in the States wrote to his senator. I was depicted as the "Beast of Berlin." The Senator, of course, got in touch with the War Department, and the War Department got in touch with me. I received a gentle slap on the wrist and the intimation that I had not been especially diplomatic. A report was requested and I confirmed everything the Senator had said, reiterating once more, in a general way, my attitude toward the Germans. I then sat down and waited for the rebuke supreme. It never came. Apparently the incident was closed.

Complicating the food, and also the public-health problem, was the influx into Berlin of refugees from Czechoslovakia, Poland, and Russia—Germans heading back to the Fatherland.

Developing the principle that all roads lead to Rome, Bismarck made Berlin the center of the German wheel. All rail and road traffic leads to the capital, and hundreds of thousands of refugees flocked in, bringing with them 25 per cent of the city's diseases, including typhus. A dangerous situation developed. Food was scarce, housing was hopeless. Something drastic had to be done.

At one time, we considered throwing a barricade around the city, but that would only have caused camps to spring up on our doorstep. Many of the refugees claimed to be Berliners. Quizzing, however, was useless, because few had any identification. The Russians tried to reroute trains around Berlin, but of course this was almost impossible since the capital was the grand terminal.

Zhukov broadcast an order to refugees to keep out of the city. We also joined in the press and radio campaign urging them to stay away and warning them that disease and hunger would be their only welcome. We stopped giving permits to come into Berlin, but none of these measures was completely successful. The only thing we really could do was to maintain control over the refugees passing through, giving them one meal at night and shipping them out the next morning. Between August and December, 1945, more than three hundred thousand persons passed through the city on that basis.

German soldiers began to appear among the civilian refugees. They had been captured by the Russians and turned loose with the order: "Go on. Get going!" The soldiers were a pathetic sight. They came into the city with tin cups and buckets tied around their necks, wearing dirty, tattered uniforms, the wounded with rude wooden splints and filthy bandages wrapped around their legs. Hollow-eyed, bones pushing through the skin, no soldiers in history ever looked more defeated and dejected than those prisoners of war released by the Russians. But they received less sympathy from their own people than they did from our soldiers. The Prussian loves a winner; he has no use for a loser.

One of the problems the Kommandatura had to deal with was the black market, and here again the profundity of the

East-West cleavage of ideas was revealed. Perhaps the term "black market" is a misnomer, because conditions in Berlin differed from those of any other city in Europe. None of the incentives that created black markets elsewhere were present. In Rome, the medium was food. In Paris, gasoline.

In Berlin, however, there was no food for surreptitious trading, except some PX goods, and we soon stopped that. No food came in from the outside, because the Red Army scraped the district and also because there was no transportation—unless you were a Red Army officer. The once swank Femina Club served big, luscious steaks, brought in by businesslike Russian officers. But Berlin saw none of the black-market activity in food carried on, say, by the German Army of Occupation in France. There was no inviting market for gasoline, either, because there were no civilian cars. One drunken G.I. did sell a jeep for ten thousand dollars, but not even an Army jeep can run on empty tanks.

What did develop was a number of barter points for the sale, or exchange, of clothing, jewelry, and personal effects. At first, the Germans left notes tacked on trees or stuck on walls, making their offers and fixing the rendezvous. Berliners exchanged ski shoes for overcoats, chairs for pants, luxury items for clothes and, if possible, for food, which was practically negligible. Barter was supposed to be for civilians only and, instead of straight swapping of goods, it was natural that money transactions should develop. To regularize this business under city control, we authorized the establishment of at least one barter market in each sector, with an official appraiser. Cash was to be used only as an emergency form of adjustment.

We immediately faced the charge that we were legalizing the black market. Over in the British sector, black marketing had been carried on in the Tiergarten, where the Germans disposed of everything from valuable paintings to silver candelabra and bicycles. The British used to raid this market, and once picked up a Russian major general and a number of Russian soldiers engaged in illicit trading.

The General's excuse was that his division had been demobilized and he was with his men buying civilian clothes and goods to take back to Russia.

We Americans were not too happy over the barter markets, although we agreed to give them a trial, hoping to control some of the wilder bartering and fraudulent practices. Paradoxically, the Russians were in favor of the markets and did not find them inconsistent with their own customs. For the first time in our dealings with them, we heard the Russians renouncing the basis of the Communist economic system and favoring free trade. We had agreed that currency could be used to cover barter items.

Allied soldiers were supposed to be excluded from the barter markets, but the Russians refused to keep their men out. They agreed to keep them from selling, but not from buying. About that time we discovered the secret of this switch to capitalistic practice and the use of sordid wealth instead of coupons. Germany had far more paper money than was necessary. During the war, Hitler had increased the Reichsbank circulation tenfold. More than seventy-three billion reichsmarks were in circulation, whereas about eight billion would have been sufficient.

We brought to Berlin plates for printing invasion money but, since there was more than enough money in circulation, we didn't use them. However, the Russians had been supplied with duplicate plates. They immediately started printing notes, actually increasing the denominations from a hundred to a thousand marks. These notes differed from ours only in having a hyphen in front of the serial number.

With the huge sums seized from German banks, these Allied notes made the Russians multimillionaires. The money could not be sent back to Russia, but was used by the troops to dominate the barter markets. Since the men received years of back pay in German or Allied currency—a lieutenant was reported to be getting US$140 per month—they were able to go on colossal sprees. Officially, the troops were encouraged to buy commodities and send them back home. Even today, the Russians will not support any plan that curbs free purchase of German commodities.

On the Russian G.I. level, the immediate goal was a watch.

Russians love watches for a number of reasons. They always have been associated in the Muscovite mind with affluence and an established, even exalted, position in life. Peasants never owned watches. A wrist watch—well! Watches soon became a universal commodity, because the troops had no confidence in Russian currency. Also, a soldier could send a watch home and his wife could barter it for a cow. Even our G.I.'s realized the fortune, in Russians eyes, represented by a watch and started selling their own and converting the money into American dollars, although our men were forbidden to enter these markets. Some Russian soldiers wore half a dozen watches. A Mickey Mouse watch was worth more than a jewel-studded trinket from Cartier. Some Russians paid the equivalent of US$1,000 for a watch.

The Russian soldiers, their pockets stuffed with spending money for the first time in their lives, weren't the only rank to enjoy this new-found prosperity. One of my detachment commanders had a Buick he had picked up somewhere on the road to Berlin. He had legally requisitioned it and, painted and fixed up, the Buick was a smart car.

One night a junior Soviet officer, carrying a suitcase, came over to the Detachment Commander's office in Steglitz, chatted a while, and then announced that he would like to buy the car.

The American was curious to know why a young officer would need a private car.

"Do you want to buy it for yourself," he asked, "or for someone else?"

The Russian didn't reply immediately. Then he said, rather hesitantly, "I have been sent by Marshal Zhukov and he offers to pay two hundred thousand reichsmarks for your car." He opened his bag and there was the money.

I can't vouch for the Russian's story, but it had the ring of truth. That's exactly how the big shots from Moscow operated and two hundred thousand reichsmarks, converted at the current rate of exchange at our Finance Office, was US$20,000— a fairly high price for a five-year-old Buick.

On a higher level, the Russians had obtained a potent weapon with this almost unlimited supply of notes. Although they forcibly requisitioned from the farmers any food that they required, they could claim that they bought it legitimately. As part of their propaganda approach to the farmers, they doubled and trebled purchase prices, giving the impression they were paying more than anyone else. Growers selling to the Russians were dazzled by false dreams of wealth. They didn't think in terms of finance integrated into German economy— as ours was—but only of a quick turnover.

If we requisitioned anything over in our part of town, we gave the owner a receipt and he presented it to the local mayor who paid him a smaller sum than the Russians would have done—in their depreciated currency.

However, the new barter market system seemed to work satisfactorily and it did check a lot of abuses. In the end, of course, this form of merchandising almost disappeared, due to lack of supplies and to alleviation of wartime shortages.

Variety spiced life at Kommandatura sessions. We had a thousand and one details to handle, all linked with the administration of Berlin, with the Russians always looking askance as a matter of policy.

One troublesome issue involved German uniforms. Thousands of German soldiers had no other clothing, but we ruled that it was inconsistent with national policies to permit former members of the *Wehrmacht* to wear uniforms symbolic of Nazi Germany. But what else could they wear? First to reach Berlin, the Russians had restricted them to nothing later than the 1932-type uniform and afterward designed a brown uniform, with a British-style beret. Inevitably, the scheme collapsed because of the shortage of materials, which the Russian had overlooked. Everyone in Berlin but the Russians sympathized with the Germans in this predicament. The men must have something to wear in winter and there was nothing in sight to replace the outlawed uniforms.

We won our point when the meeting decided to give returning soldiers two weeks either to get their uniforms dyed, or thoroughly to demilitarize them.

The comment of the Russian delegate at one point in the discussions was almost on a par with Marie Antoinette's famous advice about feeding the starving French. "No clothes?" he shrugged. "Well, let them wear underclothes."

Another subject to which the many-starred commandants of the four great powers gave considerable thought was tattooing, the difficulty arising from the fact that the Russians considered a tattoo mark an SS identification. The Russian contention was that the Germans should be allowed to remove these marks. After all, the war was over and there was no point in perpetuating guilt. The British were inclined to agree, because tattooing had been banned. We finally left the decision to the doctors, who would report any requests for the forbidden art, which they would refuse. So if a German wanted to keep his tattooed ship sailing around his waist, or his long-tressed Lorelei clutching his heart, in glorification of German womanhood, he could—or go through the long, painful operation of having the decoration removed.

The deputy commandants committed to paper a process for firing local mayors who got out of line. Here, we were treading shaky ground until we normalized procedure. The city government of Berlin was a Soviet instrument, and the mayors of the twenty boroughs were Soviet nominees. Every time a mayor was fired, the Russians claimed he had lost his job unjustly, simply because he had been appointed by the Russians before we arrived in Berlin.

Some of the mayors definitely showed their antipathy to the Western powers in the early days, tending to take orders directly from the Soviet Military Administration, and not from the sector commander. We were treated as "second stringers."

The Mayor at Steglitz gave our Military Government detachment considerable chin music and we fired him. The British fired a couple more and the French another, which placed the issue fairly before the Kommandatura. The new constitution gave the Lord Mayor power to appoint and remove, under Kommandatura supervision, and things went smoothly after that.

Lack of a written constitution also caused trouble at the Kommandatura. Procedure at our meetings had just "growed," as someone said, like the immortal Topsy. It took shape of necessity, following the one-paragraph agreement accepted in 1944 by the European Advisory Commission in London, which simply set out the idea that the city would be run by four powers in unison.

The task of writing a constitution proved very difficult, because it brought into sharp focus points of view upon which we did not agree. The original agreement specified that the Kommandatura would comprise the commandants of each sector. Signed by Clay, Zhukov, and Weeks, it read, "Military commandants of each sector." No one could tell from the Russian version whether the Kommandatura was to be made up of "the" commandant of each sector or "a" commandant of each sector. The point didn't appear significant to me, but it was an illustration of our difficulties which, projected on a larger screen, became big issues.

Moreover, the Russians held that commandants must be troop commanders, which we insisted they did not. Our policy in Berlin finally separated the office of troop commander from the Military Government. General de Beauchesne, the French commandant, also was only a military commander and did not command troops. Even the Russian contention was disproved by their commandant, Lieutenant General Smirnov, military governor. He commanded no troops except the Russian version of the MP's.

Finally, we made a curious compromise by agreeing to call the whole thing a "procedure," not a constitution. This made it more flexible, and everybody was satisfied. I must confess, however, that I still get a little dizzy when I recall some of the weird corners we cut at the Kommandatura.

Language problems continued to be formidable. Not only did each statement have to be translated, but the translations seldom agreed. Russian is a difficult language, with few fine shades of meaning, but English—used literally—can be perplexing.

A Russian officer once took a party on a tour of Soviet military installations, including the rifle range.

"This," he paused to announce, "is where we do our shooting."

There was a delighted silence, broken by a slight titter. The officer was quick to explain. "What I mean is," he said, "this is where our Russian soldiers practice their marksmanship."

CHAPTER VI

OUR first winter was mild; we got through to spring with a minimum of grief, though many of our plans were makeshift, designed to cover the narrow field of emergency and no more. The increased ration helped the German people to resist the rigors of the climate and, confounding the prophets of doom, there were no deaths from starvation which would have fanned civil discontent to dangerous proportions. In the American sector, the process of self-government we encouraged in the six boroughs made such healthy progress that by the end of winter we were able to withdraw all our Military Government detachments and let the Germans conduct their own affairs.

However, having been submerged thus far in the sea of more pressing problems, it was inevitable that the ugly head of politics should bob up as we struggled into 1946. The Russians, skillful international jugglers, always kept three balls in the air at once—political, military, and economic—but the red ball of politics seemed to be the one that came up most of the time. Russian objectives, now that appeasement was over, began to emerge in a bold, vigorous pattern.

What the Russians want in Berlin is complete political control, not the share—a quarter, to be precise—to which they originally agreed, and they want it through the German Communist party, the SED, an instrument of their own creation. When we arrived in Berlin, naturally the Russians were in control after capturing the city.

First of all, they controlled the city government because all jobs were filled by appointment and only Communists, or fellow travelers, were nominated. A casual glance at the organization chart showed many nonparty men, but they were merely a front. All key positions—the deputy lord mayor, *Magistrat,* judiciary—were filled by German Communists, trained in Moscow and shifted to Berlin as soon as the government was formed. The head of personnel for the city was a Communist. Of the twenty boroughs, personnel heads of eighteen were Communists, or Communist sympathizers, the other two being nonparty front men. No position of strategic importance was held by anyone but a Communist.

Lord Mayor Doctor Werner was a nonparty man. A fine, white-haired old gentleman and former schoolteacher, genuinely interested in helping his fellow Berliners in their hour of tragedy, he possessed little power. Actually, he was only a front man. The real power behind the job in the Berlin administration was wielded by Deputy Lord Mayor Maron, a German Communist, and a clever, unscrupulous product of Moscow's academy of distorted politics. His powers were unlimited.

One of my liaison officers once saw Maron walk into the Lord Mayor's office with a batch of papers dealing with the city's finances. Throwing them down on Doctor Werner's desk, he said, "I want these signed!"

"But I haven't read them yet," the old gentleman protested mildly. "You cannot expect me to sign them without reading them. It would be irregular."

"Sign!" commanded Communist Maron and the Lord Mayor —with a sigh—signed.

A second source of Russian power in Berlin was the trade unions. Once you control the unions, you may overthrow a government or, failing that, at least make it very unpopular with the people. The Russians introduced a new type of trade union, the FDGB (Association of Free German Trade Unions), an organization with dictatorial powers, which wasn't a union in our sense but an over-all politico-labor agency. It bore no resemblance to the unions in the United States. If an American is a garment worker, an automobile worker, or a coal miner, he has an individual craft union in which he may enroll. The German worker has no choice; he joined the Communist-controlled general labor organization.

Six key Communists, all Moscow-trained and including two notorious leaders, Jendretski and Schlimme, controlled the Berlin FDGB, which had conveniently overlapping directorates with the Soviet zone of Germany. A German workman in the Western sectors might join the FDGB, thinking it independent, only to find his union was interlocked with the FDGB in the Soviet zone, thus destroying any dream of a democratic labor setup.

A third channel of power was through control of the police force. Here again a Moscow-trained German was in office. Police Chief Markgraf was an ex-soldier, who had been taken prisoner by the Russians at Stalingrad. He was converted to communism in a prisoner-of-war camp, and proved a willing tool. Markgraf was sent back to Berlin to head the police and was given a number of key officers, all Communists. In this way, the Berlin police force was added to the Communist ranks, giving them a powerful weapon. Having control of the police is like having an army at your disposal. It takes only a few thousand policemen—and Berlin's force totaled twelve thousand—to stage a *coup d'etat*, such as robbed Czechoslovakia of her freedom.

A fourth source of power, and one vitally important to the Soviet scheme of things, was political control of the judiciary. Once you have the courts in the hollow of your hand, there is no curb on ruthlessness and illegality. The Russians had that control in Berlin, during the early stages of the occupation. And how fantastic was the setup. On the *Magistrat*, highest body of the city's judiciary, sat a man who had no legal training at all. He was a locksmith named Mittag. Even his general educational background was negligible. In the United States, I doubt if Mittag, controller of all courts, would have got through grammar school.

This judicial appointment was the most flagrant travesty the Russians had imposed on Berlin but, thick-skinned and impervious to sarcasm as they are, the wry humor of the situation eventually even dawned on the boys from Moscow. We finally laughed them out of the appointment, and they removed their

Chief Judge-Locksmith, replacing him with a more competent man.

In education and other branches of municipal government, similar Communist control was maintained. Tightening their economic grip, the Russians had created corporations that controlled hundreds of plants, siphoning almost the total industrial output of Berlin into the Soviet zone or into Russia, as exports.

This is where we came into the picture. From a sound economic viewpoint, we were not willing to pour hundreds of millions of dollars worth of food, coal, and other products into Berlin only to find they did not go toward balancing Western Germany's budget, but flowed into Soviet warehouses and coffers. However, so far as the original city government was concerned, we were sympathetic from the very beginning. We knew the government was Communist. That we could understand. The only point we insisted upon was that the people of Berlin must be given an opportunity, by democratic means, to decide what sort of government and what type of trade unions they wanted.

We strongly objected to these Russian impositions on the Berliners but, frankly, in those early days we already were a little afraid of the Communist party we had agreed to recognize—reluctantly, of course—as democratic. We were afraid because it already was showing signs of a spirit very similar to that characteristic of the former political minority, the Nazis, who grabbed control of all Germany and led the unhappy country into war against us all.

Hence all our insistence upon quadripartite government of the city and upon our share of control, according to agreement. The big struggle for Berlin started right there, when we first resisted the Communists. The Russians, operating through German members of the party, began to lose political and economic control. Russia eventually was reduced to the point where she had only one fourth of the control over Berlin, which was all that she was entitled to have, and then international friction started in earnest, making more obvious than ever before the cleavage between the East and the West.

Coincident with the shift into the political phase of the

Berlin struggle was a series of Russian changes at the Kommandatura. Colonel General Gorbatov, the first commandant, was a red-faced, fiery soldier who pounded the table, in anger flushed the color of beet borsch, and forced his will upon others, although he seldom seemed to grasp the real importance of an issue under discussion. After he left, it was reported that his inability to produce results, plus the Olympic Stadium track-meet fiasco that tickled us all—except the Russians—were the cause of his removal. I always suspected that Baranov, his deputy, was the brains of the outfit, but Baranov was a hard, taciturn officer, difficult to get along with.

Gorbatov was succeeded by Lieutenant General Smirnov, a deft verbal boxer, who frequently affected a disconcerting detachment from the matter in hand. He would approach a question with the air of a man who has a duty to perform, but who really doesn't like to bring up the subject.

Smirnov would preface an attack on one of the other commandants by smiling placatingly and saying, "I'm very sorry, but I have a disagreeable subject to discuss." Then he bored in with all the savagery and violence he could generate.

Along in April, Major General Kotikov appeared. Kotikov and I were destined to have an endless series of battles for the next three years, but when he arrived I knew almost nothing about him. All our Intelligence was able to dig up was that he had been an adviser to Colonel General Kuznetsov in Saxony and, put in charge of civil affairs, had made a name for himself as an exemplary Russian general, who firmly controlled the province.

There naturally was considerable speculation regarding the change. No American ever knew the Russian reason for changing commandants, any more than he knew the reason for any other Russian action. The newspapers in Saxony had referred to Kotikov as a "moderate," that is, he was a political man but not a rabid party member.

Kotikov proved an expert on conference technique. In startling contrast to his predecessors, he brought a new dialectical weapon to the Kommandatura. He was the first Russian commandant to use humility—and use it effectively. He would feign unfamiliarity or lack of knowledge of a subject, begging the speaker to expound more fully, please. But his humility was as unctuous as Uriah Heep's and, being as serpentine, could have as poisonous a sting.

At that time, the Kommandatura represented an interesting study in professional attitudes. General Lançon, the French commandant, was a keen logician, who spent most of his time studying languages and keeping his superiors informed of events. He usually contributed a few concise sentences to the discussions. The American and British commandants were veteran soldiers, but not too familiar with politics and economics. They couldn't be expected to know by instinct the intricacies of political Berlin. To me, it has always seemed unfair to expect regular army officers, who have devoted their lives to military tactics and generally kept away from politics, to produce a solution to the most touchy and dangerous political situation in Europe today.

Reverting to Kotikov's humility, I must tell a story that shows the word isn't known in Russian. We once had an application from some German Sisters of Charity to collect alms to which, of course, the Russians objected. I pointed out that going from house to house asking for help wasn't exactly begging: it was Christian humility in behalf of a worthy cause.

The Russians smiled condescendingly and I told them the story of the good Louis IX of France—Saint Louis, he was called by his people. One day out of each year, the King sat outside his palace gates and washed the feet of beggars passing by.

"This," I concluded my object lesson, "was to show his humility."

The story of Saint Louis was interpreted back to the Russians that the King of France used to wash his feet once a year to show his humility.

Kotikov's arrival in Berlin raised a number of intriguing questions. Was Russian policy toward the Western democracies to be softened? Or had the new Russian commandant come to Berlin with other instructions? Was he sent there because of his knowledge of politics, to help the German Communist party and the new fusion party about to be organized? None of us knew the answers to these questions, so the only thing to do was to wait. We didn't have to wait long.

Before Kotikov arrived, we had nibbled at the question of political parties. At a meeting of the deputies on January 11, 1946, the formation of a political committee was discussed for the first time. The British especially were in favor of the idea, because they were swamped with petitions for the formation of new parties and no Kommandatura authority had been established to rule on them. Some of the parties proposed sounded really screwy. There was the Democratic party and the Republican party, the Sons of Liberty and the Half-Jew party.

The French agreed with us that a political committee was needed to screen petitions, otherwise we would be overwhelmed. But the minute you mention politics, the Russians get uneasy. They enjoyed the great advantage of having their own Communist party in existence, whereas, having no particular party we favored, we were leaving the Germans to work out their own salvation.

Preferring the *status quo*, the Russians opposed the political committee idea, arguing that recognition of new parties was beyond the scope of the Kommandatura and should be decided only by the Allied Control Authority. They obviously feared that such a committee might recognize an opposition party, potentially stronger than their own Commuist party. We did create a committee, purely and simply to handle local government problems, but political parties were eschewed. The question was duly interred for the time being, with no action taken either way.

At that meeting, I felt it incumbent upon me to expound American policy on German self-government involving, also, our attitude toward political parties. Once again, I collided with our allies from behind the Iron Curtain. Reflecting General Clay's attitude, which he had twice expressed to me verbally, I announced that it was American policy to tell the Germans only what they could *not* do, not what they could do, or how to do it.

To prove our confidence in such a policy, I also announced that our Military Government detachments were being withdrawn from the six boroughs in our sector, because I was convinced the local governments had shown their ability to function efficiently and according to our concept of the principles of democracy. Somewhat vehemently, the British announced they were not withdrawing their detachments. Their spokesman said the British believed the Germans were a long way from self-government.

As far as the French were concerned, my announcement was received for information only. Astonishingly, I found an ally in the Russians, who had done their best to wreck everything else I ever proposed.

This acquiescence dazed me momentarily because here, for perhaps the first time in Berlin, American and Russian political policies were in agreement, although our two systems of government were diametrically opposed. Then the truth flashed on me. We both wanted the same thing, but we wanted it for different reasons. American policy was to give the Germans self-government, so that eventually we could withdraw from Europe. The Russians, on the other hand, favored self-government so they could control the country successfully through the German Communist party.

As some wag described the situation: Russian policy was dominated by greed, British policy by fear, French policy by national honor, and American policy by the desire to go home.

The question of political parties came up again in mid-February. Colonel Dalada, the Russian deputy, accused the British of encouraging a clandestine party, the German *Buergerpartei,* which was distributing literature throughout the city attacking both Social Democrats and Communists. Dalada said the party was headed by a rabid economist named Herr Peshotka. To my embarrassment, it developed that the party's headquarters was smack in the middle of the American sector.

Dalada was joyfully smug over his discovery of a party I didn't even know existed. "The telephone number is 24131," he added helpfully. "Call up, and I'm sure Herr Peshotka will answer the phone."

I promised to investigate. I also promised that Herr Peshotka would be out of business that very afternoon, if it turned out he actually was operating in the American sector.

Sure enough, he answered the phone when I called and admitted his activities, although he said that he had requested permission of the British and of the four commandants to operate. We found Peshotka one of those combinations of genius and crackpot, the type that always gets into trouble. He offered a program of regulated land reform and other attractive democratic ideas but, since he was operating without proper authority, I closed his office, disconnected his telephone, confiscated his literature, and arrested him. After holding Peshotka for a short time, I let him go, after instructing him to go about organizing a legal political party.

The big fight over political parties started at the very first meeting of the Kommandatura that Kotikov attended. It was the longest, brawlingest, and perhaps the least productive of all our meetings. The usual two or three pages of minutes ran into eighteen pages, for the record.

Touching off the explosion was a letter from a group of Social Democrats, who had split from the Social Democrat party, requesting recognition. In April, 1946, the following parties were operating: the KPD (Communist party, later called the SED); the SPD (Social Democratic party); and two comparatively minor parties, the CDU (Christian Democratic Union) and the LDP (Liberal Democratic party). All of these parties had been in existence before the Western Allies entered the city and had been recognized by the Russian commander of Berlin.

These parties, however, had not been recognized by the Kommandatura. But we had to concede their legality, since we had short-sightedly signed away most of our legacy in Berlin at the very outset by agreeing to recognize and accept all former orders of the Russian military commander, the German administration, and the *Magistrat*, which included the existence of all political parties established under the Russian Army.

The difference between the Communists and the Social Democrats was not easy to see. The only apparent distinction was that one was dominated by Moscow and the other by the local product. At any rate, the central committees of the two parties had decided on a merger and the establishment of one big labor party, the SED (National Unity party), which was to be the single labor party for Germany.

Even while Kotikov was sliding into the Russian commandant's chair, Herr Otto Grotewohl and a small group of henchmen among the Social Democrats were working with Communist leaders like William Pieck, now head of the East German Red government, for a merger. This would result in the complete disappearance of the old party and the creation of a new one, which would be entirely Communist. Grotewohl appeared to be in a good spot to put over the merger, since he controlled the Social Democrats' central committee.

Unexpected developments upset these sinister plans. A number of Social Democrats had no desire whatever to hook up with the Communists, and Grotewohl was howled down when he advocated the merger at a mass meeting. The splinter group then asked the Kommandatura for permission to hold a referendum to ascertain how many members wanted to join the new Communist party.

Permission to hold the referendum was given and voting was set for Sunday, March 31. Although the Russians had agreed with the other powers on the referendum, probably believing the Communists were so strong they would win anyhow, they were taking no chances. When the polls opened in the Russian sector, they were closed an hour later by the Red Army, on the grounds that the organizers had failed to comply with certain mysterious "regulations" and also because of "unsatisfactory" answers given to the Russians regarding the referendum. The few SPD members who went to the polls in the Russian sector were turned away. Sensing certain defeat, Grotewohl diplomatically issued orders to party members to stay away from the polls in all sectors.

In the French, British, and American sectors, voting was held as scheduled. There was a huge turnout, approximately 75 per cent of registered SPD members flocking to the polls and inflicting a disastrous defeat on Grotewohl's Communist followers. Voting went approximately nineteen to two against the merger and, what's more, the alternative proposal, dealing with the desirability of working closely with the Communist party, was answered with an equally strong negative.

Obviously, the next move was up to the Germans. Our view was that politics was a German question and our interest was confined to safeguarding democratic processes. Grotewohl's crowd, employing elementary sophistry, tried to cast doubt on the value of the elections, going so far as to claim that all those who had stayed away from the polls were in favor of the merger.

More important to me than the voting results was the degree of individuality expressed by the Germans themselves. This independent referendum was the first positive proof that the Germans no longer were political sheep. Whether the merger was good or bad was beside the point. Even at the top level, the American view was divided on the question. But I considered it a healthy sign that a group of individuals, who disagreed with their leadership, should insist on expressing themselves against these leaders and what they considered a wrong policy, doing so on an open and democratic basis. Had the Germans shown such independence toward the Nazis, there would have been no World War II.

So we come to the letter from the newly organized SPD committee in Berlin. Having legally won the election, the new committee leaders requested recognition as the real leaders of the Social Democrat party and sought the support of the Kommandatura. They might just as well have saved themselves the trouble of writing.

Almost endless discussion followed. The British announced categorically that they would not recognize Grotewohl and his SED group as representing the Social Democrats. We were in favor of recognizing the new SPD group, also the SED, if the merger succeeded and their principles accorded with democratic ideas. The French went along with us, but the Russians torpedoed all action by consistently refusing even to discuss the matter of recognition for the SPD.

"Until all the ramifications and details are known, we cannot make a decision," was Kotikov's pronouncement. The real reason for this inaction was that the Russians knew, as well as we did, that another "spontaneous" move had been planned for the following Sunday to rush through a semblance of a merger, however flimsy.

The Russians are not bound by ordinary codes. The Social Democrat dissidents, who had rejected Communist dictatorship so decisively, lost by a low punch. The following Sunday, according to schedule, Grotewohl's followers held a "phony" convention, where certain handpicked SPD and KPD members went through the motions of voting for the merger. Thus the SED—a purely Communist party—was born in Berlin out of wedlock, with an official birthday on Easter Sunday.

The question of recognizing the new Social Democrat committee came up again at a later meeting of the Kommandatura. Resolutely declaring they had repudiated Grotewohl and his Communist followers, the SPD sought official approval of their status. Unfortunately, the evilly gestated SED had sent a letter to the same meeting, making a similar request for recognition. Every effort we made to keep the two issues separate was a rank failure.

Stealing our thunder, Kotikov spoke first and agreed with the American contention that we should recognize both the SED and the SPD, stay out of German internal affairs, and not worry about how these parties were formed. Both, the Russian announced without a blush, were democratic, antimilitaristic, and not unfriendly to the Allies.

Boiled down to the essence, what he wanted was a "horse deal": Russia wanted us first to recognize the SED. Later, we would discuss the SPD.

The French attitude, voiced by General Lançon, came as a surprise. Let's recognize the new party, he said, but have no illusions about it. Let's recognize it as the Communist party, with a new banner and some new recruits from the old Social Democrat party.

The American chairman, Major General R. W. Barker, made one more effort to isolate the two issues. Up jumped Kotikov, armed with a sheaf of notes, indignant surprise written all over his face. It was extremely revealing how insulting a Russian commandant could be. There also was an indication in his tone that, since France had a strong Communist vote at the time, which threatened to dominate the government, a wise French envoy would toe the Kremlin line when common problems were discussed.

"I am surprised that a representative of France should speak in this way," Kotikov said, "surely you are not aware of the policy of your government."

General Lançon was very calm and very firm. "That is quite possible," he replied to the angry Russian, speaking slowly and deliberately. "But, after all, I am the French representative, not you."

The French general refused to budge, no matter how viciously Kotikov assailed him. Fortified by an incessant flow of scribbled notes from his legion of political advisers, the Russian quoted the Potsdam Agreement, attacked Lançon's attitude as being inconsistent with French policy, and generally gave the impression that he had been stabbed in the back by France, upon whom he had counted to push through his views. He talked for hours on the rights of parties, the principles of democracy, Russia's major part in "liberating" Berlin, and other less relevant subjects in a Muscovite filibuster aimed at crushing all objections with the mere weight of words.

But Lançon held firm and saved the day. The other commandants soon caught on. I happened to know that just before the Kommandatura meeting, the French commandant had received instructions from the Quai d'Orsay to oppose the idea that the new SED would be the end of the SPD, or the KPD, and also to oppose the suggestion that the new party was a merger.

Leaning over to General Barker, I whispered, "General, I think Lançon knows something we don't. It's much bigger than we thought. I suggest that you better hold out with Lançon." But this advice was unnecessary. Barker already understood the French strategy.

Kotikov's mission to Berlin was becoming clearer. From the volume of notes he carried and his generally aggressive attitude, it was obvious he had been sent by Moscow with definite orders to get the new Communist party going to control Berlin and to harass the Western Allies.

His nervous habit of massaging each individual finger, when things went badly for him in the discussions, suggested that he was being haunted by the specter of failure—and its Russian aftermath.

With the exception of a thirty-minute break at lunchtime, obtained through my insistence, we discussed the recognition issue for nearly nine hours, to the point of physical exhaustion. Kotikov did most of the haranguing, Lançon the blocking, and Barker the responding. It finally was decided to refer the recognition of both parties to the Allied Control Authority.

I find in my diary for May, 1946, the following comment on that long, unpleasant meeting: "If this type of conference is to continue, we should recognize the failure of the Kommandatura and find some other method of handling Berlin." Unfortunately, that type of conference did continue. We were going downhill fast and couldn't put on the brakes.

That was the last meeting for General Barker as American member of the Kommandatura. All through that Russian Niagara of words his successor, Major General Frank A. Keating, had sat in the back row, patiently observing and perhaps inwardly commiserating with himself.

It was the custom of departing commandants to introduce their successors, topping off the announcement with a social interlude. Around four o'clock, I had slipped out of the meeting and ordered champagne, but as the hours dragged on I grew skeptical about having a love fest after such a battle. At the end of the meeting, I said to General Barker, "I've got the champagne on ice, if you still want to invite the commandants and their deputies to your office for the the announcement."

"Why do you want to bother with champagne?" he asked, rather snappishly, an understandable mood after such a day. The last few weeks had told on the American chairman. Because of a bad back, he sat at meetings in a padded chair, with a big green pillow behind him, but always started to squirm in acute discomfort after the first half hour.

"My God," I exclaimed, "we all need a drink. After this fight, you might just as well go out on a wave of bubbles, feeling good for once."

"Okay," he said, relieved. "I'll make the announcement."

Before he could do so, Kotikov, who had heard of the impending change, as he heard of everything, asked, "Isn't this your last day at the Kommandatura, General Barker?"

"Yes, it is," Barker replied. "I was just going to invite you all over to my office to introduce my successor and have a drink on it."

Trooping wearily into Barker's office, we uncorked the champagne and passed the glasses. Barker had once said to Kotikov, "We must get along in Berlin," and the Russian had replied vindictively, "I agree, but at every turn I find you blocking me." But at this farewell party, all was friendship and light. Even Kotikov, with a glass of champagne in his hand, was extremely complimentary.

A solution to the party-recognition problem was found some time later. Washing their hands of the issue, the Allied Control Authority referred the question back to the Kommandatura, whose members, displaying Solomonic impartiality, agreed to recognize both the new SED and the SPD splinter group, on a city-wide basis only. The wisdom of that decision was manifested afterward, when we pushed through the city elections. Had the Russians succeeded in obtaining recognition of the SED only, Communist administration of Berlin would have been consolidated and perpetuated, in the absence of a strong opposition party.

While the question of recognition was rocking the Kommandatura, the Western powers were considerably disturbed by another incident that threatened to undermine the democratic structure we were attempting to erect in Berlin. Using the language of modern detective literature, I might call it, "The Case of the Four Missing Judges." Actually, there were five, but since the Russians admitted they had snatched the fifth man and brazenly defended the act, there was no mystery attached to his disappearance. The case brought into sharp focus attempts of the Communists to extend their domination of the judiciary down to the lowest level, with the NKVD, successors to the OGPU, the Soviet secret police, taking charge of the bodies.

The four victims were members of the *Amtsgerichte,* and corresponded to municipal judges in an American city. The pattern of their disappearance was identical in each case. After dark, there was a tapping on the door of the judge's house. When his wife answered, a civilian, a German uniformed policeman, and occasionally a Russian soldier asked the judge to come to the local police station. That was the last ever seen or heard of him.

In this way, we lost a judge and so did the British. The others came from the Russian sector. Our judge, whose court was in Schoneberg, lived in a community outside Berlin. In his case, a German policeman and a civilian, who never spoke a word, called for him to go to local police headquarters at Teltow. Some hours later, a Russian officer and an enlisted man appeared at his home and asked his wife for clothing, shoes, and personal effects, volunteering the information that her husband would be away for some time.

It was impossible to avoid the conclusion that the four judges had been snatched by the NKVD, although we couldn't prove it. And it was useless protesting to the Russian military in Berlin, because they did not command the NKVD, which enjoyed mysterious extraterritorial powers. Control of this beyond-the-law unit was outside Berlin, far beyond local authority. The final judge of NKVD activities must have been the man in the Kremlin.

A letter from Dr. Loewenthal, president of the *Landericht,* which is the First Court of Appeals and is responsible for the *Amtsgerichte,* complained to the Kommandatura that he was having considerable difficulty getting municipal judges to serve because of this new terror.

In answer to that strange vacancy of expression on the faces of all the Russians when the case of the missing judges was brought up before the Kommandatura, the British played a trump they had up their sleeve.

After the four judges were arrested, some of the others fled to safety. One of them gave the British a complete report on NKVD activities. He charged that the Soviet secret police threatened that, unless he showed favoritism to their Communist friends, he too would vanish. They demanded that he act as a spy and make special reports to them. He was reluctant to obey and they threatened to arrest him immediately. The judge then cannily professed to change his mind, while the Russians hung around his house, and at the first opportunity made a break for the British sector, asking protection.

This story could have been pure invention. But at the next meeting of the Kommandatura the Russians admitted arresting a fifth man, Judge Brass, in their zone. The charges against him were that he impeded and opposed the desires of the Russian Army. This is what actually happened. Criminal charges had been preferred against the local chief of police, who was a Communist and stood well with the NKVD. When the Russians demanded that the case against him be dropped, Judge Brass, a courageous German, replied that that was not his interpretation of his judicial duty. Charges had been made against the police chief, substantiated by evidence. Therefore, the judge contended, it was his duty to go ahead and try the case on its merits.

He never did. Nothing further was ever heard of Brass or the four other judges. They were either shot, or sent to a living death in a Russian concentration camp.

The Kommandatura was helpless in this ghastly case, and eventually it went to the Control Council. There Zhukov, Clay, Montgomery, and Koenig passed the matter back to the Kommandatura, instructing us to set up an investigating committee. We did, naming some of our best men, but their report could only state that, in each case, the missing judge had been arrested illegally, by persons unknown. There was a long, bitter debate on the weakness of the findings, but we all admitted the utter impossibility of getting to the truth because of Russian deviousness. There was nothing to do but drop the matter entirely, though at least the investigation produced one salutary result. It slowed down illegal arrests in the Western sectors and put some curb on the formerly omnipotent NKVD, whose snatchings in the early period were almost a nightly occurrence.

Every time I directed a remark about the missing judges at the Russians, they came back at me with the Gustav Heinrich case. Heinrich, a German, was a food official in our sector and had been arrested on my authority. His arrest had nothing to do with the case of the missing judges. Suspected of being a former member of the Gestapo, he owned the ice-skating rink at the *Sportpalast*. He was a thorough scoundrel. A lot of food was disappearing in our sector and some of Heinrich's contracts with local dealers, which I examined, seemed very shady. I collected enough evidence against him to arrest him. To protect myself against charges of "illegal arrest," I made a complete report to the Kommandatura.

The Russians immediately launched a violent attack on me. Somewhere in his crooked career, Heinrich had become a Communist, and the Russians branded his arrest a political move. They also claimed it was part of our retaliation for the arrest of the four judges. From a simple matter, involving only casual discussions at deputies' meetings, Heinrich's arrest grew into a *cause célèbre*, and finally reached the highest deliberative body, the Control Council.

When this happened, I went to see General Kotikov and put my cards on the table. I wasn't so well acquainted with him at that time as I became later.

"This Heinrich is a fake and I don't see why you're making such a fuss about him," I said. "He's just a clever rascal and he's pulling your leg more than he pulled ours. Heinrich has been stealing food for a long time and, by making an issue of his arrest, he'll make you look damn silly in the end."

Kotikov took some minutes to think this over. The Heinrich case was one way of getting back at the Americans and he couldn't bring himself to abandon such a golden opportunity without suitable deliberation.

"I know I'll have trouble convicting him in any of our courts," I admitted. "The only sure way to get him is to do it outside the American sector. I realize that what I'm offering you could make it very embarrassing for me—and for the American authorities. But, in view of your squawk, if you want him, you can have him—plus all the evidence we have."

Kotikov assured me that he had no desire to embarrass me or the United States Army. That afternoon, I turned Heinrich loose and handed him over to the Russians. We heard no more of Gustav Heinrich—dead or alive.

At that time, I got my first blast of Russian press and radio denunciation, which increased in volume and vitriolic content as the years passed. A story in an American paper, garbled either in writing or in editing, gave the cue to the Moscow newspaper *Pravda* to charge the Americans with attempting to run Berlin and curb communism. Russia's own radio in Berlin added the charge that the Americans were encouraging "reactionary" forces in Germany.

Reduced to local newspaper levels, the attack was continued in the *Taegliche Rundschau,* a German-language newspaper licensed by the Russians and expressing the official Soviet view. This paper quoted as evidence the trial of two German Communists in the American court. Actually, the case was a very simple affair. In Schoneberg, we found an active branch of the Communist party, with a secretary issuing orders to members of the local borough administration. As a matter of fact, the majority of members of the Schoneberg administration were Communists.

Making sure that my action did not constitute an attack on the party, I authorized the arrest of ten members. Only two were held for trial. I was sure that the secretary's orders came from the central city party, yet I tried hard to keep the matter on a local basis. It was a "government within a government" and violated, on several counts, our first Military Government ordinance, posted over General Eisenhower's signature, when we took over the sector.

The two men were sentenced to five years' imprisonment each, for disrespect toward Allied authority, interfering with local officials carrying out Military Government orders, and intimidation of local officials. Subsequently, I recommended that the sentences be suspended because of great pressure from the State Department, which kept crying about the possible martyrdom of the culprits.

The attack in the Communist paper was a different matter. Written before the trial of the two Communists was completed, I considered it an attempt to protect the party against a propaganda trial, in addition to being a blast at me as an enemy of the Communist party and one who was taking steps to suppress it. This was a serious charge in view of the frequently repeated basis of American policy—neither for nor against any party.

I called on Colonel Dalada and made my protest pointed and forceful. It was inconceivable, I said, that within a year of the end of the war a German editor should attack one of Russia's allies, and that this attack should be permitted in a newspaper controlled by the Russians. I demanded the immediate punishment of the Russian officer responsible for allowing the article to appear, and also punishment of the German who wrote it.

Dalada was apologetic and promised an investigation. At the next meeting of the deputies, he informed me that those responsible had been punished—a statement I strongly doubted—but I let the matter drop.

Discussing the incident outside the conference room, Dalada let drop a curious remark. "You know, Colonel," he said, "I think the newspaper mistook you for the Commandant." I am still wondering what he meant. I was the deputy commandant.

German youth posed a problem upon which there was no meeting of Eastern and Western minds in 1946. Even today, the controversy has not been settled.

All the Kommandatura powers agreed there should be no revival of anything resembling the Hitler Jugend, the spawning ground of young Nazis. In its place, the Russians favored German participation in a national youth organization, directed by a central agency in Berlin, with branches throughout the country and emphasis on political indoctrination. As the Communist party controlled the Berlin political machine at the time, it didn't require great perspicacity to see that such an organization would simply be a means of producing young Communists.

In contrast to the Russian plan to teach German youth communism, we preferred to indoctrinate them with baseball. In each borough we established a Youth House, supervised by advisory committees of doctors, teachers, and others interested in the youth movement. Here young Germans could meet, read the books and magazines we provided, and discuss all subjects of common interest—except party politics.

Tied up with these Youth Houses was a big athletic program, whereby local youths could learn to play baseball, basketball, and football with the American troops. Over one hundred thousand German kids have taken part in these games in our sector. I consider the program the best thing we ever did in Berlin to sell young Germany on American ideas of democracy and fair play.

Our athletic program was challenged immediately by the Russians. They didn't understand what we were doing, or they didn't want to understand, and voiced the open suspicion that, under the guise of sports, we were giving German children military and political training. Never in my life had I heard anything so fatuous, and I told the Russians so.

Relenting a little, they said they really didn't mind the games themselves, but did object to the fact that American soldiers were instructing the kids. Kotikov was particularly suspicious. He was convinced that it was all an insidiously clever political maneuver on our part to pervert the children in our sector.

We explained to him, very carefully, why it was only logical that American soldiers should be the instructors. They were the only men in Berlin who understood the games and therefore were the only ones who could teach the young Germans. I also pointed out that many young Americans, sons of Army officers—like young Roger Booth, a seventeen-year-old—also were devoting their time to teaching German kids our games.

Kotikov was not entirely satisfied with my explanation. He still suspected that a Louisville Slugger was a political weapon.

At the next Kommandatura meeting, while Kotikov was still stewing, we invited him to attend a baseball game.

"If you ever saw one of these games," we assured him, "you'd be sure there is nothing militaristic or political about them."

Kotikov didn't make any motion of accepting our invitation and the British commandant, General E. P. Nares, lost his patience. "As far as I'm concerned," he said, "I know of nothing less political than a game of American baseball. It's a jolly good game, too."

Someone in the back row spoke up. "Put Kotikov in at short-stop," he said.

We supplied the Russian general with complete charts and statistics, showing how our athletic program worked, what equipment we supplied, and how it was used. He professed to be satisfied and so ended the great debate on the political implications of baseball.

CHAPTER VII

IN OCTOBER, 1946, the eyes of the whole world were focused on Berlin. For the first time in thirteen years, the people of Berlin were to hold free elections, denied them by the Hitler "*Ja*" procedure, to pass judgment on the government the Russians had given them since 1945, and to indicate what form of government they wanted and the officers they preferred to conduct the government. But there were even greater international implications. The result would indicate the German people's attitude toward the occupying forces—East versus West—even more than it would decide internal politics.

The elections proved a triumph for the burgeoning democratic movement in the German capital, but probably were the most fantastic ever held in Europe. Smarting under the defeat inflicted by the SPD (Social Democrats) on the SED (Communists) at the referendum, the Russians made no secret of their determination to get their men elected, by hook or by crook, because if they didn't, Communist control of the city would be lost forever.

Subterfuges, bribes, political chicanery, intimidation, all were used to induce Berliners to vote Red. The tricks the Russians concocted made other crooked political bosses look like Boy Scouts. The Russians wooed the voters with the ardor of passionate lovers. They offered bribes, not on the niggardly scale of politicians handing out cigars, but like victorious Caesars feting the Roman masses. Their bribes were city-wide, ranging from free notebooks for schoolchildren to food and electric power to stave off the extremes of the approaching bitter winter.

And when blandishments failed, the Russians wielded the big stick on their opponents, breaking up meetings, obstructing normal electioneering activities, and playing the role of political bullies and thugs. Their prodigious effort to stuff the ballot boxes with Red votes was exceeded only by the resounding defeat they received when a record vote again repudiated the Communist party and elected a representative government for the city.

A long battle, in and out of the Kommandatura, was fought before Berliners went to the polls on Sunday, October 20. The American point of view had been expressed months before. As early as March, I had brought up the question of municipal elections, after the local government committee had failed to obtain a date because the Russians employed delaying tactics, demanding a crippling amount of preliminary work instead of getting down to business.

"Early elections," General Clay had written me, and I repeated his words at the meeting, "are an American creed." The word "creed" was in capital letters, underlined in pencil.

I told the meeting we were not satisfied with the *Magistrat* and the existing administration and that it was our belief the Germans were ready for elections. I entered a plea for early elections, to avoid increasing friction. Many political activities, I pointed out, would be perfectly legitimate if members of the municipal body were elected by the people and not appointed by the Soviet Military Government.

The best way to prepare for the elections, I suggested, was not to plunge into a mass of preliminary detail, as the Russians wanted, but to set a date—at least a target date. I added that the Russians approved of specific timing, as indicated by their use of "five-year plans."

At that stage, the only decision we could make was to refer the elections back to the local government committee. Later, in April, the question was brought up again. Discussion on this occasion lasted for hours, and Major General Kotikov delivered the most audacious speech I ever heard at a Kommandatura meeting. It might be the American creed to hold early elections, but it certainly wasn't the Russian. Their creed was simple—don't risk losing control of Berlin.

Kotikov bobbed and weaved whenever we mentioned a possible date. It was his object to torpedo the proposal completely, or to delay the date so long that the elections would lose their appeal. The United States suggested the first of July, having in mind Austria, where national elections were held six weeks after the date was set. The British suggested the first of August, and the French favored any date three months after we had made our decision.

Kotikov refused to be pinned down to any date whatsoever. During the course of a long diatribe, he made a lot of enlightening comments on Russian policy. Any notion we might have had that there was a separation between the Soviet Army and the Communist party in Germany was dispelled, once and for all.

"Suppose I said Christmas," he suggested, ridiculing our efforts to agree on a date. "That way it might be too early—or it might be too late."

I didn't quite understand that crack, but he went on to declare that it was impossible to set a date because the Russians had no proof that the Germans were ready for the elections.

Berlin was the heart of Prussia, he pointed out with the triumph of a scientist discovering a new serum, and here the most rabid elements of fascism and militarism survived. Only after elections had been held throughout Germany should the Kommandatura set a date for Berlin, governed by experience gained in other parts of the country.

Swinging over to the type of government Berlin should have and the type of men who should fill the elective offices, Kotikov let it be known that it should be a labor government. His definition of the candidates to fill the offices was "workmen"—members of the Communist party. People of any importance in a syndicate, trust, or corporation should be excluded from public office.

"I don't want to see repeated in Berlin the experience of other parts of Europe," he said significantly, indicating that he had in mind Hungary, Rumania, and other Balkan states, where the Communists hadn't done so well in the elections.

On the whole, his speech was a frank exposé of Russia's desire to perpetuate control of Berlin. If it had been left to the wily Kotikov, there never would have been open elections. I am convinced that he felt the Communists would be defeated, even though his mission to Berlin was to see that they were not. Moscow had sent him to the German capital to save the day for the Communists, who were losing ground, and he knew it.

Sokolovsky, Kotikov's superior, was not so smart. The upshot of our meeting was that the matter was referred to the Allied Control Authority. The American chairman of the Kommandatura proposed a statement indicating that the three Western powers favored the elections, with Russia dissenting. Kotikov objected, and insisted on dictating another statement, which merely signified that he disagreed with the other three powers.

Sokolovsky thought the Communists so strongly entrenched that they must win. So certain was he of this victory, that when the ACA considered our report, with its dissenting Russian opinion, Sokolovsky overruled Kotikov and went along with the other three powers, casting his vote for the elections.

By July, we had completed a temporary constitution for the city. It was a brief but good document, entirely democratic, and from the legal point of view full of flaws. But it could be used until the elected representatives wrote their own, and would serve as a basis for the forthcoming elections. Kotikov demurred when the constitution came up for acceptance. It was clear that he didn't feel he had the authority to approve such an important document and was anxious to protect himself—understandable to anyone who knew the swiftness of Soviet retribution. Consequently, the constitution was sent to the ACA and was approved.

Kotikov might have been overruled by Sokolovsky, but neither he nor his gang had given up the fight. They were not surrendering so easily, not with plenty of valuable tricks up their sleeves. The period of comradely love in Berlin had passed; savage political war raged.

Without warning, the Russians announced that all fresh fruit and vegetables collected in the Soviet zone outside Berlin would be distributed exclusively in the Soviet sector, regardless of the needs of the three Western sectors. This move fooled nobody. With the elections in mind, the Russians planned to distribute food in their sector alone to show Berliners how much better conditions were there than under the Western powers.

A second move was to boost the stock of the SED, their Communist party. Leaders would approach the Russian authorities with the request that, in view of the failure of the Western powers to feed their sectors, the Russians bring in fruit and vegetables for all four sectors. The Russians would magnanimously accede to this request, at the same time announcing that they had taken this step in deference to the wishes of the SED, the party of the people, for the good of Berlin.

I protested publicly as soon as the order was issued and saw that my protest got full publicity in the German press. After our food committee had failed to reach an agreement with the Russians, I charged over to see Kotikov. He was furious when I exposed his little plot and told him exactly what I thought about it.

"Instead of being a hero for all the work I have done to bring vegetables into the Russian sector," he screeched, "you have made me look like a villain for keeping them from the other sectors."

Though I hadn't put it so bluntly, I was glad that he got my point so readily. Then I objected strenuously to his unilateral action, reminding him that any action regarding food was reserved for the Kommandatura.

"Two can play that game," I told him. "Suppose we take unilateral action to match yours. Would you object to my bringing in fresh oranges, lemons, and grapefruit from California for the American sector only?"

This proposition threw Kotikov and his advisers into a huddle. I didn't give them a chance to answer. I answered for them. "Of course you would object," I said. "If we started that sort of thing, it would simply mean that Russians and Americans are competing for the favor of Germans, who were killing us only a few months ago, and we would win."

Kotikov, once he was cornered, admitted the soundness of my argument. "Well, frankly, yes," he replied. "I realize that America could flood Europe with food, just as I must admit that we can't bring in any food at all from Russia."

Equitable sharing of Soviet zone produce was restored. As an election weapon, the Russian plot boomeranged. Instead of getting credit for trying to feed their sector better, the Russians got the blame when the news spread. On the other hand, American intervention created a favorable impression on the Germans.

The squeeze was applied later to electric power, but in a more subtle fashion. Two weeks before the elections, the Russians ordered the Lord Mayor to distribute imported power in the Russian sector only, allowing only a very small surplus to go to the other sectors. At that time, 50 per cent of all power used in Berlin was produced locally, the other 50 per cent coming over lines from Chernowitz, near Halle, in the Russian zone.

Power also was subject to quadripartite agreement and, although the Russians had some technical explanation for this action, it didn't deceive Berliners, not with the elections coming up so soon. The shortage was attributed to the Russian desire to make the Germans think geographically. Just another way of letting them know who was boss in Berlin.

At the Kommandatura, the Russians tried to shift the blame to the British, who were ninety thousand tons behind in coal deliveries. In return, the British blamed the Russians for breaking the agreement. The French said the difficulty was due to the shortage of cast-iron fire grates. Our view was that a plan for equalizing and regularizing the use of power, based on the city's needs, was necessary. Nobody mentioned one pertinent reason for the shortage, the dismantling by the Russians of the city's most modern power plant, formerly in the British sector, which was stripped before we reached Berlin.

We introduced a ration system in the American sector that brought squawks from the VIP's when their lights went out.

Other sectors rearranged their power schedules, and we compromised on a technical study of the situation after a top-level protest was made to the ACA. Once again, the power bribe failed to influence voters in the Russian sector.

During the heat of the pre-election campaign, Colonel Dalada, Kotikov's deputy, was removed. Why, we never discovered. Grapevine reports suggested his removal was caused by his relative friendliness toward the Americans. When a Russian official shows this tendency, he is usually yanked.

This certainly was the case with Lieutenant General Smirnov and Lieutenant General Nasov, whom we got to know as intimately as anyone could know a Russian. Nasov signed his own warrant when he openly praised American business methods. A week later, he was removed because of "terrible stomach wounds received during the war."

I was sorry to see Dalada go. He had been my favorite, and we frequently visited each other's houses. When he left, he broke all precedents by inviting me, my wife, and all the family over to dinner. Generally, when a Russian official leaves under these circumstances, there are no farewell parties.

Dalada had tried to be friendly. He was a strong man when it came to presenting the Russian view, but very fair, in so far as orders from higher headquarters permitted. He had considerable freedom in making decisions, since his loyalty was unquestioned. Dalada had fought in the early days of the Revolution with Chapayev, the Russian cavalry hero who became a Soviet legend.

But he was still a Russian—and a Communist. Once, after I had gone to Switzerland to participate in an international horse show and had fared rather badly with comparatively nondescript horses, Dalada asked how I had done.

"It was awful," I confessed. "I must have finished seventeenth in one event and perhaps twelfth in another."

This shook the very soul of Dalada, the horseman.

"Oh!" he said. "I'm glad I wasn't there to see it."

It never occurred to him that a man would enter a contest unless he was sure to win. In this attitude, he expressed to perfection a guiding Russian philosophy.

The Americans had intended to give Dalada a citation, but knowing Russian idiosyncracies and suspicions, I checked with Kotikov first, to see if it would be acceptable. Kotikov, wary as usual, said that I should wait. A week later, at two o'clock in the morning, an alcoholic voice came over the telephone. Kotikov had a message.

"Be of good cheer," he said. "Colonel Dalada will probably come back to Berlin and you can give him the citation later." I heard no more about Dalada and, though I sincerely hope that I am wrong, I doubt if the proferred American compliments did him any good.

Dalada's successor was Colonel Yelizarov, a big, powerful bruiser, who had married a sister-in-law of Lenin and had forthwith become the father of an astonishing sixteen-pound baby. Yelizarov was a political expert, having been Kotikov's political adviser, but always signed himself "Colonel of the Guards." He and I always kept one hand on the trigger, but each of us tried, as far as was compatible with our missions to Berlin, to get along with each other. We didn't get very far.

Yelizarov was more Russian than caviar. He seldom smiled and when he did smile it was like ice breaking up on the Yukon in spring. Yet he, too, was not a bad fellow outside the Kommandatura. Unfortunately, however, he was an enthusiastic hunter and his sense of sportsmanship was also alien. In fact, on one occasion it was dangerously so.

The British had invited us to hunt wild pigs with them in Spandau Forest. I was standing on a knoll with my rifle, ready to take my two alloted shots if and when the pigs came out. Yelizarov was standing back about thirty yards from the edge of the forest with his driver beside him, and the British were on the other side of me.

Suddenly there was a crash in the woods. Charging out of the forest, past Yelizarov, came about a dozen pigs. The Russian grabbed his rifle and fired twice. Then he whirled around, grabbed a tommy gun, and opened up. Astonished, I hit the dirt just as Yelizarov's driver opened up with his tommy gun. The British, I discovered later, were also frantically burying their heads in leaves to escape the Russian fusillade.

When the bombardment had died down, Yelizarov had killed five pigs and wounded several others. We never got a shot. The British were especially outraged.

"The blighter!" one of them fumed. "He shot more than twice."

"Hell, no," an American said sourly. "He only shot twice. Two clips."

Yelizarov assumed his new job right in the middle of the election campaign, when the Communists were putting the heat on the electorate. In addition to rallies and meetings, newspaper articles and radio addresses, the Reds neglected no form of approach, even the German version of political baby kissing. Quite a few pre-election food parties were held at SED headquarters, supplies coming from our stocks. At the schools, they distributed cakes, cookies, and notebooks "with the compliments of the SED."

The notebooks carried this paragraph on the first page: "This paper is being given to you, dear children, rather than being used for propaganda purposes, because we know of your great need for notebook paper. Study hard and diligently, dear children, so that you may please your parents."

The British deputy, Brigadier Hinde, made a strong protest at the Kommandatura against this alleged pollution of children's minds. While I objected on principle to propagandizing kids and left the matter to the education committee to study, I did not think the notebooks would upset the world.

As October 20 approached, the campaign grew hotter. All Russian-licensed papers conducted a frantic campaign to discredit the Western powers, rather than to explain the issues. For one thing, the Americans were accused of taking reparations out of current production in the American zone, a brazen lie spread to cover the fact the Russians were taking 80 per cent of consumer goods. The American-licensed papers couldn't reply in kind; we had no countervoice. We were playing ball with them, maintaining the farce of a united Allied front. I called Kotikov's attention to the worst of these attacks, but obtained little satisfaction.

Foiled in their bribery efforts, the Russians switched over to plain thuggery to hamstring the SPD (Social Democrats) and prevent them from getting organized. In our sector, we treated all parties with impartiality and accorded equal facilities to all, allowing them to establish their headquarters in each borough. So did the French and British, although it was generally known that the British were almost openly supporting the SPD.

In the Russian sector, every conceivable trick to block SPD organization and prevent meetings was employed, a technique borrowed from election experiences in many communities in other parts of the Russian zone, where the SPD was not even permitted to present a ticket.

In a letter of complaint to the Kommandatura, SPD officials quoted examples of their futile attempts to organize in the Russian sector, where more than a million Berliners lived.

When the SPD asked permission to hold meetings, the Russians demanded that all speeches be presented to them in advance, in both German and Russian. When the copies were presented, the Russians objected to some of the speakers on security grounds, giving no details. Halls selected for meetings suddenly became unavailable. Using the time element to create confusion, the Russians would cancel meetings a few minutes before they were scheduled to open. Local borough committees were banned and, on the whole, such tactics made SPD members look foolish in the eyes of the Germans in the Russian sector.

Unwittingly, the Western members of the Kommandatura, through lack of information and a distorted presentation of the facts by the Russians, helped slap down the SPD when the letter of protest came before the meeting. I was absent that day. Accepting as fact Kotikov's assertion that equal rights were given all parties in the Russian sector, the meeting rejected the SPD complaints as unfounded and ruled that the letter clearly admitted infringement of the campaign rules laid down by the commandants.

Kotikov and the other Russians were jubilant. Not being fully informed on the subject, the Western commandants had committed a terrific blunder.

The answer came as a great shock to the SPD and encouraged

the Russians to redouble their hamstringing efforts. American and British local government officers, who had correctly advised the SPD to protest, lost plenty of face and harassed party leaders were set back on their haunches at a very critical time, when they were struggling to get the party reorganized, after losing their former leaders to the Communist party. Even our State Department was upset by the turn of events, although the setback was overcome in the long run. The incident again proved the folly of a commandant or deputy locking horns with the Russians at the Kommandatura without being prepared for the fight.

A system of Allied observers was approved to supervise the elections and check any irregularities. This was one of the few great victories for Allied co-operation, and twenty four-man teams toured Berlin with complete freedom of movement, something that had never happened before. The arrangement was marred by only one regrettable incident, when a Russian guard shot an American civilian observer.

In the Western sectors, pre-election activity was intense, businesslike, and quiet. Voters were perfectly aware of the issues involved and speakers were incisive in repartee. I recall one meeting in Tempelhof, which was addressed by a man called Alex Swolinsky, who looked like a grocery clerk without his apron, but was very earthy. He was one of the SPD's most outspoken speakers against the Communists.

While he was talking, he was heckled by a Communist, who asked, "What about the western boundaries of Germany and the Ruhr?" A slap at the Western powers.

Swolinsky stopped short and then retorted, "I hadn't intended speaking about boundaries, but if this gentleman wants me to do so, I might be willing to discuss the question he has raised. However, I hope that he isn't so stiff-necked that, while he's screaming about our western boundaries, he's unable to speak about the territory taken from Germany on our eastern boundaries."

"You'll have to go and talk to the Russians about that!" the heckler shouted.

Happily, Swolinsky pounced. "You and your party can do

the talking to the Russians," he said. "Most of you speak better Russian than I do!"

The Soviet sector was frantic. I went over one day and you'd think that every house was packed with Communists. The entire sector reminded me of a newsreel version of the Red Square celebrating the October Revolution, with Red banners and huge slogans strung across the streets. The Communist propaganda department must have been working all night to trim up that sector. Of course, that is good Communist technique. One man can tack up a thousand posters and, instinctively, you think there are thousands of sympathizers with the slogans. The vote showed the reverse to be true.

A last-minute hiatus threatened to disturb the delicate balance of this contentious situation. And I am quoting from notes of a Kommandatura meeting held at three o'clock in the morning. The elections were set for Sunday, October 20. At midnight the previous Friday, I was with friends at the Lakeside Club when I received an urgent telephone call from General Jean Ganeval, French commandant and current chairman, saying Kotikov was very excited about some phase of the elections and demanded a meeting at ten o'clock on Saturday morning.

The committee in charge of the elections had ruled that, to prevent fraud, voters should carry their ration cards to the polls for identification. General Ganeval said Kotikov thought this was a mistake, which also was my opinion. I suggested that Ganeval tell the Russian that, if anything was to be done, it should be done at once, because the ration-card order would be published in the next morning's papers and broadcast throughout the city.

The order came to be given because of an extraordinary discovery in the French sector. The voting list there contained 125,000 names, but 40,000 persons in one borough had received from two to five voting slips each! The election committee decided that, if voters were required to present their ration cards, duplicate voting would be impossible.

Our first reaction was that the Communists were tampering with the vote. Our commandant agreed it was a damn fool order about the ration cards, but it was too late to cancel it without confusion. I learned the Russians had already instructed the Lord Mayor to countermand the order and that this had been done in the Russian sector.

The problem was how to reach the voters, so that as few as possible would be turned away from the polls. Ganeval called a special meeting of the Kommandatura at three o'clock on Saturday morning. Kotikov hurried over, nervous and sweating profusely. The American commandant was not available, so I represented him. There was no doubt in my mind that Kotikov feared the ration-card order would knock out a large number of "phony" Communist votes. Ganeval also was concerned with these votes, which he assumed were scattered all over the city by this time. I imagine they were, too, because the SED had used every trick in the bag.

My opinion was that the confusion of recalling the ration-card order would do more harm than good to parties friendly to Western ideas of democracy. Kotikov claimed the order was illegal, and would thwart the purpose of a democratic election. What he said wasn't important, but it was important that he wasn't going to allow the order to apply in the Russian sector. It appeared that voters would carry their rations cards as identification in the three Western sectors, but not in the Russian.

The vital question at this frenzied dawn meeting was: Should we call off the elections, so that any frauds could be checked in advance of voting, or should we hold them on one basis or another, and do the challenging afterward? Uppermost in our minds was the certainty that we must not reveal to the Germans that the Allies—on the eve of the elections—were completely divided among themselves.

Finally, around four A.M., I pointed out that while we were talking, the newspapers were going to press. In a matter of minutes, we agreed to cancel the order, giving the *Magistrat* instructions to proclaim the fact. Not waiting for us, the Russian newspapers already had "killed" the order. The American and French newspapers had been held for a decision, and the "kill" order went out to them. The British thought their paper had already gone to press. The net result of newspaper action, plus radio plugging and an official announcement by the *Magistrat,* reduced the confusion to insignificance.

The extraordinary meeting ended at six A.M. Understandably, Kotikov was delighted. Ganeval's fears were dispelled; the British hadn't made a strong stand; and my opinion was that, although the ration-card order would have checked a few false votes, it would have done great harm to legitimate voters —an assumption that proved correct.

After such a strenuous night, a drink was more than welcome —even at six A.M. Gathered in the French chairman's office, I was surprised to find myself unusually popular with Kotikov, who did not try to disguise his satisfaction over gaining a tremendous victory, which he had not, over the Western powers.

"Someday I'm going to pick something where I can lick you," I said, obligingly playing up to his exuberance. "You always win."

Turning to the others, Kotikov announced spaciously, "Colonel Howley reminds me of the man who has another man down and is kicking him, but always claims the man he has down is winning the fight."

Berlin went to the polls. There was a record turnout, a far greater percentage than in any election I ever knew. The result is history: defeat of the Communists and a tremendous blow to Russian prestige and to the party they sponsored, the SED.

The results were as follows:

SPD	(Social Democrats)	48.7 per cent	63 seats
CDU	(Christian Democrats)	22.2 per cent	29 seats
SED	(Communists)	19.8 per cent	26 seats
LPD	(Liberal Democrats)	9.3 per cent	12 seats

The defeat of the SED was so crushing it was beyond challenge. The vote was actually smaller than the Communist party drew in Berlin before the rise of Hitler. Even in Russia's own sector, the SED got only 21 per cent of the votes.

After the elections, I saw Kotikov and the other Russians at the Kommandatura. They were downcast; it was as great a personal defeat in a campaign they had directed with such devious fervor as it was a party defeat. The Russians brought up the question of the elections, but we spared their feelings and made no comment on the landslide.

Kotikov reciprocated by opening the meeting with an inquest, enumerating a long list of alleged abuses. He mentioned incorrect appointment of officials and incorrect election lists, violations of the principle of the secret ballot and orders regarding pre-election campaigns, as well as illegal use of propaganda at the polling stations.

The emphasis he placed upon these incidents led me to wonder what the final verdict would be in reporting the fiasco to Moscow. Not unexpectedly, Kotikov made no mention of the flagrant Russian transgressions, brought into the open at the Kommandatura.

He next asked for the views of his colleagues, a procedure so proper that it was amusing—in view of the general political hijacking that had gone on in the Russian sector. The British and French commandants expressed their satisfaction at the course of the elections, adding a word of commendation for the inspection teams. As acting American commandant, I replied in a similar vein, speaking warmly of Allied co-operation. It had been a model election and would compare favorably with elections in countries more accustomed to democratic procedure than Germany.

I pointed out that, though a week had elapsed since the elections, not a single complaint had been made by any central political party organization concerning either irregularities or results. I made the American stand as strong as possible, in the hope of discouraging any unfavorable comment from Kotikov, who still had not expressed his views on the results of the elections. I sat down and waited.

Surprisingly, the storm failed to break. Again, Comrade Kotikov was very correct. "I agree with my colleagues in noting the results of the elections," he said. "Before we close the meeting, I wish to commend the local government committees and the inspection teams for a job well done."

The defeat of the Russians and their party was due to a combination of circumstances. In reality it was a vote for the West against the East—the East being represented by the Russian-sponsored SED, and the West by all other parties considered friendly toward the three Western powers. The conduct of the raping, looting, and murdering Russian Army in Berlin had reacted against all Communists in the minds of the voters; the party, in spite of bribery, fraudulent voting, and intimidation, lost ground. Instead of the SED combining the Communist party with the best elements of the Socialist party, it was simply the old Communist gang, with a few Social Democrat renegades.

The official American view on German politics was that we favored no party and stood against no party, but only a fool would suggest that the United States could be indifferent to a Communist victory in Berlin. Before the elections, I definitely fought against the SED with my own secret weapon, which I called "aggressive neutrality." We had installed our own radio station in order to have a free voice in the city. We authorized an afternoon paper, *Der Abend,* and supplied it with sufficient paper for a circulation of a hundred thousand. We increased the circulation of *Der Taggesspiegel,* another of our newspapers, to four hundred thousand, saw to it that Western, particularly American, ideas were expressed and expressed forcefully.

American tactics are successful tactics, and there's nothing like neutrality when applied aggressively. The trick was to find the weakness of the Communists and the SED. Once that was accomplished, the rest was simple. The weakness was that their whole structure was based on falsehood, intimidation, and phony Utopian promises. The formation of the SED as a spontaneous amalgamation of two great labor parties was false. It was an artificially created *coup,* to present the SED as representative of the people against reactionary elements. This, in itself, was a lie. The SED does not exclude Nazis from membership. In the Russian sector of Berlin today, 142 Nazis who were fired from the American sector are in Russian official employ.

One of the lies—it could, perhaps, have been extremely wishful thinking—spread by Colonel Sergei Tulpanov, the Russian political commissar, in a clumsy effort to align the German clergy with the SED, was that the Americans would be out of

Berlin two months after the elections, which, he also stated, would prove a complete repudiation of American policy in Berlin. From this lie, which I traced to a conversation with Bishop Dibelius, developed rumors of alarming proportions.

I was besieged by terrified Germans, who remembered only too well the early days, when the Russian Army controlled Berlin and not even a cheap wrist watch was safe on a girl's arm. They were appalled by the suggestion that the days of "Com Frau" might return.

During the entire course of my campaign, I never directly corrected a rumor detrimental to the United States. Instead, I issued a positive release on the subject, which shed light on the falsehood. In this case, I told the Berlin press that the United States was not withdrawing, that we were staying in Berlin and would stay there twenty years, if necessary, to help them along the road to democracy. I told them we were in favor of turning government control back to the Germans as fast as they were prepared to handle it, and that we were shipping into Berlin sixty million dollars' worth of food a year to feed the city. That alone should show that we were not quitting.

Whether my frank approach to the people, through the press, killed the rumor I cannot say, but the evil chatter died down. On the day of the elections, not a single word detrimental to the United States was circulated, in strong contrast to the early spring, when the Russian rumor mill was at white heat, grinding out lies so vicious and so numerous that our prestige stood at low-water mark.

CHAPTER VIII

HARDLY had the excitement of the elections died away when another Russian crisis rocked Berlin, causing considerable public alarm and producing strong protests from nearly every political party and public organization. All evidence showed that the move producing the crisis had been planned for some time, but the Russians had postponed action until after the elections for fear of arousing public opinion and losing votes. Now that the Communists had been defeated, the Russians moved swiftly.

On the night following the elections—October 21—the homes of German technicians in the Russian sector were visited by Russian secret police, accompanied by German interpreters. When they answered the door, the technicians were given two minutes to make a fateful decision: whether or not to take their families with them to Russia. Naturally, there was no question if the technicians themselves would go. That was all arranged. However, if they indicated they wanted to take their families, the Russians gave them two hours to get ready. If they chose to leave their families behind, they departed at once.

As far as I know, there is no evidence that these German technicians were atomic experts, although a number of them were experts in the field of electronics. They were employed in a Russian electrical factory, making everything from vacuum cleaners to radar detecting devices. More than a year before, the Russians had thoughtfully assembled the best technicians in Berlin under one "roof" by offering them better rations and better houses in the Russian sector. Some of them had signed contracts to work in the USSR, but whether they were forced to sign the contracts is not known. I have my own opinion, however.

In any case, by daybreak on October 22, over four hundred of them had been spirited out of Berlin. The Russians moved them in trucks to a railroad station in the Soviet sector, household goods and everything, and shipped them off to Russia that same night. The technicians went in special passenger trains and their furniture in special freight trains, waiting for them at the station. Several "deserted" during a stop at Frankfurt-on-Oder and reported later they had been put on the train and given an excellent meal. Then, as the train sped eastward, they were handed contracts to sign. I say it grudgingly, but Operation Technical must have been a model police operation. No fuss, no noise, no bother.

Three days later, at a meeting of the Kommandatura, the British protested strongly against the action as a violation of basic human rights. Unfortunately, General Keating, who was then the American commandant, was in a sticky spot. In the early days of the occupation, we ourselves had taken a number of German scientists and technicians to the United States, and we were hardly in a strong position to condemn the Russian action without knowing more about it.

Moreover, the men involved lived in the Russian sector. If they had come from other sectors, we could have challenged the Russians. As it was, some of the technicians had signed up to go to Russia and the majority were in no position to tell us whether or not they had been forcibly taken—at that moment being on trains speeding toward Moscow. So far as we knew, not a single man had put up physical resistance. They certainly had not been dragged through the streets by the hair, or driven at the point of bayonets. Actually, there was no proof that force had been used at all, although the way the decision was put to them clearly constituted *force majeure*. Some even had moved voluntarily into the Russian sector, simply swallowing the Soviet bait.

Keating therefore requested "more information" of the Russians, although he associated himself in principle with the British protest. Kotikov said he had no more information, that all he knew was what he read in the newspapers—unconsciously quoting Will Rogers.

"What newspapers?" we asked with interest.

Kotikov demurred. Finally he said *Taegliche Rundschau,* the voice of Moscow in Berlin. The Russians had always insisted it was a Red Army newspaper, though, curiously, it was printed in German. In any case, the *Taegliche Rundschau* had published a routine article saying that a number of German technicians had signed contracts to work in Russia, where living conditions were better.

We got nowhere at the Kommandatura, and eventually the subject was referred to the Allied Control Council. There it was dropped like a hot rock when Russians unexpectedly turned on the Americans and British, accusing us of removing technicians under similar circumstances. The Russian general silenced demands for further information by saying bluntly, "I am not asking the Americans and British at what hour of the day or night they took their technicians. Why are you so concerned about the hour at which I took mine?" Unfortunately, nobody could think of a reasonable answer. The Germans who had gone to America had gone voluntarily, but the Russians claimed their technicians had gone voluntarily, too.

It was Kotikov, as usual, who provided the sequel. Several weeks after the British protest at the Kommandatura, Kotikov invited the political leaders of Berlin, with the exception of the Social Democrats, to his headquarters in the Soviet sector. There they found the Russian general sitting on a platform at one end of the room. Facing him, with his back to the "audience," was a German technician.

"Are you sure you want to go to Russia to work at your profession?" Kotikov asked him.

"*Jawohl,*" the technician replied.

"Why do you want to go to Russia?"

"Because in Russia I will have wonderful equipment and an opportunity to perfect my science."

"Aren't you afraid the Russians will chop your hands and feet off?"

"No. That's reactionary press talk."

Kotikov rose and smiled triumphantly. The political leaders filed silently out of the room. A few hours later, one of them came to my office and gave me an account of the meeting.

"What was your reaction?" I asked him.

"We could hardly keep from laughing," he said.

I do not consider myself an infallible prognosticator. Yet, in view of the State Department's apparent reluctance to recognize what was happening, I feel compelled to refer to an entry in my diary, made in late October, 1946.

"The whole thing," I noted, "reminds me of the tragic foreign policy of Russia, which has . . . so conclusively proved their immaturity diplomatically and their unpreparedness for the role which has been thrust upon them in international affairs. They have, in less than two years, converted the American admiration and love, which was built up during the war by their magnificent resistance, to a hatred of their stubborn, uncompromising greed.

"They have caused American policy to turn toward a soft peace for Germany instead of a hard peace. This in itself has divided the Western Allies. The French feel that they have been sold down the river; the British, who are depending economically more and more on us, have had to go along with the American view. Russia can be blamed for the tragedies which are going to follow from our having lost the peace."

The defeat of the Communists at the polls weighed heavily on the Russians. They were morose and took the voters' rebuff personally, absenting themselves from Allied cocktail parties and other social functions. The screws on the iron collar with which they had tried to strangle Berlin were coming loose. It was obvious they had to find a new way of imposing their will.

For two weeks, the Russians lay low, assessing the situation. Then they realized that it wasn't so bad as it first appeared. Although the elections had named the top city officials, they still had all the machinery of government in their hands through their appointed Red stooges. Here was a weapon they could use to obstruct the smooth functioning of the government machine and drive out the elected officials.

At the end of November, the new City Assembly was thrown

into consternation by an order from Kotikov, notifying the solons that no member of the *Magistrat* could take his position in the city government without prior approval of the Kommandatura, and no changes could be made in the *Magistrat* organization without such approval. Kotikov had issued this order unilaterally, being chairman at the time.

The City Assembly was in a dither and called an emergency meeting to discuss the predicament. Their assumption was that, according to the constitution, when they elected members of the *Magistrat* these members took office immediately. They could be removed by a unanimous vote of the Kommandatura, but it was not necessary to have a prior unanimous vote in order to be seated.

It was clear from the start what the Russians were aiming at —retention of their unilateral control by use of the veto of elected officials. Kotikov started another long filibuster at the Kommandatura to confuse us, discoursing on abstruse constitutional interpretations, but I brought him back to the point. He was furious.

I told him that he was not empowered to issue such an order and, furthermore, I considered it another attempt to rob the people of Berlin of the limited degree of self-government accorded by the elections. According to his interpretation, any commandant could prevent a duly elected official from taking office, without even bothering to give a reason. The City Assembly would then be reduced to the status of an advisory body, not a democratically elected council.

After the meeting, I took care that the City Assembly fully understood the American view. That body therefore voted that the new *Magistrat* should be seated and forthwith ran into the first obstacle. Acting on Russian instructions, Lord Mayor Dr. Werner, head of the *Magistrat*, refused to vacate office. The newly elected Lord Mayor was Dr. Otto Ostrowski, a Social Democrat, and former mayor of Wilmersdorf. Werner sent a message that if Ostrowski attempted to enter the City Government Building, he would be thrown out.

If we failed to break this impasse, confusion in the city would reach the danger point, also bringing into the open—before all the Germans—the fight between the so-called Allies. We could do nothing physical to help the newly elected officials, not even protect them from the goon squads and rabid Communist mobs rounded up by the Russians and trucked to the City Government Building to beat up Social Democrats. The City Government, the *Magistrat,* and the Assembly Hall were all in the Soviet sector.

The best we could do was to compromise, evolving a plan to allow the old, appointed *Magistrat* to "resign," in exchange for supporting the Russian objection to three new members. The main question was referred to the ACA for decision—a long, dilatory process, which wasn't completed for months.

Meanwhile, the Russians firmly refused to relax control of the city's institutions. Two months after the elections, the new government was still unseated, the Russians refusing to permit it to take office in their sector while maintaining the old SED-dominated administration on the grounds that they were still "investigating" certain of the elected candidates, who would be permitted to take office only after they were approved.

That "investigation" device was a dilly. The way the Russians employed it, not only did it disrupt city machinery, but gave us a perpetual headache at the Kommandatura. The struggle continued until the blockade was imposed.

The procedure was to select a certain SPD official and, ignoring the fact that he had been legally elected by the voters, trump up a bunch of charges against him and then demand an investigation by the Kommandatura. If the man was removed, the Russians still had their own deputy. At one time, we had before us a dozen cases of democratic leaders out of favor with the Russians. I issued orders to American committeemen that no investigation for reprimand should be held without my approval.

When he brought another case before us, I told Kotikov straight out, "I won't agree to this investigation. You've got nine or ten going as it is. You're always having these investigations. As far as I can see, these men are doing a good job. You've never suggested we investigate one of your Communist officials."

I never minced words in referring to the SED, or to the Communists. The "certain party" camouflage, used by the milder British, was childlike diplomacy at these tough Berlin meetings.

My advice, based on long experience, was in one particularly unfortunate instance ignored on a higher level at the Kommandatura and, to our lasting shame, we pulled a colossal boner and walked right into one of those "investigation" traps baited by Kotikov, much to the General's surprise and joy.

A new American commandant, whose tenure was destined to be shortlived and whose name I prefer to omit on grounds of compassion, arrived in Berlin with virtually no equipment except a set of wondrous notions about what dandy fellows the Russians were. In practically no time at all, he had handed Kotikov the entire Berlin school system.

The Russians had already succeeded in dominating the educational system by placing Communists in all key positions except that of the head of education, held by Dr. Nestriepke. Nestriepke, although he was not a particularly smart politician and was in fact a good example of the absent-minded professor, alone opposed communization of the school system. It therefore was desirable, from Kotikov's point of view, to get rid of him eventually and to replace him with Wildangel, the deputy head of education and a completely reliable Russian tool.

As was customary with him, Kotikov had about a dozen duly elected non-Communist officials under attack at the time, including Nestriepke. Kotikov, however, was willing at this point to settle for a reprimand as the first step in pulling the rug out from under Nestriepke. I, however, had refused to reprimand Nestriepke, although Kotikov insisted he was violating Kommandatura orders. This patently was not true.

The new American general arrived just about the time Kotikov was ready to drop the issue. The day before his first Kommandatura meeting, I briefed the new commandant on the situation. To my great distress, he refused to believe it was purely a Russian political maneuver. A State Department representative, who attended the briefing, also was inclined to scoff at the idea. The next morning, before the meeting, the new general questioned my head of education, who told him the same things I had told him. Later the education expert said that, for some reason, he could not make the General understand what he was driving at.

The French chairman, General Ganeval, opened the meeting by briefly summing up the situation. The British were next, but General Herbert, the British commandant, was also a new arrival, and admitted he wasn't well acquainted with the Berlin situation. He asked to hear his colleague's views.

The new American commandant lost no time in letting his opinion be known.

"I'm used to the Germans," he blustered. "I know them from the last war. They'll twist us and take advantage of us whenever they can. I propose we remove this man from office!"

If a thunderbolt had landed on the conference table, the effect could not have been more devastating. That an American official should recommend removal of an elected official, without trial, stunned me.

When I was able to speak, I leaned over and whispered to the Commandant, "My God, General, now we're really in hot water. You're green to what's been happening in Berlin for months. The Russians would have been contented with a reprimand, but you're firing the man without trial. What's even worse, the whole education system of Berlin now goes into the hands of the Communists."

Kotikov thanked the new American general very prettily and accepted his proposal that Nestriepke be removed. The French and British shrugged "yes" rather indifferently. The French representatives were frequently torn between their historic distaste for Germans and their temporal dislike for Russians. In this case it apparently didn't make much difference to them which way they voted. The new British general obviously didn't understand the situation. As for the Russians, Kotikov couldn't have been happier—or more surprised—if we had given him the state of Pennsylvania.

But even with this unexpected gift, the Russian wasn't satisfied. He wanted more. "I thank you all for your understanding," he said, "and now I propose we issue an official reprimand to Mr. Shafer, the American head of the education committee, who has been responsible for misleading us in this matter so long."

That was too much for me. A thunderous "no!" was the answer to that proposition. I wasn't going to see Paul Shafer, my officer, pilloried by the Russians for performing his duties. The matter was dropped.

The news of our blunder traveled quickly around Berlin and the alert American correspondents immediately demanded a press conference. Clay insisted that the new commandant face the newspapermen. We had pulled a Class A boner all right, but the job now was to save our skins with the press. Many of the permanent correspondents were well informed on the principles of Military Government and were out to get the American commandant. How well they succeeded! I've never seen a man's hide taken off with such ruthlessness and "hung on the barn door." Questions, sharp and pointed, shot from every direction and there were moments when I wanted to run and hide. After one particularly difficult series of questions, the General said desperately, "After all, I'm only human!"

To which one cynical correspondent in the front row retorted, "Ah, how true."

After the conference, some of the more mature correspondents apologized for the gadfly tactics of the others. The Nestriepke affair was caused by misplaced faith; the American commandant had too much confidence in his Russian opposite number. He was taken to the cleaners because he didn't know communism and didn't understand Russian tactics. This was one of the last sacrifices to the false god of Getting Along with the Russians.

Finding the Social Democrats were slowly insinuating their way into their elected positions, despite Communist obstruction, the Russians turned their big guns on the new lord mayor, Dr. Ostrowski. Not a man of great moral strength but a good politician, Ostrowski collided head on with Red opposition. He found the Communist machinery of government working against him and could make no headway, because he was powerless to remove a single appointed official. His first efforts to clean up the administration brought a sharp order from the Russians not to interfere.

As head of the winning party, his hands were tied. Although, with 48 per cent of the votes, the SPD had theoretical control of the city, in reality all they controlled were the *Magistrat,* comprising eighteen departments, the offices of the lord mayor, and some positions in the boroughs. All the other posts, down to the menial jobs, were filled by Communists, who held him in contempt.

"What I would like," he told me wistfully one day, "is a Kommandatura clarification of the term 'leading city official.' Here I am, elected lord mayor of Berlin, and when I enter the City Hall in the Russian sector, even the charwomen don't answer when I say good morning."

From the outset, the Russians did their best to discredit Ostrowski and the new *Magistrat,* hamstringing the elected government and robbing it of legislative independence. By cajolery or threat, they sought to undermine the resistance of the new officials and to win them over. In their "investigations," they descended to lurid depths in uncovering family skeletons and unsavory personal details.

The results of this new Russian policy were violent in the City Assembly, where the Social Democrats began to lose the cohesion that had carried the party to victory at the elections. Confusion replaced unity and members started to squabble among themselves. The Russians were anything but reticent about their suspicions of the new lord mayor.

"My name is Ostrowski," he said to me, "but the Russians say it ought to be Westrowski. As far as I'm concerned, I'd like to change it to Centrowski. That's where I stand."

But he wasn't strong enough to resist Russian pressure for long. A high Russian official, presumably Kotikov, warned him that he must stop opposing the Communists or he would lose his job.

Two or three nights a week, Ostrokski would be summoned to Soviet headquarters. One night the Russians would ply him with liquor, overwhelming the Lord Mayor with good fellow-ship. The next night, they would put out the welcome mat for sure and greet him with smiles, honeyed words, and tattered platitudes about the solidarity of labor. The third night would be another thing again—they would work him over in earnest, giving the unfortunate German one of those terrible mental third degrees, in which the NKVD boys are experts.

His private life was bared and he was threatened with exposure unless he conformed. One of the charges, which would damn him forever politically if it happened to be correct, was that he was a former Nazi sympathizer. Ostrowski denied this. During the war, he had divorced his wife, who was part Jewish. This act, said the Russians, showed that he had Nazi leanings and to the embittered Berlin mind of that period, it wouldn't take much emphasis to drive the charge home. The British authorities had investigated Ostrowski's background before he was elected lord mayor. His divorce seemed a personal affair to us, entirely unrelated to politics. But it showed how deep the Russians would dig for political pay dirt.

Ostrowski yielded and agreed to support the SED. At Russian insistence, he put it in writing. This rapprochement was effected without the knowledge of his party, the SPD, but when the news became public there were violent scenes in the City Assembly. The other SPD leaders attacked Ostrowski, calling him renegade and traitor. Ostrowski attempted to defend himself, pointing out that his term of office would expire the following February, and the only way to get any legislation passed in the few remaining months was to co-operate with the Communists.

In his defense, the SED leaders made long, windy speeches that only demonstrated how completely he was in their pocket. On April 11, 1947, his action was put to the vote and disavowed by eighty votes against twenty.

I called in both Ostrowski and the SPD leaders to hear their views first hand. Ostrowski defended his action and justified his co-operation with the Communists on the familiar grounds of expediency. Heatedly, the SPD leaders maintained they couldn't work too closely with the Communists for fear of being swallowed up in the process, only too well aware of the fate of the Socialist party in France. Their very existence depended upon continued resistance to Moscow's dictatorial plans and strategy.

I informed both sides that, as far as American policy was concerned, the election of the lord mayor was purely a matter for the German people, and that we had no intention of either defending Ostrowski or of supporting another candidate. The only conditions we made were that the lord mayor be competent and not a Nazi.

Faced with impeachment by his own Social Democratic party, Ostrowski resigned, and his resignation came before the next meeting of the Kommandatura. Ordinarily, this resignation would have been simply routine, but the Russians, who must have anticipated it, saw a new means of clinging to power and blocking further democratic encroachment on the Communist-monopolized city government.

Ostrowski had been told by the Russians they would accept his resignation, but I knew they wouldn't. And they didn't. Instead, they tried to exploit it as another bargaining point. The three Western commandants agreed to accept the resignation, leaving the City Assembly to choose his successor. Kotikov asked for time to "study the matter," garnishing the request with a four-hour harangue denouncing the SPD government.

We pointed out to Kotikov that it was a simple question. We had Ostrowski's letter of resignation, as well as a letter from the City Assembly announcing it. Therefore the Kommandatura had no right to refuse it. The Russian continued to be stubborn, attempting to raise constitutional objections, and finally, out of sheer courtesy to him—a phrase I'm sure he wouldn't appreciate—we agreed to postpone final action until the next special meeting.

Imagine our astonishment when the Russian-licensed newspapers appeared the next day with front-page stories repeating the attacks made by Kotikov at the meeting, and accusing the American commandant and the other Western powers of meddling in politics and of instigating Ostrowski's resignation. It was an entirely unwarranted lambasting of an elected government. The other charges were too ridiculous to worry about, except in their relation to the Germans.

Again I called in the press to let the German people know where we stood. I repeated that the election of a lord mayor was their business, not ours, and categorically denied we were involved in politics, as the Russians charged. I remarked caustically that there would be considerably less trouble in Berlin if another power did less mixing in politics. On the whole, I think the Russians realized they had made a mistake by that newspaper attack.

Although it was inevitable that they would have to accept Ostrowski's resignation sooner or later, the Russians continued to stall. Kotikov offered to bargain: he would accept the resignation on the condition that Ostrowski's successor be approved in advance by the Kommandatura or, in other words, that we hand the issue over to the mercy of Kotikov's veto. We absolutely refused to submit to this blackmail. You can't accept the principle of prior approval of a government or of legislation, where there exists the Russian veto. But Kotikov's offer again underlined Russian political technique. It is impossible to negotiate an agreement with them without strings, or without leaving the door open for further concessions.

From the Kommandatura, the question was forwarded to the co-ordinating authority, where the Russian proposal was rejected. From there, it went to the highest authority of all—the Allied Control Council—where General Clay, Marshal Sokolovsky, General Koenig, and General Sir Brian Robertson, the new British commander, studied it and, repudiating all lower-level decisions, agreed to accept Ostrowski's resignation but ruled that his successor would have to be approved in advance by the Kommandatura.

This decision got quite a reaction in the world press, the Russians praising the Control Council and the Western press declaring democracy had been "sold short." It was a great blow to me, because I had maintained consistently that the Russians would try to control Berlin's elected government by means of the veto, and there was no antidote except abolition of that power.

Dr. Ernst Reuter was nominated as the new lord mayor. The Russian press attacks, the stalling, the baffling little jigsaw pieces of intrigue scattered all over Berlin began to fit together. The Russians didn't want Reuter, and all their efforts had been directed toward obtaining prior veto power to prevent his election.

Dr. Reuter is a courageous political leader, a man of powerful intellect, and an experienced and capable municipal administrator. He is a man able to meet the SED leaders on their own ground, because he understands the devious workings of the Communist mind. In 1922, he was a member of the German Communist party and rose to eminence. Reuter conferred with Stalin and key men of the party in Moscow. Disillusioned, he rejected communism as a false philosophy, resigned from the party, and joined the Social Democrats.

When Hitler rose to power, Reuter was mayor of Madgeburg, and soon incurred the wrath of the Nazis for his outspoken criticism. He fled to Turkey during the war and remained there until the Nazi grip was broken. Returning to Berlin, he obtained a post in the *Magistrat*. Moscow never forgave Reuter for forsaking the Red cause. At the *Magistrat*, he was constantly under Russian pressure, which, in turn, was applied to the SPD on an intensified scale when they learned that Reuter was their candidate for the biggest job in Berlin.

These attacks definitely weakened the SPD, whose leaders were not permitted to answer back to an occupying power. After the first shock of the Russian offensive, they were inclined to consider nominating a less vigorous man than the Kremlin's arch enemy, in order to protect their position and safeguard the gains they had made in the City Government.

But Berliners were in no mood for another surrender. My statement that the American forces were not withdrawing, but would stay and continue to defend the German right to a democratic government, had a heartening effect. This new spirit emboldened the SPD to put forth Reuter's name, veto or no veto. Backing his nomination was the vote of the City Assembly, on June 24, 1947, electing him lord mayor by an overwhelming majority. He got 82 per cent of the votes, the remaining 18 going to the Communist opposition.

Three days later, the Russians applied the veto through Kotikov. The question again went up to the Control Council and back, with the decision attached that, in view of the Russian veto, Reuter could not be approved as the new lord mayor of the city of Berlin.

Politically, this period was a new low for American prestige. The Council's decision gave final proof—if any were needed— that appeasement of the Russians was futile. It proved that any government set up according to Moscow specifications could never be better than a puppet.

According to all democratic conceptions and to the definitely expressed preference of the City Assembly, Dr. Reuter should have been lord mayor, although by Control Council ruling— and Russian obstruction—he never could take his seat in the City Assembly.

Among the many able SPD leaders was Frau Louise Schroeder, who won the nomination as deputy lord mayor on the Reuter ticket, and was the first woman in Prussian history to be elected to such an office.

Frau Schroeder is one of the brave women of modern history. In the face of Russian threats and indignities, she was fearless. Unlike the caricatured weighty, dimpled German *hausfrau,* she was a tiny, gray-haired woman approaching her sixties, pleasant but firmly determined in character. In her younger days, she had been an energetic suffragist, not the belligerent Carrie Chapman Catt type but a woman who worked persuasively toward the goal. In 1932, Frau Schroeder was one of the first women members of the Reichstag and enjoyed an excellent reputation.

When Dr. Reuter was officially barred from office, the duties of Berlin's chief executive fell on the small but firm shoulders of Frau Schroeder, who became acting lord mayor, an office she continued to hold until December 7, 1948, when, in view of continued Russian obstruction, elections were authorized for West Berlin alone and Reuter again was elected.

This extraordinary woman had no qualms in attending to the

duties of her office in the Russian sector where, on occasion, the Reds used goon squads, and again brought in crowds of sympathizers in tanks and trucks to beat up Social Democrats right on the City Hall steps.

A typical case of goon-squad assault involved an SPD leader, who was stepping into his small car when a thug yelled, "Let's beat up the reactionary!" and slammed the door as he was entering, trapping the man and injuring his thigh.

Frau Leber, another member of the small group of women elected to the City Assembly, was badly beaten up and had to be sent to the hospital. Her husband was decapitated for his part in the disastrous summer *Putsch* of 1944, when an attempt was made to assassinate Hitler. In her husband's name alone, Frau Leber deserved better from her countrymen.

At first, Frau Schroeder was recognized by all the powers, including the Russians, as acting lord mayor and signed her name as such on official documents. The Russians eventually realized that, although they had blocked Reuter, this tiny, petticoated figure also was a symbol of the Social Democrats and that a woman was carrying out the program of the party. Accordingly, they withdrew recognition of Frau Schroeder as acting lord mayor and recognized her only as deputy. The rest of us accepted her as a substitute for Reuter.

She passed from sector to sector, keeping both her official dignity and her sense of humor. One day, when she called on me in the American sector, I asked how she managed to preserve her dual official status.

"Well, Colonel Howley," she explained with a smile, "I have two hats. When I go into the Russian sector, I wear my deputy lord mayor's hat. When I come to see you, I put on my acting lord mayor's hat."

I glanced at the becoming creation topping her gray hair. It didn't look like the impressive fore-and-aft headgear worn by the Lord Mayor of London, the only dressy civic dignitary I had ever seen.

"That doesn't look like a lord mayor's hat to me," I kidded.

"Oh, this," she answered, touching the hat lightly. "Well, it's my new bonnet. An American friend sent it to me from New York. Wasn't that kind?"

Although Frau Schroeder did her intelligent best to accommodate conflicting attitudes, official communication with the City Government grew hopelessly involved. We couldn't address anything to the Lord Mayor in the Russian sector, because the Russians always returned the communication with the explanation that no such official existed.

With this absurd difficulty in mind, I was very emphatic to Kotikov at the Kommandatura.

"If you want to abandon all Military Government, it's okay by me," I told him. "But if you want the Kommandatura to issue any orders at all to the City Government, you better find some way of doing it. You can send orders over there addressed to the City Government, to *Magistrat,* or anywhere you like, but let us get our orders over there."

Kotikov hemmed and hawed. He didn't want to sacrifice one iota of the advantage he had gained on the veto deal, but he was able to realize the futility of the situation. We got an agreement out of him to let us address all orders to the *Magistrat,* who would act as post office and determine their final destination.

In establishing a democratic basis for public organizations, we also had trouble with the FDBG, the over-all labor organization that had been established under Russian sponsorship before we arrived in Berlin. At Potsdam, the powers agreed to the principle of democratic trade unions. With the FDBG, we had no ordinary problem. It was a union of unions, combining the horizontal and vertical structures of the AF of L and the CIO. With a made-in-Moscow label, the FDBG operated from top to bottom, instead of the reverse, as we prefer in democratic organizations.

The union was completely dominated by Communists. Moscow-trained Jedretski and others on the executive committee also were key members of the executive committee of the Russian zonal organization, although an Allied Control Authority directive forbade the Berlin FDBG being a part of the Russian zonal plan. For some time we tried to obtain information about the FDBG, its constitution, its election procedure. According to the Kommandatura setup, even the Bird Fanciers' Association had to present their rules to us, but this huge labor organization, which claimed two hundred thousand members, defied the Kommandatura.

At meetings, Kotikov always put us off with the contention that the FDBG "isn't your business." This was pretty abrupt treatment, even for Kotikov, but it proved that the union was an organization obeying Communist orders. In the absence of any information, we were placed in the position of giving approval although we knew nothing about it. Just as the word "Allied" on Russian-printed invasion money gave that currency respectability, our apparent acquiescence gave recognition to the FDBG.

Our major insistence was on the principle of democratic election. The FDBG had held some sort of elections, but we never learned how they were conducted. Berlin had craft unions, such as the metal workers—the largest—garment workers, and transport workers, and we maintained that these should be represented individually on the executive committee of the FDBG. The Russian idea was the exact reverse. No union individuality was permitted; they preferred a fusion so inextricably organized that the "safe" men at the top controlled everything.

The time came for new elections, and the Kommandatura proposed that, of the thirty seats on the FDBG executive committee, eighteen should be elected directly by member trade unions and the other twelve elected at large. We thought this an equitable arrangement, representative of labor rights in general, not of one particular union. Back from the FDBG came another Russian circumvention procedure, accepting the proposed eighteen individual seats but increasing the committee to forty-five, thus permitting the "election" of twenty-seven members-at-large—that is to say, politically acceptable members —completely outvoting the democratic nucleus.

Even so, we were not unwilling to go along with the Russian proposal. We agreed to accept a committee of forty-five, provided we were told the basis upon which the members-at-large would be judged, and that a uniform system of delegates in ratio to members would be employed for the entire city. That was reasonable enough and actually involved our surrendering three of the points originally advanced. The meeting broke up with no agreement. Kotikov's decision was blunt. We had no right to interfere in the internal affairs of democratic institutions such as trade unions, he announced, and the FDBG would maintain the *status quo*.

Employing his favorite post-meeting weapon, Kotikov made an all-out attack in next morning's *Taegliche Rundschau* on the good will and intentions of the Western powers. That decided me. Again, I invited the press in, and while I did not answer any of his insults directly, or make derogatory remarks about the Russians, I carefully explained the American viewpoint on the question of trade unions and described exactly what had happened at the meeting.

Running my eyes over my press audience, I was astonished to find two extremely unnewspaperly-looking strangers, who identified themselves as SED committee members. Their names were Goering and Bernhardt. After the meeting, I took them to my office with my labor adviser, Major Abe Kramer. Both men said they were relieved to learn that I did not desire the abolition of the FDBG, as the Russians charged.

I explained that, if necessary, the Americans could be tough and dissolve the FDBG, but that we didn't desire to do so. I was confident, I added, that it was possible to reach another solution of the problem.

Up to that point, I had been diplomatic and even conciliatory. Then I gave them the works. I had learned that morning that the FDBG had called a special action meeting. Among the measures discussed was an attack on me as representative of "reactionary" Americans attempting to suppress a democratic organization. The proposed attack didn't worry me. By this time I had acquired crocodile-hide resistance to verbal barbs, tipped with Russian poison.

The second measure, however, did arouse me. To enforce their terms, the FDBG was prepared to go as far as calling a general strike. I got up firmly on my hind legs. "If the FDBG dares take such an unlawful action, we'll fight to the finish.

We won't starve," I told them. "We have all the food in the world and I can always bring in more." At this, the two emissaries shifted uneasily in their chairs.

"But we will keep that food for the American sector—only. There will be people dead in the streets. But they won't be Americans. They will be Germans. And I will hold you, and your organization, responsible for their murder. The margin between life and death on the present rations allowed you by your Russian masters is so small that you'll have thousands of deaths on your hands. That would kill your organization forever in the eyes of your people. Think it over!"

There was no general strike. The American conception received wide and favorable publicity. Leaders of the SPD came around to our view and started to show a little more stamina in resisting Communist demands.

And Panin, the Russian political adviser, quietly approached the French labor adviser to see if a compromise could be reached. The French had been least involved in the fight, though they supported the American and British view.

No compromise was possible on Russian terms, and important developments were taking place within labor ranks. A revolution broke up the central conference of the FDBG, held in the Russian sector, when for the first time individual unions were given a voice in proceedings. Sensing the trend of the meeting, the Communists denied seats to many delegates. At least 120, suspected of rebel tendencies, were shut out of the hall.

But this action was useless. There was an immediate split and from it emerged the UGO, an independent trade-union organization, which carried with it a large part of the FDBG membership and eventually replaced the Communist organization as the mouthpiece of Berlin labor. Basically, UGO came nearer our interpretation of the Potsdam decision on trade unions and so received our support. The British and French followed our lead and UGO became a recognized union in the Western sectors.

CHAPTER IX

ON DECEMBER 1, 1947, I officially became American commandant of the Allied Kommandatura, Berlin, ninth in the line of succession. With the exception of General Clay, who was still American military governor of Germany and commanding general of the American forces, I was the only top-rank official left of the group that originally entered the city after its fall, two and a half years before. During that period, key American personnel had changed three or four times more frequently than the Russian, whose leaders sagely believed in continuity of office.

Promotion from deputy to commandant took a long time. Change after change occurred among the commandants, but I remained director of the Office of Military Government of the U.S. Sector of Berlin, and deputy commandant. Military Government had been decimated. Our only continuity was a thin thread, based on a few old hands who remained to see the job through. Only eight of the original 150 experts were left, and none of the 180 specially trained enlisted men. I was still a colonel, although former commandants had the rank of major general.

There were times when I was ready to quit. I had consistently fought against appeasement of the Russians and against allowing the Communist party in Berlin preferential treatment. This attitude was not calculated to win me any popularity awards in certain milk-toast sections of the United States where, every time I touched a Russian, someone screamed. But it did help make many Americans realize that Communists are "until death" enemies.

During the months of September and October, 1947, I had

a series of five conferences with General Clay. While the conferences probably seemed unimportant to him as commanding general, they reaffirmed my own feeling that my thinking was in complete disagreement with American policy in Berlin and, logically, I could expect no personal advancement.

At the first conference with Clay, I was on the mat for having thrown a handful of Communists in jail overnight when they called a mass meeting in Kreuzberg without the approval of Military Government. They knew the rules, and I had the German police pick them up in a café before the crowd gathered. The next day the Russians protested.

My talk with Clay indicated that he was unaware that the original SHAEF order requiring advance approval of "meetings"—technically a gathering of three or more persons—was still in effect. Clay accused me of running a Gestapo city. I told him I wasn't and walked out.

Back at my office, I reviewed the facts and wrote the General confirming what I had told him at the conference. That letter probably was a bad idea, because I was called on the mat a second time and invited to go home if I couldn't follow the orders of the Commanding General. Naturally, I assured Clay that I could follow his orders, that I had followed them for more than two years, and that when I couldn't, I would be the first to request a release. The meeting was stormy but, as I was leaving, Clay said, "I want you to know, Frank, that I wouldn't call you up here if I didn't think the world of you." That made me feel better.

A couple of weeks later, I conferred with him again over a staff study I had drawn up dealing with steps to curb communism in Berlin. Because I think as I do, the first paragraph indicated the false premise on which Military Government was operating in Berlin. I pointed out that Russia was neither a friend nor an ally and further noted that the Communist party was not a democratic party.

Clay and I had another argument, most of the details of which I have forgotten, and I decided to go home to Philadelphia to learn more about our democracy at its historic source. I was fed up.

Two days before my departure, Clay called me in again and broke the ice by asking a routine question about a member of my political-affairs section. I answered, but he didn't appear to be listening. Apparently, he had something much more important on his mind.

When I got up to leave, he suddenly asked, "Frank, how would you like to come back on active duty as commandant?"

Clay can be irresistible. I did go to the United States, but three weeks later I was back in Berlin as commandant.

When I returned, the Kommandatura scene was unchanged. I will describe it. Outside the building four poles flew the American, British, French, and Russian flags. At the first meeting after my appointment as commandant, there was a British chairman, so the Union Jack was on the right. The flags rotated monthly with the chairmanship.

Inside the Kommandatura, the four commandants sat at a rectangular table, the British chairman at the head. On his right was the French representative, across the table the Russian, and next to him the American. Beside each commandant sat his deputy and his political adviser, and around the room were groups of experts, who either whispered suggestions to their chiefs or passed up notes.

In the building were smaller conference rooms, where the committees met to handle routine work, issue agreed orders directly to the Berlin government, and iron out details on disagreed orders or papers of great importance. These were sent to the deputies, who met twice a month in the main conference room and screened them for presentation to the commandants' meeting. When I was made commandant I appointed my former assistant, Colonel William T. Babcock, as my deputy.

In this plainly furnished room, more like a business executive's office than a council chamber as portentous in world implications as the Hall of Mirrors at Versailles, more international conferences have been held than in any other room in the world today. Since I attended the first meeting of the Kommandatura in July, 1945, I have engaged in more quadripartite discussions than any other American, living or dead.

To get through the mass of business, we developed a streamlined procedure that made the machinery of the Council of Foreign Ministers appear crude and amateurish. We were forced to reduce everything to bare essentials; otherwise we would have been swamped by bitter international wrangling.

Translation was time consuming but, of course, unavoidable. Behind the commandants stood the interpreters selected by the Kommandatura Chiefs of Staff to handle different parts of the discussion. When an American spoke, his remarks were translated into French by the interpreter behind the French commandant, and into Russian from French by the interpreter behind the Russian commandant. The Russian interpreter understood no English, but spoke excellent French and Russian.

Early in the proceedings, we learned to cut out individual translations. I understand French extremely well and often beat the French interpreter in telling the American commandant what the French general had to say. But I soon found this caused confusion, instead of clarification. It was better to wait for the official translation to come down the line. The delay gave the Commandant time to arrange his ideas for compression into the few sentences required. Each man spoke in short "takes," to facilitate translation.

The definitive American symbol "O.K." was accepted and used by all the powers, including the Russians. On the rare occasions when he did assent to a proposal, Kotikov's "hokay!" came booming across the table, although most of his decisions were confined to *"nyet!"*

During the debate and discussion, national psychology determined the manner in which ideas were expressed. The Americans were always practical. "Let's stop talking about theory and decide what we want to do, and how we want to do it," was our guiding motive. This attitude was aimed directly at the Russians, who talked for hours, to crush everybody else by weight of words, and then slyly attempted to slip in a new proposal.

The French were impersonal, applying to another's proposal the brilliant light of logic. The British, oddly enough—and this applied to the three commandants I knew—were the most emotional of the four. They made a fetish of fair play and honesty and were inclined to show great annoyance at anything smacking of twisted truth. Inevitably, the British were constantly annoyed by the Russians, who had no hesitation in twisting facts, figures, and even the words of their colleagues to suit their needs.

The flow of notes from advisers was like rivers flowing into a lake. I doubt if we could have lasted without those notes, suggesting, sometimes probing, and often shattering arguments. I recall a few notes passed at various meetings.

From a State Department representative: "If we accept Soviet paragraph 2, it seems to me we are forfeiting all possibility of objecting to the present law again, for the Soviets will never agree to any 'remarks' we might propose. Don't you agree this is a trap?"

From the chief of the American political branch: "Colonel, your introductory remarks were fine, but that last remark about the Soviet AG's was over the center field since Kotikov's face is red all the way up to his ears."

From another member of the American staff: "A political wisecrack concerning the activities of the Communist party being discussed by Kotikov would be to refer to the party's co-operation with the Nazis when Hitler came into power."

Not all our sessions were as straightforward as I have outlined. I can only wish they were!

After some months of scowling, following the Berlin elections, Kotikov began to smile again. It was an interesting development for two reasons. One was that Kotikov habitually smiled just before trying to hit you over the head, and the other was that his teeth had miraculously blossomed out in new caps and fillings.

The Russians had struck gold somewhere. In place of the stainless-steel dentistry to which they had previously been accustomed, more and more of them now appeared with German gold in their mouths. The Germans especially should have been comforted by this change, inasmuch as the *Wehrmacht*, at one point in the war, professed to be quite sure that the Russians sharpened their stainless-steel teeth with files in order to improve their biting.

I personally had never been bitten by a Russian, but I half-believed the *Wehrmacht* theory some months later when Kotikov presented the Kommandatura with a list of "crimes" that American soldiers had allegedly committed against the civil population of Berlin. It was the usual Russian smoke screen, except for one thing. As Kotikov went down the list, monotonously reciting the charges for more than an hour, he repeatedly referred to instances where soldiers had bitten old German ladies. Most of the cases were claimed to have originated in the British sector. One was supposed to involve two American soldiers who had broken into a house in Kurfuerstendamm, and attacked and bitten an old lady of sixty-two.

I couldn't believe I was hearing right, and by the time he had finished, I was almost helpless from sheer incredulity. His mustache bristling, the British commandant huffed over Kotikov's charges, saying they were ridiculous and entirely untrue. Moreover, it was none of Kotikov's business, because the British were fully capable of keeping order in their own sector.

Finally it was my turn to speak.

"Well," I began, "I am forty-five years old and I have never seen an American over five bite anybody. All of the ladies seem to be in their late sixties and American soldiers seem to like to bite old ladies over sixty."

As I spoke, the British and French commandants were having difficulty stifling their laughter, and Kotikov, sensing that something was wrong, was getting fidgety. After a hasty whispered conference with his colleagues, he shifted gears. He denied he had said "biting." His interpreter had not translated correctly. What he had meant was that American soldiers had been "beating" old ladies, not "biting" them. The story set all Berlin laughing.

Later, I sent one of my aides out during a recess to ask the interpreter, a rather pretty Russian girl, whether Kotikov had said "biting" or "beating."

"Biting," she said, snapping her white teeth to emphasize the point.

A sequel to this incident was provided when my aide called

at the interpreters' office some time later, on another matter, and looked around for the girl. She had been removed.

As the year 1947 drew to a close, relations between the Western powers and Russia deteriorated rapidly. Merging of the American and British zones in Germany into a single unit—Bizonia—for economic purposes, and our pooling of resources and imports had added fuel to Russian resentment. From all levels downward, from the Control Council through the Kommandatura, they attacked the move. The vehemence of these attacks proved how good the bizonal idea was.

Russia's economic plan in Germany was to control all industry, drawing off through spurious German corporations 80 per cent of all consumer goods. What industry they were unable to control, they disorganized to such an extent that no one else could benefit. Less than 5 per cent of consumer goods went to the West, but as Bizonia developed, a larger percentage went there.

Sokolovsky's attack in the Allied Control Council was shaped to fit the local situation. The British and Americans were accused of tying in their sectors with the Western bizonal areas. The Russians said this was a violation of the quadrilateral agreement. This was sheer nonsense because, in the first place, each sector always had been tied to its zone.

The first food agreement, signed on July 10, 1945, provided that each zone should supply food for its sector. No steps had been taken to place our sectors strictly under Bizonia. We simply invited German officials to visit Bizonia agencies to purchase food and consumer goods. Only half a dozen German officials from the *Magistrat* accepted the invitation, but at the time the Russians were leveling charges at us, 120 members of the city government were in the Russian zone, collecting food and making business arrangements. The whole purpose of the attack was to discredit Anglo-American economic measures, which we were forced to adopt bilaterally, because the Russians and the French refused to act with us on a quadripartite basis.

Passing months clearly indicated that, after their political defeat at the hands of the Berlin electorate, the Russians had determined on other ways of driving the Western powers out of the city. A cloud, faintly outlined on the horizon, was the blockade, but the full storm was yet to break. Meanwhile, they were probing and testing along other lines, and we were resisting. I will not enumerate the methods by which we started to assert ourselves, but in hundreds of small ways—and in some big ones, too—we stood up for what we thought was right and refused to play mat for Russian boot scraping.

At one point, in an obvious move to test our reaction to force, they sent several truckloads of soldiers to the German Railway Administration Building, the nerve center of rail operations in and out of Berlin. The building itself, while in the American sector, was occupied by Russian officers and men who ran the railroads, which were under Russian control by agreement. Now, however, they had posted armed sentries around the building.

We were taken by surprise. Nevertheless, I did not propose to allow armed Russian soldiers to parade around the American sector, waving guns in American faces. Accordingly, I laid a plan. The Russian guards usually arrived about eleven P.M. to take up their nocturnal stations around the Administration Building. Our plan was to send an American guard down around nine o'clock to turn them back when they arrived.

Shortly before nine, one of my men called in.

"We're here, all right," he said. "But so are the Russians. They came early tonight."

Obviously, they had learned of our plan either by tapping our telephones, which they did regularly, or from one of the innumerable spies they had planted in the American sector, including my own office. One afternoon not long before, I had addressed a staff meeting and by nightfall Kotikov had a full report on everything I said. This time he had outfoxed me, temporarily.

However, we deployed for action. We set up machine guns and the men lay on their bellies in the shadows, ready to turn back any more Russians who might show up. In the face of the machine guns, the Russian guard withdrew into the building, but before long three truckloads of Russian infantry drove up. The Russians insisted they were going to school in the building and we insisted they were not. The ones who were inside could come out, we said firmly, but no one on the outside could go in.

I had called General Clay meanwhile and had said I thought we ought to send more men and more machine guns, just in case. Clay was attending a West Point reunion party, but he was not feeling particularly sociable when it came to the Russians.

"Double the guard," he said.

The extra guard arrived promptly, with more machine guns. Just as promptly the Russian infantry withdrew. But there were still armed Russians inside the building. About one o'clock in the morning, Kotikov called.

"How is Mrs. Howley?" he asked sweetly.

"Fine," I said, becoming suspicious immediately. Kotikov always got excessively polite when he wanted something.

"By the way," he said finally, "an awkward situation has developed in our building."

"Your building?" I said.

"Well, the German Railway Administration Building," he said. "We thought you ought to know that American soldiers are down there and one of them has just stuck a tommy gun in General Petrov's stomach."

It later developed that Petrov, one of the Russian generals in charge of the railroads, had refused to identify himself when challenged by an American soldier.

"Well," I said, "I will certainly investigate the matter. I will call you in the morning."

"Oh, no!" Kotikov cried wildly. "Shooting may break out." He repeated it three times.

"Our soldiers are well disciplined," I said curtly. "I trust yours are, too." And I hung up.

Kotikov could realize a *fait accompli* faster than he would recognize his own mother. The Russian troops withdrew the next morning.

This was one of the major attempts to intimidate us, but Soviet secret police and their German agents were constantly pin-pricking Western patience and increasing German fears by snatching suspects from our sectors. Although Sokolovsky, from the authoritative heights of Russian command, announced that there would be no more snatching, the NKVD boys were busy at work again within a week. Hundreds of people disappeared, in spite of everything we could do. Kotikov admitted to me that four men had been taken on his own orders, and held incommunicado. His excuse that they were spies was very shallow.

Russian secret police and their German stool pigeons were everywhere. Little seeped through the net of espionage cast over the city. When NKVD agents were not busy snatching, I was bombarded with written requests for the surrender of persons, real or fictitious, they claimed were hiding in the American sector. Many of these requests were fabricated to put us off the scent and keep us preoccupied while the Russians were busy elsewhere.

From my files, I select just one case. Kotikov, through his deputy, Yelizarov, wrote me as follows:

> The Soviet Kommandatura has learned that the USSR citizen Dmitry Ivanovich Plaksin, born in 1920, who had committed a criminal offense, is a fugitive from justice hiding in the U.S. Sector of Berlin and is living at the home of Citizeness Uvanitzka, at No. 22 Siegfriedstrasse, Tempelhof.
>
> The accomplice in the crimes committed by Plaksin is the German woman Lizabeth Michalik, resident of the village Gross-Koeris, who, having abandoned her four small children, has also fled to the U.S. Sector and is hiding at the same address.
>
> I request that you issue an order to the effect that Plaksin and his accomplice, the German woman Michalik, who are hiding at the address indicated above, be turned over into the hands of Soviet justice.

As usual, Yelizarov signed himself dashingly, "Colonel of the Guards."

I suspected the case from the first. No specific means of identification were suggested in the letter, merely the names, and our efforts to find the persons mentioned were not successful. Or, to make it stronger, it was all a complete waste of time, because I am convinced the couple never existed.

Officially, I reported our findings to Kotikov:

Investigation shows that there has been no one at 22 Siegfried-strasse, Tempelhof, who fits the description of Plaksin, nor has there been any German woman fitting the description of Frau Michalik. Inquiry in the neighborhood indicates that neither of these persons is there.

The case was dropped.

The Russians weren't always so formal in their search for "criminals" in our sectors and I had to issue a public warning to residents of the American sector, telling them what to do in case of a kidnaping.

A car would run down a street, men in civilian clothes would jump out and grab their victim, then race over the Russian border. In one case, German agents looking for a certain woman on political charges first seized her sister in the Russian sector and got from her where the "criminal" could be found in our sector. They picked her up on the street, and her screams, as the car raced for Russian territory, were the last heard of her.

We arrested nine German police officers, most of them captains in civilian clothes, prowling around the American sector carrying pistols. The policemen said they were acting on Soviet instructions and were looking for a man they claimed was an enemy of Russia. Two were women, evidently intended to give a disarming civilian appearance to the mission. Under examination, the Germans—all Communists—admitted they had no intention of arresting the "enemy of Russia"; they were going to beat him to death with a hammer.

When their trial started, I received a letter from Kotikov frankly admitting he had sent them into our sector. He said they were innocent of any crime, having merely carried out his orders, and demanded that they be released to him. If they were tried, he added, he wanted the assurance that they would be given a fair trial. I wrote back saying I was shocked to obtain confirmation from him that, as the prisoners said, he had sent them into our sector. This action was a direct contravention of the agreement we had regarding arrests. I pointed out that he knew if he wanted the suspect, he could get him by contacting me, but not by sending his own goons into the American sector.

However, he could assure himself of a fair trial by sending an observer and selecting the defense lawyers.

Officially, no Russians appeared at the trial. According to our laws, it was difficult to prove conspiracy, but the nine were jailed for carrying arms.

Synchronized with such terrorist acts against Germans, the Russian radio and newspaper propaganda campaign was stepped up to fortissimo. The foulest abuse was heaped on the Western powers, especially the American Army.

A vicious pamphlet, titled "Gangsters at Work," was distributed throughout Berlin, slipped under doors and passed from hand to hand. Bearing the imprint of the Communist party, it purported to contain quotations from American newspapers, distorted according to Red technique to blackguard the American Army. We were all a bunch of thugs, said the pamphlet. As soon as I saw a copy, I instructed my Public Safety people to find out exactly who was behind its distribution.

Visits were made to two SED headquarters in our sector and, when the Public Safety men failed to obtain the desired information, they searched the premises and inspected the files. These visits were investigations, not raids.

The City Assembly was in session at the time and the Social Democrats were attacking the SED, demanding that a protest be sent to the Kommandatura against the snatchings taking place throughout the city. Frau Leber, out of hospital after her brutal beating, had delivered an excellent speech on the subject of habeas corpus and the right of the individual to freedom from illegal arrest, directing her remarks against the Russians.

Before a vote could be taken Maron, the former Red deputy lord mayor displaced by Frau Schroeder, now a City Assembly member, jumped to his feet and announced dramatically that a raid was taking place—at that very moment—against one of the democratic parties of the East. Savage American MP's with fixed bayonets were arresting workmen, breaking windows, and intimidating party members. The Assembly, moved by the Red's violent picture, accepted his version without investigation and unanimously voted a strong protest to the Kommandatura. There, the Russians lost no time in enlarging on the incident.

Before we had an opportunity to reply, the Russians and their Assembly stooge, Maron, had managed to hoodwink the other Assemblymen and confuse the real issue to such an extent that neither the Assembly nor the Kommandatura could take action against the Russians for their city-wide abductions. We had to drop the charges.

But I refused to drop the question of that infamous booklet, "Gangsters at Work." I conferred with Major General George P. Hays, deputy military governor, and he instructed me to summon the two city heads of the SED and challenge them with responsibility for publishing it. If they denied it, he instructed me to require that they announce the fact in the press. If they admitted authorship, I was to put them under arrest and try them under an appropriate Military Government directive. I saw Clay later, and he agreed with his deputy's suggestion, except for arresting them. Such action, he said, would make the two men appear as martyrs and would bring Russian retaliation.

The leaders, Litke and Mattern, obeyed my summons and I interviewed them singly, with only one American witness. They both admitted producing the booklet, which had been read by a committee of twelve before it was sent to the Russian commandant for approval. It was then printed in the Russian sector at Communist expense. Litke, a former Social Democrat who had bolted to the Communists, blatantly denied it was aimed at any Americans, military or civilian. Later he qualified his statement. If it was aimed at the Americans, he said, it was against reactionaries and imperialists, not fine American soldiers.

It was Saturday afternoon when I interviewed the pair, and few people were around. As a precaution, I stationed two armed guards in the next room, in case the Communists started something. Up to this point, the SED leaders apparently thought they had been very clever and would escape punishment. Then, flanked by my advisers, I told them my terms. On their own admission, I pointed out, they had violated directives issued by the occupying powers, specifically disobeyed at least three U.S. Military Government orders, and so were subject to immediate arrest and trial, with the prospect of a ten-year jail sentence.

After some verbal blasting, I said I would not arrest them but would send them back to party headquarters. I gave them three days to produce a satisfactory written explanation for the pamphlet. By noon on Tuesday, I had the letter. It was mild, saying much more between the lines than in the written context. The German and American press raised such a clamor that 150 attended the conference I called, at which I produced the letter and our explanation. I got it over, all right, that the real "Gangsters at Work" were the SED people, not the Americans.

By this time, the people of Berlin surely were the most propaganda-hardened in the world. Even if they had managed to survive Hitler's high-pressure machine during the war, the blasts they had received since must have deafened them, or turned them all into cynics. But the Russians didn't figure that way. Temporarily deserting their stupid campaign of American vilification, since their efforts had failed even to dent the city's skepticism, the Russians tried the old dodge of wooing the people into believing that their sector was a suburb of Paradise, by offering more food and vastly improved living conditions.

Without consulting the Kommandatura, whose case history is based on the original food agreement, modified from time to time, Kotikov issued an order announcing concessions for workers in the Russian sector. Under this order, 150,000 workers would receive a hot noonday meal. Employed housewives were promised a day off every month, pay was to be raised and, on the whole, an attractive working program was promised, discriminating against the other three sectors.

None of these measures deceived us. The free meal increased the workers' rations by 516 calories, bringing them up to 2,500 calories in many cases, but there was no altruism involved. The food bounty wasn't offered to alleviate suffering in the semistarvation categories, but to increase production, which had been falling off. The 150,000 workers affected were slaving either directly for the Russians, or indirectly for the 336 German firms manufacturing goods for Soviet export. It was just another step up in the Russian plan to regain economic and political control of Berlin and get the Western powers out.

We had tried for a long time at the Kommandatura to increase rations in the city, but had never been able to agree because the Russians always quoted the iron-clad Moscow ration. By unilaterally boosting food in their sector and adopting the role of the city's best friend, the Russians had stolen a march on us and placed the Western powers in the awkward position of apparently standing in the way of more food for Berlin.

Before the next Kommandatura meeting, I conferred with General Ganeval and General Herbert to discuss countermeasures. We could increase pay on a city-wide basis, adopt the new Soviet principle of equal pay for equal work, favoring women and children, and increase the rations for two thirds of the people, totally eclipsing the Russian offer. General Clay agreed with me that we couldn't make the increase unless the French were willing, and their stocks were low.

The reservation in our minds was whether a bold move on our part would drive the Russians to equally bold retaliation. They could stop the trains bringing two thousand tons of food a day into Berlin. I favored the move, as I did other bold moves. I favored throwing the Reds out of the radio station they occupied in the British sector. If they limited products from Berlin to the West, I favored cutting off products shipped to the East. If they made arrests in our sector, then we should make arrests in theirs. If they cut our telephone wires, we could cut theirs and also pull the power switches, which went through our sector into theirs. Countermeasures are the only thing the Russians understand and respect.

As matters developed, there was no need to be so drastic. The next meeting of the Kommandatura differed from others only in the fact that we actually reached an important agreement on the food question. Berliners were to eat better. On the surface, the agreement indicated a successful degree of co-operation among the powers. On the contrary, it was a very vicious battle, in which Russia tried to make the Western powers the villains of the piece, who were trying to starve the city.

Our proposals, made on a city-wide basis, were to give children in Category IV and adults in Category III an increase of two hundred calories a day. This plan would have helped the people who needed food most, housewives and families of workers who were shown by medical records to be undernourished. Workers in Russian plants were getting as high as 2,500 calories, but we were not interested in feeding them to increase Soviet production.

These prospective increases were announced in the press before the meeting. French food stocks were low, even in France, and Ganeval had to communicate with Paris for permission to go along with us. It is certain that the Russians knew from their agents in the French government exactly how far he was authorized to go and, consequently, were prepared for the meeting.

Ganeval duly made our joint proposal, increasing Categories III and IV by two hundred calories, affecting two thirds of the population. Formally, we and the British agreed. But the Russians did not. They proposed a blanket increase of two hundred calories, affecting the city's entire population of 3,200,000.

This maneuver put us in a tough spot. Ganeval didn't have the authority from his government to promise the extra tons of food. But if he said no to the Russian offer, the Russian-licensed press would promptly blame him and the other Western powers for refusing the "generous" aid of the Soviets and we would have lost yet another round in the propaganda game.

Kotikov didn't attend this meeting. If he had, I could picture him leaning back in his chair, gazing smugly at his three colleagues. He was represented by Yelizarov, who blandly waited for our reaction to his unexpected proposal. When it came his turn to speak, the French general sputtered and stammered. The British commandant sputtered and puffed. When my turn came, I spread honey liberally over my words.

"I think we all should express our gratitude to the Russians for their generous offer," I said, "and I am sure that the people of Berlin will appreciate it."

Yelizarov looked almost human at this nosegay.

After a suitable pause, I continued, "But I think at this stage it would be more practical if we approved the French proposal. We are all willing to go that far immediately in increasing food rations. If we accept it, two million Germans will start enjoying the new rations almost at once. You can't expect us to make an all-or-nothing decision at this meeting. As for the additional increase proposed by the Russians, I think we should give it further study and take it up again at the next meeting."

Both my French and British colleagues pounced on this suggestion as a way out. But not the Russians. They responded with a definite *"nyet!"* It was a case of all or nothing with them.

My own opinion is that they really preferred nothing, because their proposal meant another drain on their food resources, and they had hoped to scare us out of making an increase. They evidently had figured out that we would be unable to meet our commitments in view of the strained French food situation. In any case, they were trying their best to steal all the credit for this gift to Berlin and were absolutely determined that not a shadow of credit should go to the Western powers.

After a long and bitter argument, during which I again lectured the Russians on the ethics of using food as a political propaganda weapon, we reached an agreement that didn't altogether please me, but it was a compromise between the two viewpoints and helped stock the city's larder. Reluctantly, as far as I was concerned, we gave 100 more calories to the two workers' categories, as well as 150 calories to the housewives' class and 250 calories to the children's category.

But the very moment we were discussing these questions, vainly attempting to persuade Russia to co-operate in the quadripartite administration of Berlin, the stage was being set for the greatest act of all—the walkout.

Since the beginning of the year, the Russians had been putting on the squeeze. Control had been tightened on the movement of persons and goods between Berlin and Western Germany, and between Berlin and the Soviet zone. The Helmstedt line was the check point for entry into the city. In accordance with Allied Control procedure, all Germans had to carry an approved pass to travel from one zone to another. The Russians now began insisting that these passes must carry the handwritten—not stamped—signature of a Military Government authority before they would be recognized.

There were other restrictions—a new one almost every day—all plainly indicating that they were designed for nuisance value only, not practical usage.

Giving a new twist to a very old game, the Russians began to interfere with the export of goods to the West. By May 1, 1948, these exports had practically vanished. At one time in the past, 17 per cent of all goods produced in the Western sectors, ranging from radio tubes to cosmetics, were going to the Western zones, but after the squeeze was on this amount was reduced to less than 5 per cent.

The Russians used every means their devious Oriental minds could devise to maintain their strangle hold. Factories wishing to co-operate with the West found their power shut off. Shipping permits were refused. Since the Russians operated the railroads, by agreement, no manufacturer could dispatch goods to the West by rail. In January, 1948, the Russians had insisted that all factories must first obtain a Soviet permit before they could ship out goods by water, rail, or road—all of which the Russians controlled. All manner of hindrances were strewn in the path of manufacturers attempting to deal independently with the Western powers.

For instance, Telefunken, the big electrical concern, was continually plagued by the Russians with demands for their source of materials and the destination of their shipments. As an excuse for this prying, the Russians pleaded that they were trying their best to control black-market activities in their zone.

In another move to hamper the Western powers, the Russians blocked our parcel-post service by refusing to carry our parcels on the Russian-controlled railroad. The *Reichspost* was left with thousands of packages addressed to the West and no means of delivering them. At one time, before we took over delivery ourselves, 650,000 packages were stacked up. To handle their own service, the Russians established a new parcel-post office in their sector.

All these irritating actions were taken without consultation with the other powers and in complete disregard of quadripartite agreements. At the Kommandatura, Kotikov brazenly paraded complete indifference to signed pacts.

I set down here an illuminating excerpt from the official minutes of a meeting held three weeks before the final breakup, during which we protested against interference with the parcel-post service. The excerpt is a perfect illustration of Russian bad faith. The antagonists in this case were Herbert, the British commandant, and Kotikov. The exchange follows:

> *British:* Last time I said there was one question of major importance to which I wished an answer. [Herbert was referring to the parcel-post question.] You can divide it into two, if you like. The first part can be answered quite simply by "yes" or "no." Does the Soviet delegation adhere to the various treaties providing for quadripartite government of Berlin?
>
> *Russian:* Would you please ask the second question? I will answer them at once.
>
> *British:* I have had a smoke screen thrown out before by asking too many questions at once and I would like to have an answer to this one now, thank you. If you cannot answer "yes" or "no" to this simple question, it will be very significant.
>
> *Russian:* I would like to ask General Herbert not to worry about that and to ask his second question.
>
> *British:* I am asking for an answer to a simple question and I propose to go on asking it until I get it, or until you refuse to give it. If you refuse to give it, we will know what the answer is.
>
> *Russian:* If General Herbert has not listened attentively to my first statement, that is not my fault. At the end of that statement there is a very direct reply to the question put by General Herbert.
>
> *British:* General Kotikov is still declining to reply to me. He refers to some statement. Perhaps he will give it. If it is more than a plain "yes" or "no," I shall consider it to be an unsatisfactory answer.
>
> *Russian:* I just wanted to repeat the end of my first statement,

but because of the ultimatum I have received I cannot do that now. General Herbert probably knows that the Soviet delegation does not consider it possible to answer any ultimatums of this kind.

British: There is no question of any ultimatum. I merely said that if his answer was not given in a certain form it would be an unsatisfactory answer. I asked General Kotikov to repeat the portion of his statement to which he has referred.

Russian: That is quite another thing. That is a more or less form of request. I will willingly comply with it. At the end of my first statement I said, "As to the question of the quardripartite management of the City of Berlin, the position of the Soviet delegation on this question is well known."

British: It is exactly because the position of the Soviet delegation is *not* well known that I have asked my question. I am asking him what appears to me to be an extraordinarily easy question to answer, and if he was a witness in the witness box I would describe him as the most evasive witness I have ever heard.

Russian: I don't know anything about the traditions in a British court. . . . Let us discuss the question of parcels now.

British: I do not wish to be treated like a small boy and told that I may have my sweet in due course, when Father Kotikov is ready to give it to me. There is to my mind no object in discussing the matter of parcels when this major item is not settled, and I propose that the matter be withdrawn. I think we have heard quite enough from the Soviet for one day.

And so it went. You might as well try to pin down a jellyfish as to try impaling a Russian on a reasonable question.

These unilateral activities were followed by new attacks on the Western powers. As early as April, Kotikov began a series of tirades in the Kommandatura, accusing us of preventing its smooth functioning and attempting to end quadripartite government of Berlin. Any action we took unfavorable to the Russians was interpreted in this light. To me, Kotikov's attacks seemed all part of the new campaign by the Russians to "kill" the Kommandatura, blame the West for its demise, and then try to drive us all out of the city.

I went to Major General Walsh, the United States Intelligence chief in Berlin, and told him frankly the Russians were getting ready for this *coup*. I supported my statement with references to the meetings I had attended, where it was patent to the least prejudiced that the Russians were building up a case, step by verbal step, to make their action plausible.

General Clay appeared to think that there was nothing unusual in the Russian attitude at that time. Other commanders had pooh-poohed the idea, but Walsh forwarded my report to Washington.

I was later summoned by James W. Riddleberger, assistant in Berlin to Ambassador Murphy. After seeing General Walsh, I had repeated to a State Department man, Perry Laukhuff, what I had told the General and he had prepared a report for Washington.

Laukhuff, with all the inconclusiveness and circumlocution of a government official, indicated that "it would appear a possible responsible assumption" and "subject to later observation and study" the Russians were embarking upon a course for blaming the Western powers for what they were going to do, namely, kill the Kommandatura and take other steps to drive the Western powers out of Berlin.

Riddleberger asked me if the report by Laukhuff wasn't too extreme.

"Too extreme?" I gasped. "Why, if anything, it's too weak!" praying I wasn't overestimating Russian perfidy.

Kotikov, I am sure, had his orders from the Kremlin. I knew he had received them, just as surely as though I had read them myself. He was to terminate the elected city government. He was to separate the Russian sector from quadripartite control. He was to break up the Kommandatura by introducing a carefully prepared "walkout" subject, on which the Russians could claim we had insulted them, or had otherwise made the Kommandatura inoperable. After these nicely timed preliminaries, the Russians would clamp on a blockade to force us out of the city.

At the Kommandatura, Kotikov stepped up his attacks in both frequency and virulence. At every opportunity, he blasted the Western powers for the failure of quadripartite government, and the inability of the Kommandatura to function smoothly. Always in the tail of his attacks was the stinger: we were solely to blame, not Russia.

At the next meeting, Kotikov was flanked by Yelizarov, his deputy, on one side, and a new political adviser, Maximov, on the other. Maximov was a big, rawboned joker who had been Vishinsky's secretary. Kotikov was now a mere puppet, or perhaps I should say a parrot, reduced to reading papers written for him by Maximov and Yelizarov. On one amusing occasion, he had to ask Maximov's permission to agree that the meeting was over.

Kotikov went through his customary routine, mouthing the same old charges against the Western powers and raising his clamor to a hysterical pitch. He absolutely refused to talk rationally or to discuss intelligently any of the subjects on the agenda. I shook my head sadly. This, I said to myself, is the end.

The fateful day came on June 16, 1948—two meetings after most of us thought it would come. The Russians walked out. The blockade of Berlin was almost a reality.

CHAPTER X

T IS no use pretending I wasn't relieved when the Russians walked out of the Kommandatura. The walkout brought one nightmare to an end, although it conceived another—the blockade. Neither did I favor the breakup of Kommandatura machinery and all its loss implied to the government of Berlin, but Kotikov and his crew of saboteurs had made this catastrophe inevitable.

For months, the made-in-Moscow saber had hung over our heads, poised to fall at the signal of a *"nyet!"* The Russians had worked, carefully and patiently, to create the circumstances that would induce the desired climax, but, when the saber finally fell, we were not caught beneath the blade. Intelligent reading of the signs and portents had forewarned us, and the Russian weapon cut a deep notch only in the conference table, not in the combined determination of the Western powers.

The Russian *coup* was planned with all the dramatic finesse of a Bolshoi Theater production, lacking only stage properties. The London Conference of the Council of Foreign Ministers, held in December, 1947, had failed. Russia had put forward a plan for a centralized German government, which it didn't take a State Department official to recognize as puppet. This government would have been saddled with the task of paying ten billion dollars in reparations to Russia, and Moscow already had collected eight billion dollars in reparations in the strip tease of Germany.

On March 20, 1948, Sokolovsky staged the first Russian walkout at a meeting of the four-nation Allied Control Council and succeeded in *de facto* liquidation of the supreme Allied authority of Germany.

Three days before, the *Volkskongress* had met in the Russian sector of Berlin, and from the conference had emerged the framework for what the Russians styled the "People's Government of Germany." At the Council meeting, Sokolovsky demanded full support for this new government, which the Western speakers branded as bogus and unrepresentative of the majority will of the German people.

The Russian also asked to know what decisions had been reached by the Western allies regarding the work of the London Conference. General Clay replied that there was no necessity for the Council to go into the proceedings of the Conference, since they had been the subject of notes exchanged between the United States and the Soviet Union.

Apparently this perfectly logical refusal was Sokolovsky's cue. Reading a long-prepared statement, he terminated the Council meeting with this announcement:

> A situation is being created in which only the Soviet delegation can report before the Control Council, while the U.S. and British delegates refuse to give a report to the Control Council on their actions in the zones of Germany occupied by them. These delegations thus far only prove that they are breaking the agreement on control machinery in Germany and are taking responsibility for the disruption of this agreement. . . .
>
> It is clear that the action being taken or to be taken in the Western occupation zones of Germany in implementation of the unilateral decisions of the London Conference cannot be recognized as rightful action. Since the British and the United States members refuse to report before the Control Council on matters discussed at the London Conference, I see no sense in continuing today's meeting and declare it adjourned.

Thereupon, Sokolovsky left the meeting. The Kommandatura walkout was still to come, although it lacked the sense of international consequence permeating the Control Council session. There had been previous Kommandatura meetings where important matters appeared to be the peg on which the Russians would hang their excuse for picking up their portfolios and leaving. But the actual breakdown developed on a minor point.

On June 16, the meeting opened at ten in the morning. Kotikov did not attend because of "illness." His place was taken by Yelizarov, supported by the sinister Maximov. Kommandatura meetings were getting longer and longer, the Russians spinning on like phonographs in verbal trials of strength to wear us down. Twelve- and fourteen-hour meetings were common, with only half an hour's break for food. During this brief respite, the Russians always exchanged one mask for another— smiles for glowers.

We argued heatedly about a number of things, the debate swirling even more inconclusively than usual. Yelizarov laid his favorite chestnuts on the table, on which no agreement was conceivable. Hours passed, and still nothing had been accomplished. I was growing more and more uncomfortable. A lark sang in the June sky outside the conference-room window. While the discussions droned, I watched the bird make graceful spirals in the blue and longed desperately to exchange places with the sweet singer.

At 7 P.M. an unusual thing occurred. In walked a strange commissar, a man I had never seen before and have never seen since, and sat down on the Russian side of the table. He added an exotic note, with the embroidered Ukrainian blouse he wore under his civilian coat. The stranger didn't say a word aloud, he merely leaned over and whispered something to Yelizarov and Maximov.

An emotion very close to excitement shook the two usually frozen-faced Russians, and Yelizarov asked for a recess. While the rest of us went upstairs to the dining room for a sandwich and a cup of coffee, the Russians and their fancy-dress visitor trooped back to their own part of the building.

Looking out of the dining-room window a few minutes later, I saw Maximov striding nervously up and down, puffing a black cigarette in a long holder. The mystery man joined him for a minute, then got into his big, black Horsch car and drove off. Something big was in the air. That was definite. I began to sort over the possibilities. Had the Russians got wind of the impending secret currency reform the Western powers were going to introduce in their own zones? If they had, such information would give them a very good excuse for a walkout, because we had carefully refrained from consulting them on the matter. On reconsideration, however, I argued myself into the viewpoint that the Russians weren't going to walk out at all right now. Even if they did know about the currency scheme, Howley told Howley, they would wait until we actually announced it before acting. As it happened, they knew nothing about our currency plans and didn't act until they were announced.

When the meeting resumed, Yelizarov launched a blistering attack on the Western powers on another subject entirely— trade unions. With our encouragement, the rank and file of German unions had thrown off Communist top-level control and had created UGO, an independent organization operating on democratic lines.

The debate lasted until ten P.M. and, when the subject was finally dropped from the agenda, I was nearly spent. I was convinced there would be no fireworks. After twelve solid hours of bickering, it didn't seem likely that the Russians would walk out. So I made plans to leave the meeting, leaving my deputy, Colonel Babcock, sitting in for me. This procedure had been authorized by my immediate superiors weeks before—a fact never mentioned in subsequent attacks on me. For instance, it was never mentioned to General Clay. During eight years of Army service, I never shifted responsibility for my actions to higher headquarters.

My reason for leaving the meeting was perfectly understandable. The Russians worked until one, two, or three in the morning and slept until noon if they felt like it. In the American Army we get up early. My office in Berlin opened at eight thirty A.M., and I was always there on time.

At ten forty-five that evening, I proposed that we end the meeting at eleven. Thirteen hours had passed since the session opened, and we were all weary. The Russians refused and Yelizarov dragged out the chestnut of all chestnuts. For the umpteenth time, we were going to discuss Kotikov's "Fourteen Points for the Amelioration of Working Conditions of the Workers of Berlin." We had argued about this plan for eight months straight and had never reached a decision, because the

Russians consistently refused to discuss the program point by point. We either had to swallow all fourteen points at once, or none at all. That we would never do. In addition, the Kommandatura had no power to act on several of the points because the Allied Control Authority was the supreme arbiter on labor questions.

Realizing the futility of going over all the tiresome old arguments again, I requested permission from the French chairman, General Ganeval, to be excused. I had a heavy day ahead of me and had to get some rest.

"It is now a quarter past eleven," I said. "Half an hour ago, I suggested that we end our meeting. I'm tired. I'm going home and I'm going to bed. With your permission, General, I will leave my deputy, Colonel Babcock, to represent me."

Ganeval graciously gave me permission, and I left the conference room. There was a subsequent report that I slammed the door on my way out. I did not. The door stuck and I simply yanked it open. After I left, Maximov started an excited whispered conversation with Yelizarov. It was Yelizarov's turn to speak. He stood up and suddenly slammed his papers down on the table.

"I consider it impossible to continue this meeting after an action that I can only claim as a hooligan action on the part of Colonel Howley," he shouted. "I consider we should finish."

At that point, Ganeval tactfully offered to close the meeting, but Yelizarov would have none of it. "If Colonel Howley will not excuse himself, I will not remain here any more," he announced.

About eight minutes had elapsed. Yelizarov started to move toward the door, and Ganeval reminded him that I had been properly excused from the meeting. The Russian kept right on going.

What happened after this is confused. The official minutes of the meeting are not clear. There was a terrific hubbub, and the interpreter system broke down. The French chairman did manage to get in a remark that the Russians were acting improperly and that it was Yelizarov, not Colonel Howley, who was being rude. He also tried to get out of the Russian a suggestion for the date of the next meeting. By this time Yelizarov was only ten feet from the door, violently propelled by Maximov, who had his hands on the Deputy's hips.

Yelizarov turned to say something before he left, but his words were lost in the confusion. Maximov pushed him through the door. Some say he simply called out a final *"nyet!"* Others contend he said, "Not until Colonel Howley does something!"

The Russians out of the room, the French chairman brought the meeting to a close. "This meeting," he ruled, "is not closed because Colonel Howley went home, since he was replaced by his deputy, which has happened before, but because of the departure of the Soviet delegation."

On my way home from the Kommandatura, I stopped at the Press Camp, my custom after all meetings, to give the American correspondents a briefing on our discussions. This normally took half an hour. Just as I was about to start speaking, Babcock called up excitedly and told me what had happened in those eight history-making minutes. Well, I thought resignedly, the break has come at last. It seemed a poor issue the Russians had selected, but it had served its purpose.

Going back to the correspondents, I indicated that this was the breakup of the Kommandatura the Russians had been planning for months, and warned that it would be followed by further unilateral actions designed to destroy quadripartite government and get us out of Berlin.

"But if any jokers think they're going to get the British, French, and Americans out of Berlin," I told the correspondents, "they have another think coming."

However clearcut was the evidence—grossly distorted in subsequent attacks on me—that I was not responsible for breaking up the Kommandatura, I found myself frying on an unexpectedly hot griddle.

After the press conference, I went immediately to the telephone and called General Clay at home. He was in the throes of a delicate negotiation with the French on currency reform and was hopping mad about the Kommandatura walkout. He wanted to see me right away.

Then I called Major General Hays, to tell him of the incident. Hays was more philosophic. "Don't worry," he said kindly, "they've been building up to this. If it hadn't been this incident, it would have been something else."

No sooner had I hung up then General Brownjohn, the British deputy military governor, called Hays. Brownjohn told him that I had precipitated the break by walking out of the meeting. For some reason, best known to themselves and completely unjustified by the facts, the British held me at fault.

On the other hand, the French stood behind me 100 per cent. Ganeval, at the conclusion of the meeting, had declared quite frankly where the responsibility for the breakup lay, and he had no intention of retracting his statement.

My own attitude was reflected in a notation I made in my diary:

> The status of the Kommandatura is now the same as the status of the Allied Control Authority—no one knows whether it exists or not. When it suits the Russians, they will say it does exist, and when it does not suit them they will say it does not exist.
>
> Personally, I say it is good riddance of bad rubbish. I think it has been a disgrace for an American representative to sit for six months and listen to the abuse of the American people, the American Army, and all our concepts of democracy.

Officially, General Clay thought otherwise. When I arrived to report on the incident at the Kommandatura, he was steaming.

"You have done a terrible thing," he said.

I remained discreetly silent.

"And the worst of it is," he added, "you're not even sorry about it."

"You're damn right I'm not," I snapped.

The next day we had another session. This time I sat in a chair, while Clay paced up and down in front of me. I tried to explain that I had taken all I could stand from the Russians.

"Your job is to sit there and take it," Clay said.

"I thought my job was to keep them from stealing the city

of Berlin," I retorted angrily. Probably, I should have been fired on the spot for insubordination. Fortunately, Clay understood my impatience.

"Wise Guy" Sokolovsky wasn't pleased either. He wrote Clay that I had refused in "an offending and rude way to deal with suggestions submitted by the Soviet Commandant, referring to material and legal improvement of the situation of workers and employees of industry and traffic in Berlin, leaving the meeting room after a series of unseemly phrases against the Soviet representative.

"This unworthy behavior of Colonel Howley," Sokolovsky continued, "which is contrary to the elementary rules of decency and the proceedings of the work of the quadripartite organization, breaks the work of the Allied Commandants in Berlin and must be designated as inadmissible."

But in spite of all these verbal flourishes, the Russians realized they had pulled a boner. The first explanation—backed by a fusillade of insults directed at me—that the Kommandatura had been broken up because I went home, didn't sound valid. The Russians belatedly discovered the flimsiness of their excuse and, when the Western allies announced their currency reform, found themselves in the unenviable position of the hunter who shoots his gun in the air and watches the deer run by. They had terminated the Kommandatura on no more serious grounds than the fact that the Russian commandant was peeved because the American commandant had left the conference room properly after listening to thirteen hours of Russian abuse.

They quickly switched alibis. The Kommandatura, it was officially announced, had collapsed because of our "illegal" currency measures. Once again, the Russians proved themselves capable of disposing of yesterday and liquidating history overnight.

On the night of June 18, two days after the Kommandatura walkout, we had announced our currency reform and caught the Russians napping. Although the question had been discussed at the Control Council months before, and the Russians must have been aware that the Western powers had currency reform in mind, they were not prepared with countermeasures. We were in favor of a unified currency for Germany—as was logically envisaged by the Potsdam agreement—but not on Russian terms. The Russians had stubbornly insisted they should have the exclusive privilege of printing all German money in their zone, at Leipzig, and eventually came to believe that, if they held out long enough, the other powers would yield the point.

Currency reform was imperative. Inflation in the Western zones had reached such proportions that it threatened to prevent any substantial revival of German economy. To prevent this catastrophe and provide a basis for healthy economic recovery, the three Western powers took the drastic step of revaluating the reichsmark to one tenth of its former value. We were reluctant to initiate such a measure, but this step was taken only after we were convinced that quadripartite agreement on a unified currency was entirely impossible. Our action, we were fully aware, was bound to cause personal hardship to the Germans in the Western zones, but the people's reaction to revaluation was favorable. They believed intensely that anything was better than the greatly inflated reichsmark.

On the night of our currency announcement General Ganeval, the French chairman, called a meeting of the Kommandatura for the following morning, to discuss the effects of Western currency reform on Berlin. We wanted to know what the Russians thought. Our official announcement pointed out specifically that the new measures applied only to the three Western zones of occupation and not to Berlin, controlled by the four-power Allied Kommandatura. Yelizarov, the acting Russian commandant, answered the invitation to the meeting by letter. "Owing to pressure of business," he would not be able to attend.

His letter sounded Moscow's new note of four-power discordance in relations with the Western powers. Yelizarov declared, "The new currency reform plan in Western Germany is not only contrary to the Potsdam agreement and to other agreements with Soviet Russia, but is designed to split Germany."

Meanwhile, we learned of the frantic efforts of the Russians to introduce a new currency in their own Eastern zone. They were driven to take this action because we had refused to surrender to them on the basic principle of currency reform at the Control Council, where they not only demanded control of the printing plants, but attached a couple of other strings that would have made currency reform just another powerful Soviet tool.

Had we allowed them to print the new money at Leipzig, as they insisted, we never would have known how much was printed, nor would they have given us any exact information about the general currency situation in the Eastern zone. We would have been right back where we started in 1945, when the Russians duplicated our invasion currency plates and printed billions of marks—exactly how many billions, they never told us—aggravating inflation. The result was that the United States was backing phony Russian money with good U.S. dollars, though not a single rouble backed the Russian issue. We had no intention of being caught again.

If we had given them the plates for the new currency, the Russians undoubtedly would have printed their additional billions, with which they would legitimately buy Ruhr iron and coal, as well as other German products, at no more than printing costs—all at the expense of German economy and the European Recovery Program. In a nutshell, they would have been able to "buy" reparations from current production by using this spurious currency, while the United States continued to pour money and goods into the German economy.

In order to protect ourselves against the impending currency reform in the Eastern zone, which we guessed might include Berlin, although we had meticulously excluded the city from the scope of our scheme, we laid plans to extend Western currency to Berlin—if necessary.

If ever there was a "top-secret" operation, this was it. Of necessity, our currency plan enjoyed the highest security in order to prevent a disastrous leakage of our plans. We flew into Berlin from Frankfurt ten planeloads of the new Western currency, disguised as ordinary military cargo, to hide it from the prying eyes of Russian-employed German agents who might have been snooping at Tempelhof airfield. Altogether, we had a fund of 250,000,000 crisp, new *Deutsche* marks—as we called them—ready for emergencies. Under the supervision of our own finance officers, we recruited a dozen carefully screened German finance experts, whose task was to study the problems of introducing currency reform in Berlin with the least possible disorganization of economic life.

This was a strictly cloak-and-dagger affair, with all the trimmings. At York House, a Military Government building in the British sector, we established a "cage" where the German experts ate, worked, and slept on the problems. And it was a cage in the strictest sense of the word. We couldn't afford to allow the slightest hint of our intentions to reach the Russians. We had no intention of introducing the West mark into Berlin unless the Russians attempted first to introduce their East mark, but we had to be ready just in case. The men were allowed no outside contacts; they were instructed to tell their families that they were going to Frankfurt to work on a Military Government job. To strengthen the illusion, we drove them from their homes in the direction of Tempelhof airfield, then doubled back to York House. No key physicists, with the dark secrets of the atom bomb locked in their brains, were guarded and shrouded more carefully.

On June 23, the Russians announced the introduction of their new currency into Berlin. Sokolovsky issued an order to the Berlin city government that plans should be made at once to convert the old reichsmarks into new East marks and that the new East mark would be the only recognized currency in the city. Any German found in possession of West marks would be subject to arrest and punishment, he announced.

Sokolovsky went so far as to state that Berlin no longer would be considered quadripartite in structure, but would become an economic part of the Soviet zone. Hence, at all levels —Soviet Zonal German Authorities, Soviet Zonal Command, and Soviet Command in Berlin—the Russians were attempting to take over the city by currency proclamation. The big grab was on.

The new Russian currency, rushed into circulation and enforced wherever people would accept it, was impracticable. To begin with, it was worthless, whereas Western currency was integrated with the German ecomony through such channels as wages, rent, and food. And it wasn't newly printed currency at all.

In their haste to forestall us, the Russians had stumbled in with a lot of old, worn reichsmarks, with thumb-sized stamps stuck on to distinguish them as East marks. The stamps were held on with cheap potato glue, which usually lasted three or four exchanges before dropping off. The notes then became nonnegotiable without their identifying symbol.

The Germans, whose pockets were being rapidly emptied, wryly dubbed the Russian currency "wallpaper marks." In the Russian sector, the change-over was made with considerable confusion. Long lines of Germans fought outside Russian exchange depots to get to the windows first and obtain the most durable of the tattered currency. Adding to the general chaos, the Russian propaganda machine went into action, insinuating by rumor or thundering over Soviet Radio Berlin and in the Russian-licensed papers that any Berliner accepting the West mark would be considered "an enemy of German economy" and "a traitor to German unity."

The city government felt the dead hand of the new currency almost at once. On the Russian assurance that the city funds in reichsmarks, banked in the Soviet sector, would be converted into East marks, it was agreed that the city budget should be collected in this currency. But the more acceptable and negotiable West mark acquired such a premium value that the Russians reneged and refused to cover the reserves. Overnight, the city government was bankrupt.

Fortunately, we were prepared for this emergency. The following day, June 24, we countered by announcing the extension of Western currency reform to Western Berlin. That made two new currencies in the capital. In fact, Berlin had two of almost everything—to the comprehensible perplexity of Berliners.

Currency conversion in the Western sectors worked smoothly and efficiently. Our only real difficulty was in providing some form of proof that residents of the Western sectors had converted their old money into new West marks. A Western Berliner, or an Eastern resident who accepted our currency, walked right into jail if he went into the Soviet sector, where he might work, or into the Soviet zone outside Berlin, because we stamped a large "B" on his identity card when he converted to Western money.

At first, we considered not stamping the cards at all but keeping them for two days and returning them when the exchange was complete. This procedure would have had frightful results. Not only would two and a quarter million people have had no identity cards, an absolute necessity in strife-torn Berlin, but two and a quarter million identity cards would have been filed away at borough police stations and it would have been harder to return them than to collect them.

"The Germans have never shown the ability to run a hat-check room at a party and return the right hat," one commandant remarked sardonically. "Then how can you expect them to get the right identity cards back to the right people?"

We eventually devised a plan whereby the people who did not exchange their old marks for new West marks still had to go to their local police station and get their cards stamped with a "B." That gave them a perfect out. If they were arrested by the Russians, they could say that their card had been stamped at the police station, where they had to go in accordance with Military Government orders.

Swiftly unrolling more red tape, the Russians stole our identification plan. They started frantically stamping identity cards of people who exchanged money into their currency, but the move collapsed on a single point. They had been issuing East marks long before they began stamping cards. Berliners had their answer ready when they were picked up: "I received my quota of East marks the first day, when you weren't stamping identity cards."

It is impossible to overemphasize the general confusion that the Russians attempted to create in Berlin on the week end of June 23, preparatory to the imposition of the total blockade, which was to start officially the next day. While they were doing their best to stampede the Germans into refusing the Western currency measures, the full weight of their propaganda was flung into the campaign to force us out of Berlin.

"The Western powers have sacrificed their right to remain in Berlin, the capital of divided Germany," was their theme song. "The Russians are ready and willing to feed the city in order that the plunderers, the reactionaries, of the West can get out of Berlin while their skins are whole," they promised wholeheartedly.

This was a new propaganda line, no more calculated to impress the Germans than the previous Moscow assertion that the United States was tottering on the verge of economic collapse.

About this time new American cars—Buicks, Fords, Chevrolets—began to appear in Berlin in great numbers. As one German remarked to me, "If this is American economic collapse, then Germany certainly would like to have a lot of it."

Having lost their prosperity appeal, the Russians had turned to the "oppression of minorities" line. Germans were told at length of the terrible conditions under which the American Negro lived. Soviet-licensed newspapers blandly used material from old American books on slavery as modern evidence. I know of one writer who lifted a complete editorial right out of *Uncle Tom's Cabin*. Publication dates meant nothing to the Moscow-trained propagandists.

Here they ran into easily controvertible facts. Negroes worked in Military Government on exactly the same basis as white members. General Clay had a Negro honor guard—handsome men, all over six feet. They were excellently trained, smartly uniformed, and, when they appeared on parade, Russian propaganda about the sorry lot of the American Negro looked pretty silly, just as silly as the new line that the Russians were ready to feed the Germans, while we bolted with the loot.

On the eve of the blockade, the City Assembly met at the City Hall, in the Russian sector, to discuss the predicament facing Berlin.

The city fathers had two pistols pointed at their heads. Sokolovsky had proclaimed that economically Berlin was part of the

Soviet zone and ordered them to accept this decision and adopt the East mark. On the other hand, the three Western powers had ordered the city government not to obey this unilateral Soviet order since it breached the city constitution, agreements at the Allied Kommandatura, and agreements signed at the highest authority, the Allied Control Council.

To make sure that the city fathers knew their own minds and would reach an appropriate decision, a crowd of five thousand jostled outside the building, hooting and trying to intimidate Assembly members. The majority of the demonstrators were professional Communists, wearing party badges, and had been brought to the scene in Russian military trucks—all "made in the U.S.A." and given to Russia under Lend-Lease. City officials were mobbed on the street, and even inside the building, while loud-speakers harangued the crowd outside. Russian-sector police stood by idly. They had their orders, I was told, to "keep hands off and let the mob have its way!" The office of Soviet Police Chief Markgraf was next door to the City Hall, but calls for police protection were ignored.

Denied police assistance, Assembly officers did manage to clear the floor of interlopers and to open discussion. The Communist minority of 18 per cent instantly demanded that the Russian order be implemented and obeyed, climaxing their speeches with wild attacks on the Western powers. Boldly, in view of the massed menace outside, the three democratic parties—Social Democrats, Liberal Democrats, and Christian Democrats—stood up for the rights of the city, embodied in the international agreements. They stoutly insisted that the Assembly must abide by the constitution that Russia and the other three powers had given Berlin.

After a debate lasting four hours, the meeting ended with the announcement that the Assembly could not accept the Russian order, thereby intimating their ultimate refusal to see Berlin incorporated into the Russian zone.

Strange things were happening outside while the Assemblymen were making this decision. Despite the efforts of agitators to start a riot and incite the mob to break windows and attack democratic leaders as they left the building, when the meeting finally ended most of the crowd had vanished. Only a few hundred diehards remained, and from their ranks sneaked a typical Russian-paid goon squad. Under the noses of the inactive police, they started beating up Assemblymen, injuring five who had shown the courage to stand out against the Russian edict. Satisfied, the hired thugs then scurried down their ratholes.

So the Assembly meeting ended with a major defeat for the Russians, as well as for their riot organizers. Berlin's elected representatives refused to be bullied by Sokolovsky into breaking agreements with the Western powers, and organized efforts to generate public indignation had failed ignominiously, even among their own Communist sympathizers.

The Muscovite mind then swung over to the next phase, one that had been long contemplated and refined in concept. The Germans refused to be propagandized or intimidated into accepting the will of Russia. All right. We'll try starving them, the mind decided, and the blockade was on in full force the next day. The Russian reason was the only excuse available at the time—the Western currency reform.

Their action was not unexpected. The blockade was beginning to take shape as early as April, after the Allied Control Council walkout. Pressure started in many irritating ways, building up in intensity until the final clamping down on all communications with the West. Using one feeble excuse or another, the Russians asserted "technical difficulties" required certain controls on the railroads. Our trains and trucks had to meet their constantly changing requirements. Procedures at checking points became more complicated. Passes weren't honored. The Russians demanded the right to search all our trains going in and out of the Western zones. This search generally took place at night and was carried out by heavy-booted Russian guards, striding noisily up and down passenger trains and snapping their flashlights in the faces of American women and children. The guards insisted that they had to check every passenger and every piece of luggage. Traveling became a nightmare.

General Clay decided to deny them this search power and issued orders that the guards were not to be allowed on passenger trains. As a result, the Russians refused to allow our passenger trains to move, and later this prohibition was extended to our freight trains. From that point on, military rail traffic between Berlin and the Western zones was discontinued. And from that point on, the forerunner of the great Allied airlift, which in the succeeding strenuous months fed the Western sectors of Berlin, began to operate. Deprived of rail facilities, the three Western powers resorted to air for transporting passengers and freight. Dependents, who wanted to go home in view of the gathering storm, were flown out.

Russian obstruction methods followed the same pattern on the roads. Why not? They had got away with stopping the railroads. The *Autobahn*, the only main road in and out of Berlin to the West, was our chief road link. At first, the Russians would block it and stop our traffic, pleading the need for immediate repairs. Later, they would reopen the *Autobahn* and permit us limited use, until they discovered that some bridge also needed repairs, and the road would be closed again.

Eventually, the *Autobahn* was closed entirely to Western traffic. The reason the Russians offered was that the bridge across the Elbe at Dessau needed repairing. (Incidentally, American engineers had built this bridge.) But we had to accept the excuse, and American cars, instead of using their own bridge, had to make a long detour along a poor dirt road and cross the river by hand ferry, two at a time. These initial phases of the wrath to come were like the slowly tightening movements of a giant boa constrictor—almost imperceptible at the instant of movement but gradually working up to complete constriction.

I had called on Kotikov one day, perhaps our last meeting before the Kommandatura walkout, to find out the reason for the restrictions on shipments of goods out of Berlin. The Russians claimed there was a lot of black-market activity, and therefore any rail shipments out of the Western sectors, either by military or by civilian train, must receive detailed approval of every item.

General Clay had instructed me to make the call. "Go over and see Kotikov," he said, "and try to find out if the Russians are just trying to annoy us, or if they really have a black-market problem. Tell him if he has anything reasonable to suggest, we might be able to work out something."

I explained my errand to Kotikov, adding quite frankly, "We don't want to cause you unnecessary trouble and we hope that you aren't trying to cause us trouble."

He asked my ideas on the subject; the Russians always asked you to express your opinion first. I gave him a number of suggestions, all practical ways of avoiding the train holdups the Russians claimed they had to make looking for German saboteurs, black marketeers, and illegal cargo, even going to the extent of suggesting that we put a desk in one of our sector stations in Berlin, where Soviet officers could examine German passenger credentials.

"Then the trains won't have to stop up at the Elbe in the middle of the night," I concluded, "and you won't have to go through any fighting with us over the principle of stopping them."

Kotikov could not make an immediate decision. He seldom could—on anything. "I'll have to take this up with my superiors," was all he could say.

He stalled for a week. When I called up his office, I couldn't reach him for several days after that. In the end, he called me and passed on a message through his interpreter.

"Tell Colonel Howley that there really isn't anything for me to discuss with him," he said.

As we had known for a long time, Kotikov's message meant that his superiors were not interested in a solution to that particular part of our transportation problem, because that little blockade was part of the preparations for the big blockade.

The big show would start when the Russians decided not to allow food, freight, and coal trains to come in to supply all the German people in the three Western sectors.

The Russians had seen our planes coming in daily, landing supplies for the few thousand Americans, British, and French in Berlin, and conceded that we would continue this service for our immediate needs. But they assumed comfortably that we couldn't do it for the large German population. They were content to sit back, with cynical satisfaction, and watch the results of their evil work. How wrong they were.

CHAPTER XI

JUNE 24, 1948, is one of the most infamous dates in the history of civilization. It should have been marked in red on Stalin's personal calendar, and possibly was, because the blockade imposed on Berlin that day bore the unmistakable imprint of the Kremlin in the callousness of its concept and the ruthlessness of its execution. The Russians tried to murder an entire city to gain a political advantage.

Following the iron chain of restrictions aimed at the Western powers, a week of Communist-fomented political turmoil, and the series of arrogant and coercive orders from Sokolovsky, the Russian zone commander, the blockade was clamped tight on Berlin in a badly gauged effort to break the spirit of the Germans. There had been a partial blockade for nearly three months, but it didn't reach brutal totality until early that June morning. Berlin was in a state of siege, and the Germans called it "hunger blockade."

In rapid succession, the Russians stopped all rail and road traffic into Berlin, then extended the ban to include canal-borne traffic. Every train, car, or barge coming into the city, or leaving it, was stopped by Russian guards. Nothing on the surface was allowed to move east or west across the Elbe River. Power was cut off from West Berlin. This included both power imported and paid for under Allied agreement, and power produced at the big plant in the Russian sector from our joint stockpiles of coal.

The Russian High Command announced that all food brought into Berlin by truck from their zone would be distributed in their sector only. Drug supplies in the Russian sector were seized and deliveries to the Western sectors blocked. All

196

deposits in the *Stadtkontor* Bank, located in the Russian sector but serving all Berlin, were seized and frozen. Not the smallest detail was overlooked in this comprehensive criminal plan to shut off the Eastern zone of Germany from the West and to isolate completely the three Western sectors of Berlin. Overnight, the city became a remote island, isolated one hundred miles within hostile Russian waters.

In view of the cataclysmic consequences these actions portended for Berlin, this must sound like a strange confession. I am unable to recall clearly the details of what happened on that fateful morning. Events had followed such a whirlwind course that it was difficult to keep one's feet on the ground in the swirling storm, or one's mind concentrated on anything but the larger issue—how to save Berlin from starvation.

Midnight, the hour Tchaikowsky paraded his skeletons in the *Danse Macabre*, was the favorite Russian hour for action. It was the time they chose to announce and begin the blockade. General Clay was first to learn the news, when the Russians started stopping traffic crossing the Elbe, and I was informed later. I was called at my house about daybreak, when the first physical signs of the blockade became apparent in Berlin. I must admit that I had been called so often, during other hectic nights, about Russian emergencies that even the final step in their anti-West onslaught failed to stir me sufficiently to photograph sharp impressions on my mind. One of the minor irreverent oaths in Berlin at the time was: "For crises' sake!"

It didn't take long for news of the blockade to spread through the city. As usual, I drove that Thursday morning from my house in Gelferstrasse, in the rear of Clay's headquarters, along Grünewaldstrasse to my office, not far from the Grünewald, using my open black Horsch. My theory was that an open car was the best answer in the world to possible assassins. If they wanted to shoot me, there I was, out in the open, not hidden away in a bullet-proof limousine packed with guards. But no one ever took a shot at me.

And I do remember the faces of the Germans along the streets, looking up at me with the greatest anxiety as I drove past. Those who hadn't learned the news first hand had heard it over the Soviet radio, which broadcast hour after hour, recounting what Moscow had done and what the Western powers were expected to do—evacuate Berlin immediately.

At my office, I made a rapid appraisal of the situation and of the enormity of our job. Approximately 2,250,000 Germans lived in the three Western sectors. The Western Allies, including military, civilians, and dependents, did not exceed twenty thousand, but all were potential victims of the Russian threat.

Berlin would suffer a severe economic setback. Before the blockade, the city had struggled into life again with a reviving industry. Living conditions, judged by Western standards, were hard, but the future was not entirely dark and devoid of hope for Berliners. The administration was functioning in spite of the deadlock splitting Russia and the Western powers. All this painfully built edifice of rehabilitation might collapse under the Russian pressure.

The three Western sectors seethed with excitement when the people fully realized they were in a state of siege and that, for the time being at least, we were entirely on our own resources. Berliners, though inured to crises since the little paperhanger beat his way to the top in 1933, at last lost their stoic calm, and it was easy to feel the shock sweeping the city. The Western powers had amassed large stocks of food, coal, medical supplies, and other necessities for just such an emergency, but it would be ridiculous to claim that we were not anxious about the future.

Synchronized with the blockade, the Russians loosed the most terrific terror campaign Berlin had yet experienced in the propaganda war. While the radio and the newspapers continued to blast the Western Allies, they also struck hard at German fears, in an attempt to stampede the people against us.

On top of threatened starvation, frightening rumors were spread that the dreaded Mongolian troops, the soldiers who had sacked the city with all the Asiatic savagery of Ghenghis Khan's hordes, were coming back. To give color to these rumors, Russian troops maneuvered close to the city's boundaries, in plain sight of the Germans. Remembering the evil excesses of the early days, terror filled the hearts of the German women who had survived the first Mongol invasion.

Some of our women also were frightened. Mattern, the most rabid of the German Communist leaders, announced in a Soviet-licensed newspaper that when the Russians took over Berlin, American families would be held in concentration camps for "further disposition." Everybody knew what that meant. If soldiers march in and drag you off to work in a salt mine, or to die in a concentration camp, fear is a natural reaction—but you at least know your fate. However, even with their diabolical "further disposition" threat, the Russians didn't scare us into quitting, and they didn't scare the German people into turning against us.

Outside Berlin and throughout Germany, the Soviet radio blared even more vicious reports. Riots had started in the streets of the capital, stores were being looted, houses were burning, Western troops had fired on German mobs, hundreds of dead were lying where they had fallen, the three Western sectors were in a state of chaos, and—the Americans, British, and French were preparing to leave the city, having asked the Russians to expedite their departure.

Colonel Robert Willard, U.S. troop commander in Berlin, was the first to call me. Willard wanted to know if I needed military help, and I told him that I didn't. He had two battalions of well-trained fighting troops at his disposal.

Soviet radio lies reached our zonal headquarters at Frankfurt. Major General Clarence R. Huebner, commander of the U.S. forces in Germany, phoned me directly, ignoring channels. "Howley, we've just heard the news over the Russian radio," he said. "What's the real situation? If you want any troops, we'll rush them in right away. Just tell us what you need."

"What you've heard is all Russian bushwah," I replied, thanking him for his offer. "There's absolutely no rioting in our sectors. The situation is tense, but I've got it in hand and I think we'll be able to handle it ourselves."

I admit the Russian military maneuvers just outside the city disturbed me as much as they did the Germans. The Russians might well follow up the blockade by moving into Berlin. The few battalions of Allied troops would be helpless against the large Red Army on our doorstep.

Since the subway ran through our sector, the Russians could move in a division as easily as you can take a train from Brooklyn to Times Square, and we wouldn't know what was happening until the men started pouring out of the subway entrance like commuters on the 8:09. But I still didn't consider the situation serious enough to warrant calling for a division of American troops from Frankfurt.

On that first day of the blockade I forced myself to dismiss military threats from mind because of the imperative job on hand—plans for defeating the blockade. I was in touch with General Clay all day. I went on the air, and spoke through the newspapers, to explain American intentions to the German people.

"We are not getting out of Berlin," I promised. "We are going to stay. I don't know the answer to the present problem—not yet—but this much I do know. The American people will not stand by and allow the German people to starve."

And to give the Russians something to chew on besides black bread, I added, "We have heard a lot about your military intentions. Well, this is all I have to say on the subject. If you do try to come into our sector, you better be well prepared. We are ready for you."

Perhaps I was speaking out of turn, presumptuously trying to read the mind of Washington. But, when you are faced with a long-planned attempt to create absolute chaos you can't wait until the issue goes all the way to Pennsylvania Avenue for a decision. You've got to make an appraisal of the determination of the American people yourself. My appraisal differed from Sokolovsky's—he was convinced that we wouldn't resist—but I was justified when mine was adopted as the national policy. Clay called me later in the day and said that he was in full agreement with the announcement I had made.

Contrary to Russian expectations of early collapse and mass evacuation, we were well prepared to demonstrate that determination and carry out that promise to the German people. First of all, the Russians had badly underestimated the extent of our preparations for withstanding a siege. We had ample stocks of food and other stores in the Western sectors, having been providentially warned by the slow and obvious course of preblockade activities. The great Sokolovsky didn't know what any of his junior officers could have told him. He thought we had only two weeks' supply of food, which would soon see us hightailing out of Berlin, whereas actually we had thirty-six days' food, thirty days' coal, and many other stores of vital importance. This foresight alone gave us a long breathing space and essential time to think.

Second, though neither the Russians nor the rest of the world knew it, we were lying in wait with "Operation Counterpunch." On March 25, three months before the blockade hit us, my experts and I had drawn up a plan anticipating just such an emergency. We didn't know precisely what form the emergency would take, but we labeled the plan "Basic Assumption," the assumption being that the Russians would split their sector from the other three.

The plan provided for the building up of food and coal stocks and included the emergency use of what little power we had in West Berlin and the creation of a temporary administration in the Western sectors with all departments—legal, public health, administration, even information, including the use of our radio station for counterpropaganda.

I showed my "Basic Assumption" plan, in great secrecy, to the French and British commandants, General Ganeval and General Herbert, at a meeting in my home. Their reactions were white on one side and black on the other.

Ganeval looked at the plan carefully. "I can't believe that the Russians would do such a cruel thing," he said, "but it is a possibility. I'm glad to know that the first steps to counteract it have been taken."

Herbert—always the pessimist of the Kommandatura—was gloom personified. "They won't do it," he announced. "And even if they do, we never could hold out." Lugubriously, he predicted that the Russians would drive us out of Berlin by October. The first was his "washout" date.

When I defended the soundness of my plan, he raised more

objections. "My records show that we can't produce enough power to keep the Western sectors going," he said, referring to the capacity of the power plant in the Western sector.

I had him there, because I was fully armed with my own figures. "With careful rationing," I replied, "we have enough coal to produce one third of our normal requirements in summer and one fourth in winter. We can keep the sewers and the water wells pumping, because we need only 110 tons of coal a day for that, and we have that amount, too."

But Herbert would not be convinced that we could stay in Berlin on limited supplies, even when I showed him that we had sufficient emergency stocks to hold out until we could get a permanent supply system working—which actually was only a matter of days, when the airlift started.

At any rate, we proceeded with our arrangements, based largely upon my plan. And thanks to this preplanning, which gave us ample coal stocks, within a few hours of the time the Russians cut off the power supply, we were able to meet 50 per cent of our power requirements. Water and sewage continued to be pumped, solving a vital health problem, trolley cars continued to run, and certain essential industries were supplied.

A rationing system was instituted within two days, and 75 per cent of nonessential industries were deprived of power, although in some inexplicable way they managed to operate on a limited scale and thus avoided turning their workmen, jobless, into the streets.

German households were reduced to only two periods of two hours each per day. Allied occupation personnel and their families were allowed two longer periods, morning and night, so they could cook two hot meals on their electric ranges. Since 80 per cent of the city cooked with gas, we started coal economies by reducing the pressure.

While we were husbanding our resources and devising other ways of ensuring the city's survival, the most powerful station in the city, Soviet Radio Berlin, supported by the Soviet-licensed press, shifted into high gear in an attempt to create the panic that the first day's propaganda offensive had failed to achieve.

"German babies in the Western sectors are dying for lack

of milk," the radio screeched, stressing the fact that the Russians had all the cows in Berlin and so no such calamity could occur in the Russian sector. Over our radio, stepped up according to "Operation Counterpunch," we announced that German mothers could go to their regular stores and get condensed and powdered milk for their babies, and we gave them a new formula, which medical advisers assured us would be much better for the children. Soviet Radio Berlin charged that we weren't pumping the sewers. We answered that one, too.

Then the Russians concentrated on the water supply and in this instance they almost succeeded. The episode showed how easily even tough-minded people panic. As soon as the gutteral voice had announced that the water was going off, a shortage developed in certain sections of the city. *Hausfraus* rushed to their faucets and began filling bathtubs, washtubs, buckets, anything they could lay their hands on. These women had been through water shortages during the war, when Allied bombs smashed the city mains, and they weren't taking any chances. As a consequence of this sharply increased demand, the supply began to fail.

We were on the spot for sure; what the voice had predicted had happened. But we countered in a manner that astonished the Russians. "Forget about the water shortage!" we urged the women over the air. "Give your baby a bath. All of you take baths. Use as much water as you want. There's plenty of it!" Reassured, the women soon stopped hoarding water and the supply returned to normal.

"Operation Counterpunch" was by no means merely a mass of conservancy measures. It also provided for telling counterpunches in kind for vindictive Russian measures—a procedure I had always strongly advocated, but on which I had got little support. The Berlin subway, though running through our sector, was of primary interest to the Russian sector and the Russian zone. One of my first steps after the blockade was to notify the Russians that we intended cutting their subway power line, thus compelling them to furnish their own power. Depriving us of our imported power recoiled disastrously on their export program. Most of this power formerly had been consumed by industrial plants producing exclusively for the Russians. The flow of exports ceased.

The counterpunch that pleased me most was directed at Sokolovsky himself. To my unbounded delight, I discovered that the gas for the Russian commander's house, in the Russian suburb, came from a plant in the American sector, and I promptly turned it off. Sokolovsky had to go house hunting. While he was moving, for some doubtlessly logical Muscovite reason, the Russians tried to spirit a truckload of his furniture through the American sector, but we captured it.

The airlift—"Operation Vittles"—began on June 26. There is little that I can add here by way of tribute to the magnificent performance of the American and British airmen who made it possible. They flew in the darkness as well as in the sun, in storms as well as in good weather. Seventy of them were killed, but they were heroes, every one, and they saved Berlin.

The airlift was born of necessity, a product of improvisation and inspiration. Its creation overnight was the boldest and most spectacular supply operation in the history of aviation. Yet it had a most modest birth. On the afternoon of Saturday, June 26, General Clay called a staff conference to discuss the state of the blockade and efforts to break it.

"Frank," he said, "I'm ordering some planes in. There won't be many, but they will be planes. How fast can you get ready to accept them, and what do you want brought in first?"

"We'll accept cargoes as fast as they come in," I replied, "and we'll have flour first, please." I instantly chose flour because it is a famine food of high food value and is easily handled. I must admit that at first I was dubious about the practicality of the airlift. I couldn't quite visualize how planes could supply 920,000 German families.

That night we telephoned American zonal headquarters at Frankfurt-am-Main, 220 miles away, and by Monday we had two hundred tons of flour to start our new blockade stockpiles.

I was down at Tempelhof airfield that first morning to see the planes arrive. They were wartime twin-engined C-47 transports—"Gooney Birds," the pilots called them with affectionate contempt. Old, tired, and patched, the planes had been hastily collected from military airfields in the Western zones of Germany and rushed into the Berlin service. Many veterans still wore their camouflage paint from North Africa. Each plane had brought in two and a half tons of flour in a two-hour flight from Frankfurt.

They wobbled into Tempelhof, coming down clumsily through the bomb-shattered buildings around the field, a sight that would have made a spick-and-span air parade officer die of apoplexy, but they were the most beautiful things I had ever seen. As the planes touched down, and bags of flour began to spill out of their bellies, I realized that this was the beginning of something wonderful—a way to crack the blockade. I went back to my office almost breathless with elation, like a man who has made a great discovery and cannot hide his joy.

The perfect crime the Kremlin had planned was doomed. Although the Reds had succeeded in cutting us off completely by land, depriving us of the *Autobahn*, the railroad, and the canals, which they had stipulated we could use when we first entered Berlin, the blockade had one flaw: the Kremlin had not counted on the airlift. The narrow air corridor from the Western zones into Berlin, which had been conceded to us along with the other communication facilities now blocked, was still open. The Reds couldn't close it. Moscow didn't control the skies.

Once the vast possibilities of an airlift became apparent, we sat down to work out plans for developing it. While the men in the air had their problems, we on the ground had ours, too. With British and French experts, the pick of Military Government staffs in Berlin, we started to figure out an imponderable no one in history had ever attempted. What was the absolute minimum weight of supplies needed to keep two and a quarter million people alive and contented—so they wouldn't riot—and what should this minimum consist of? If you've ever had a difficult housekeeping problem for a large family, faced with the possibility that some member, dissatisfied with your food, might start throwing dishes at you, then you have a miniature parallel of Berlin on a domestic scale.

To work this out, experts of the three Western powers started with my "Basic Assumption" plan, which already had broken the ground. It normally took twenty thousand tons of supplies to keep the three Western sectors running. My plan was to reduce this to four thousand tons a day, the barest minimum to support the occupation authorities on an austerity basis and maintain minimum stockpiles for the German population. This tonnage included food, coal, medicine, and all essentials to feed the people, keep vital industries intact, and maintain public services.

The three Western commandants and their corps of experts differed gravely among themselves, although in the end the British and the French went along with us. Our problem was this: Could we maintain our position in Berlin with four thousand tons a day? After he had studied my figures, General Ganeval agreed that we could. General Herbert maintained that we couldn't. Herbert and I had some terrific head-on fights, far beyond mere academic disputes. Tension was high and I considered his defeatist approach destructive to Western unity.

I maintained that if I were ordered to stay in Berlin with four thousand tons a day, three thousand tons a day, or any number of tons a day, I would stay. Furthermore, I was convinced that the Germans would stand by us. I was sure that if a small minority should wish to go over to the Communists and accept Soviet dictatorship, German leaders in the Western sectors would see that they were sternly disciplined and kept in line. It is a matter of record that, when we had our full provisioning plan operating, less than one hundred thousand Germans in the three Western sectors succumbed to the blandishments of the Russians and obtained food in the Russian sector. Many of these backsliders lived in our sectors, but worked in the Russian domain.

Herbert continued to adhere to the gloomy prediction he had made back in March, when I first showed him and Ganeval my "Basic Assumption" plan. He kept repeating his conviction that October 1 would be our "washout" date.

"By that time," he insisted, "the people of Berlin will be so fed up with short rations that they'll start rioting. Then we'll all have to leave Berlin, unless the Soviets consent to drop the blockade," he added pontifically.

This was a shockingly defeatist attitude on the part of one of our allies. To be sure, some of the Germans themselves shared his opinion, but I am sure that it wasn't the official British viewpoint, since "Operation Vittles" (known to them as "Operation Plain Fare") was to become a joint U.S.–British project. It was simply one jaundiced British officer's viewpoint and ignored the confidence of the others. American policy on the question never changed from the very first; neither did my personal viewpoint.

Fortunately, the aid and comfort these violent discussions might have brought the Russians never reached them. At that time, the Kommandatura was composed only of the three Western powers. After the Russian walkout, a Russian clerical staff had remained in the building for a few weeks, collecting their papers, but the building wasn't used again for meetings until the end of the year. The three Western commandants gathered at each other's offices, where they could express their views frankly.

Happily, our differences didn't prevent us working together as an Allied team. Our joint technicians slaved day and night on calculations, cutting corners on minor details, and looking far and searchingly into the future. Plans made in early July, when the airlift started, carried us as far as the next February. We had to take the long view.

For August, September, and October, we figured on a minimum of 3,475 tons a day, consisting of food, coal for utilities, coal for laundries and bakeries, newsprint for our papers, and medical supplies for drugstores and hospitals. For December, 1948, we estimated our winter needs would be 4,360 tons, although we didn't know at that time whether we ever would be given sufficient air transport to take care of what then appeared huge loads. The days of ten and twelve thousand tons weren't even dreamed of.

We had other problems. Manifestly, the daily tonnages we had mapped out for relief of the city needed a correspondingly large volume of air transport, and we had only two airfields—

Tempelhof, in our sector, and Gatow, in the British sector. The first step was to provide additional receiving facilities, so the construction of a third field at Tegel, in the French sector, was begun.

This was constructed on wasteland. By leveling hills and excavating thousands of tons of sand, the U.S. Engineers, under Colonel Whitaker, put down two runways that would handle the largest aircraft we had. German workers completed the project in record time. The other two fields were improved, with reinforced and lengthened runways, loading and unloading aprons, ramps, and platforms to increase delivery tonnage. Twenty thousand Germans worked, under our engineers, and worked the clock around, to get the fields ready.

From its inception, the airlift was a U.S.–British operation, the French taking no part in transporting supplies but being responsible for loading and unloading at their bases and at the Tegel field. When the participating American and British air forces were integrated into a Combined Airlift Task Force on October 20, 1948, under Major General Tunner (U.S.), commanding officer, and Air Marshal Williams (British), deputy commander, planes began shuttling in freight to these three fields from eight bases in Western Germany: Rhein-Main, near Frankfurt-am-Main, and Wiesbaden, in the American zone; and Fassberg, Celle, Wunstorf, Lubeck, Fuhisbuttel, and Schleswig Land in the British zone, all within a 275-mile radius. American aircraft carried 77 per cent of the net tonnage.

A favorite crack around Berlin in the early days was the one about the three undefeated generals. According to the Poles, it was General Mud. The Russians had General Winter. And we had old General Distance—until the airlift came along.

Early transport efforts provided us with valuable experience, which helped to improve cargo handling. To construct and rehabilitate the Berlin fields, we had to fly in all equipment and material, ranging from bulldozers, cranes, and dredges to shovels and asphalt. In a few weeks, almost miraculously, we had these three big fields in order. Ground organization grew so efficient that, at the peak of our program, it took only thirteen minutes to unload ten tons of cargo from a C-54, the biggest type we used, sweep out the plane, and get it back into the air again on its way to a West German base.

The airlift was a reality by the first week in July, acquiring strength with every succeeding day. That first month, we brought in fifty thousand tons of food for civil consumption, a fraction of what we were to achieve when the lift got into its stride, but enough to convince the Russians that we meant business and to prove to the Germans that, if they stood by us, we could feed them. By rearranging the city's rations, we reduced total daily food requirements to 1,178 tons and, at the same time, were able to retain our thirty-six-day reserve stocks.

It is conceivable that the Russians credited us with the ability to bring in food for the city. We had been doing it for months, but what they didn't count on was coal. Who ever heard of supplying a city with coal by air? It was all incredible and impossible to them. Yet we did it, because coal was vital to our existence, extending all the way down from power to bakeries. Berliners had to have bread. We once considered flying in bread, prepared in Army bakeries in our zone, but the loaves proved too bulky. Bringing in bread meant bringing in water, because one third of the loaf is water. It was more sensible to fly in flour and coal. Berlin had water. I quote this as an instance of how fine we cut our loads.

Before the blockade, we shipped in six thousand tons of coal a day by rail, but we reduced this to an emergency total of fifteen hundred tons a day. Of course, the first air deliveries didn't approach this amount, but our stocks enabled us to carry on until we reached the desired tonnage.

The arrival of the coal planes at Tempelhof was the most popular spectacle in the city. Black diamonds, flown two hundred miles in million-dollar military planes, costlier cases than Cartier diamonds ever boasted, became an actuality, not a figure of speech. The fuel was packed in Army duffel bags, the type the G.I. lugs around. We found that these bags didn't get so dirty as bags made of more porous material. To simplify unloading, we tried dropping coal from the bomb bays of B-29's, but this type of bombing wasn't as successful as General Curtis

LeMay's raids on Japanese cities, and we abandoned it as impractical.

While we were building up our supplies, the German people themselves neglected no opportunity to supplement the bare rations we were allowing them. Before the blockade, Berliners had done large-scale foraging for food in the Russian zone, coming back with fruit and vegetables, and sometimes even coal and briquettes. At one stage, the forager traffic was so heavy that trucks were used. And, even though the Russians applied the same rigid restrictions to this source of supply as they did to ours, an appreciable quantity of food seeped through the Soviet wall.

Inevitably, a widespread and efficient smuggling organization sprang up. All sorts of banned food appeared openly for the first time in the black market. One day a German came to my office with an offer: "Colonel, if you'll provide me with the necessary trucks," he said, "I'll bring in any quantity of food you want. It's all a question of knowing the way."

By that remark, I inferred that the German meant running the blockade was possible if somebody was paid—that is, the Russian guards; and if others were shot—that is, those who wouldn't be bribed.

"No," I had to say, as a matter of policy, "that's not the American way. We're going to stick it out. The airlift is doing fine and we can bring in all the food we need."

I was fairly conversant with some of the tricks of the blockade runners. One was very neat indeed, and brought truckloads of food into the Western sectors all the way from beyond the Elbe River. By some underground means, the German smugglers had provided themselves with sets of duplicate papers. Loading their trucks in the Western zones, they crossed the border near Helmstedt and passed the Russian check point by exhibiting papers showing the cargo was consigned to a firm in the Russian sector. Once safely inside the guard ring around Berlin, they switched papers, entered the Western sectors, and disposed of their food.

I once got a sharp reprimand from Kotikov when we seized half a dozen trucks passing through our sector. At that time, we didn't forbid the Russians use of arterial highways passing through the American sector. Our police were rightly suspicious of these trucks, and held them up. Kotikov was furious, and appended to his complaint at the illegality of our action the fact that the trucks contained fish, which would spoil unless the trucks were returned immediately.

A few days before, the Russians had seized forty trucks of smuggled food, trying to get into the Western sectors, and I wasn't at all pleased. Not that I approved officially of smuggling, but I thought I might as well close my eyes to its existence. We might need the smugglers later. Who could tell? So I wrote Kotikov, thanking him for informing me of the contents of the trucks we had stopped. I promised him that a careful record would be kept and, when the blockade was lifted, a proper adjustment would be made. In the meantime, I added, the fish wouldn't spoil; it would be distributed immediately to the German people in our sectors who, I felt sure, I said, would enjoy it because they hadn't had any fresh fish since the Russians brutally imposed the blockade.

The new home of black-market activities was in Potsdamerplatz, a "no man's land" where the boundaries of the four sectors converged in the dead center of Berlin. Crowds flocked there daily. From their side of the square, the Russians made a number of raids to suppress illegal trading, but the first time their police appeared, the Germans picked up stones and drove them back over the Soviet boundary.

The Russian police returned three hours later, led by their chief, who was attacked so furiously in his car that he had to turn back. Then the police fired into the crowd. We never knew the exact number of casualties, but four wounded Germans were taken to our hospitals. After that brush, Russian troops took up positions along the boundary and there were some nasty incidents, which might have revived the shootings of the early days of our occupation, had we not taken steps to make the square a neutral area.

These raids were given great prominence in the Soviet-licensed press, but my opinion is that they were induced by the mounting sense of frustration among the Russians, who were in search of an alibi. They wanted to blame the black market for falling living standards in the Russian sector and the Russian zone, and also wanted to stop black marketing in order to control distribution of food and commodities through their own channels. They were furious because smuggled goods were getting into Berlin in spite of the blockade, causing their East mark to sag to a three-to-one exchange for our West mark.

As we struggled through the initial phases of the blockade, meeting the challenge of Moscow resolutely and with encouraging results, the Russians redoubled their pressure on the city government, the majority of whose members were in sympathy with the Western powers.

City finances were in a desperate state, and we hesitated to take any positive steps to correct the fiscal situation. The Russians, unhampered, pressed their advantage to the utmost. To embarrass the administration, they refused to make their own East marks available to the city government. Every week, the city leaders had to go to Soviet military headquarters at Karlshorst and beg for money to meet the payroll. They got it—doled out at the rate of ten million marks at a time.

In the Western sectors, we realized at the beginning of the blockade that we had to make some concessions to the new Russian currency and started accepting East marks on a limited basis. Thus we were able, on occasions, to match the Russian contribution from the sale of food and tax collections in East marks.

Fortunately for us all, the spirit of the democratic leaders of the government remained unbroken by these humiliations. The City Assembly voted on July 26 to suspend Police Chief Markgraf, the Moscow-trained official who obeyed only his master's voice. In his place, the Assembly recognized his deputy, Dr. Johannes Stumm. The Russians already had fired Stumm and named a pliable Communist in his place, but the city government stood by its guns. Stumm was their man and, although the Russians refused to accept his appointment, the three Western powers now comprising the Kommandatura approved him.

But the long-harassed city government began to split asunder. The issue was forced by Kotikov who, under an early blockade order by Sokolovsky ending the existence of the three Western sectors, had been made commandant of Berlin. He ordered an immediate investigation of the Berlin police which, in Moscow, would have been called a purge. Four hundred police were fired and replaced by Communists.

Unable to enforce his orders, Stumm left his office in the Soviet sector and established headquarters in the West. Of the two thousand members of the Soviet sector police, eleven hundred followed him over the boundary to work on the new force he started to organize. But Markgraf continued as chief in the Russian sector.

The cleavage in the administration widened. Because of Russian influence, City Assemblyman Fuellsack, another Social Democrat, and head of the Central Food Office, also bolted, transferring his office to our sector. The final breaking point, which gave Berlin two city governments, was near.

In the middle of August, Dr. Reuter, the Lord Mayor without office, called on me and said the City Assembly had been convened for that day. What, he asked, should they do? Communist headquarters at Kreuzberg had called a mass meeting and stores and factories in the Soviet sector were closing down so that a huge demonstration could be organized to march against the *Magistrat* and the Assembly.

The Russians thought that the meeting would be called off rather than face the mob. I hoped it wouldn't be canceled, in order to justify the Assembly in moving city government headquarters out of the Russian sector entirely.

"It would be better for the city government not to be scared out," I told Reuter. "By all means hold the meeting, but if you have to leave, then leave under pressure from the Communist stooges. If you ask for sanctuary in our sector, it should be clear then that you were forced out of the Russian sector by the Communists."

Nevertheless, the meeting was called off because of the threatening mob gathered in front of the building. Social Democrat leaders then wrote to Kotikov, seeking the assurance that they would be protected from violence if they called another meeting. Kotikov, who knew they were prepared to move into our sectors, replied in a letter full of sophistry and cynicism, embodied in embarrassing questions. The Assembly leaders read between the lines and deferred action once again.

Dr. Otto Suhr, head of the *Magistrat* and a Social Democrat leader, later came to ask my advice on the desirability of holding another meeting. He felt that, to perform its duty to Berlin's electors, the Assembly should meet without too much delay. His visit came at a very delicate stage in the affairs of the blockaded city. On August 2, the Western envoys in Moscow held their first meeting with Stalin to discuss the Berlin situation and the four military governors of Germany were having almost daily meetings in Berlin. All these discussions proved abortive, but I couldn't know this fact at the time.

My visitor said that his party, the SPD, favored meeting in the regular City Hall in the Russian sector despite the fact that Kotikov had not promised them police protection, and also despite the fact that the city government had received no official assurance that Berlin's problems had been solved in Moscow. The other two democratic parties, the CDU (Christian Democrats) and the LDP (Liberal Democrats) were afraid to hold such a meeting, remembering too vividly the cudgeling in the past.

I told Dr. Suhr that such a decision lay within the purview of the city government and was no concern of Military Government. When we returned government to the people of Berlin, giving them the right to elect their own officials and to conduct their own affairs, we had meant what we said.

One point was crystal clear. It was the Russian intention to make the city government inoperative, and not to snatch the democratic leaders in one fell swoop and ship them off to concentration camps.

"If the Russians can frighten the city government out of office, that will please them more than anything else," I said. "Therefore, it's important that you don't allow them to scare you into shirking your duty. Hold your meeting, by all means, even if violence does break out. In that case, it will be obvious to all the world that the Russians are preventing a democratic government from functioning."

The Assembly did meet on September 6, in the City Hall in the Russian sector. It was the last meeting that body ever held there, because of a series of nightmare happenings that would be written off as incredible—any place in the world except in Berlin.

The meeting was scheduled for noon. The Communists had ordered a crowd of party members and factory workers to demonstrate outside the building, but only about a thousand turned up. This meant that an unusually large percentage of goon squads was present. After the Assemblymen gathered and were prepared to start their session, the goon squads went into action and hammered down the doors. The mob swarmed through the building, shouting and cursing, occupied the Assembly chamber, and drove out the Assemblymen.

Unable to meet at their traditional headquarters, the democratic members of the Assembly—numbering about one hundred—moved into the British sector and called a meeting for that afternoon at the Taberna Academica Building. No Communists attended, but one of their stooges put in an appearance as an observer. The Communists seats remained vacant from that day on. They wisely stayed in the Russian sector to form part of the new rump government the Russians were cooking up to shove down the throats of the people in Eastern Berlin.

The Taberna was an old building, not like the comfortable and historic City Hall, which had dignified Berlin for many years. At first, the Assemblymen had no chairs or desks, and did business standing, but the Assembly was able to function. The initial step had been taken in splitting the city government between East and West, and the Assembly immediately made plans for new elections. An early resolution set a date for these elections—November 15, later changed to December 5.

While the Assemblymen were seeking shelter in the British sector, extraordinary scenes were taking place in the City Hall. As Kotikov had failed to furnish protection to the Assembly, Dr. Ferdinand Friedensburg, who temporarily was acting lord mayor, asked the Berlin Western police to send over a number of men in civilian clothes to keep order in the City Hall when the meeting started. A party of forty-six was assigned to the job.

Soviet Police Chief Markgraf got wind of this request and two hundred "Markgraf police," as they were called by the Germans, surrounded the building and then started combing the City Hall for the Western police, or "Strum police," as the Russians called them. The forty-six thereupon sought refuge in the American, British, and French liaison offices, which we maintained in the building.

Our liaison officers tried to protect the police, but there was little they could do. It was a bad show, to say the least. Deputy Police Chief Wagner, who commanded the Soviet police, was obeying orders directly from the Russian liaison officer, Major Krochkin. Forcing their way into the American liaison office, the Soviet police pushed aside our officer and seized twenty Western police who had huddled in the room.

The men were handcuffed and dragged, sobbing and screaming, out of the room, while an American lieutenant stood helplessly aside in the face of tommy guns brandished by Russian soldiers, brought in by the Russian liaison officer to help the police.

The remaining twenty-six Western police spent the night in the British and French offices, where they had fled. Russian troops and police drew a ring around the building and demanded that these men be turned over, but no attempt was made to take them.

Twenty hours later, the unfortunate police were still trapped in the building. Finally, on the night of September 7, the French military governor, General Koenig, obtained a promise from Sokolovsky that the police would be permitted to return to the Western sectors. The French commandant, Ganeval, thereupon contacted Kotikov early the next morning and told him of Sokolovsky's promise. Kotikov assured him that the men would be released immediately.

Ganeval sent over two French trucks to pick up the men, but the Russian troops refused to let them leave the City Hall. Ganeval finally reached Kotikov at four o'clock in the morning and the Russian gave his word of honor that the men would be released and allowed to return to the Western sectors.

The two French trucks went back to the City Hall. With

Kotikov's personal guarantee and Sokolovsky's promise—the highest you could get, except from Stalin—the Western police emerged from the building. As they filed out, the Russians arrested them at gunpoint and took them off to prison in the Soviet sector. Three of the men subsequently received long prison terms from the Russians and the others were eventually released. So much for Russian promises.

Berliners did not take these outrages calmly. If the Russians thought the blockade was breaking their spirit, they were due for a sad awakening. Three days after the city government was driven out of the Russian sector—September 9—nearly three hundred thousand Germans assembled in Platz der Republik, outside the old *Reichstag* building in the British sector, to protest against Communist attempts to take over the city government and against the Russian attempt to starve them into submission. It was the biggest democratic demonstration in the political history of Berlin, and men and women from all walks of life stood in the rain to cheer their leaders, Ernst Reuter, Otto Suhr, and Franz Neumann. *"Freiheit!"* (freedom) was the cry from thousands of throats as the speakers said, "We call upon the world for support in our struggle for democracy. We've been through this once before. We've had one single dictatorial party and we don't want another. Let the Communists get control and they will lead us to ruin!"

The crowd, passive enough at the beginning, began to stir uneasily, and finally broke up into groups. Several thousand paraded to the Allied Control Authority to present a petition to the commanders. Others left on different missions. Several youths were noticed scaling the Brandenburg Gate at the entrance to the Russian sector, bent on reaching a Red flag fluttering there.

Once at the top, they tore down the flag, scrambled to the ground with it, and grimly started to burn it. At the same moment, seven Russian guards at a Soviet war memorial nearby rushed over, grabbed their flag and fired into the mass of people. A great, frightening roar went up from the crowd. With remarkable presence of mind and great coolness, the British deputy provost marshal walked calmly over to the Russians and, with his swagger stick, pushed them away from the threatening Germans.

A jeepload of Russian troops appeared and the men were saved from mauling, or worse, by the British, who put a squad of MP's around the monument. Some of the mob surged over into the Russian side of the gate, yelling, "Let's drive the Russians back to Moscow!" and, "Let's drive the Communists out of Berlin!"

The Russians fired again. Reports differed on how many Germans were killed but four were buried the following week, after a long, impressive funeral procession. Then, as suddenly as it had started, the Brandenburg Gate fury was over. But it made a deep impression on my mind. The Russians were re-building a terrific hate balance in the German ledger.

CHAPTER XII

MY FOURTH and last winter in Berlin was approaching. There is nothing poetic about Berlin winters. The city lies as far north as Labrador, and the weather becomes quite as bitter. Each fall brought the threat of another food crisis, contingent upon the weather and the bare adequacy of the ration the population was receiving.

We had survived two mild winters and one severe season, in 1947—during that terrible time two thousand Germans froze to death. And that was in the relatively carefree days before the blockade, when trainloads of food came into Berlin regularly. What would happen if the coming months proved severe, now that we were reduced to the meager limits of air supply?

It was a question I dared not attempt to answer when I surveyed the situation. If the winter were severe, the consequences of Russia's starvation policy would be calamitous, now that the city's needs were slashed to only four thousand tons of supplies a day. If we had a prolonged spell of bad flying weather, which would reduce deliveries and force us to cut rations, the result would be almost as disastrous.

Two signs alone were encouraging. The Germans were standing up well under the siege, and the airlift was developing so rapidly that within the next few months we could look toward greater tonnages—six, seven, perhaps eight thousand tons a day. Those valiant old carriers, the C-47's, that had rushed to our aid in the early days of our need, were withdrawn. From Western Germany came C-54's, four-engine planes with a pay load of ten tons. The British also brought in bigger planes, Tudors and Yorks, almost the size of ours, and began developing tanker planes to bring in gasoline, kerosene, and Diesel oil in bulk.

Our reliance on the airlift increased, and so did deliveries.

Most people living near airports regard the noise of the planes as a public nuisance. To me, Tempelhof was a stirring symphony. The roar of incoming planes, dropping supplies and rushing back for more, was great music in my ears. The engines seemed to repeat, "We're licking the blockade! We're licking the blockade!"

Every load that hit the ground meant another hole in the Russian stockade around Berlin and another assurance of survival. As a demonstration of our capacity and our resources, 897 airlift flights were flown on Air Force Day, September 18, 1948, while Berliners still seethed against the Communists for driving out the elected city government.

By this time, the Russians had realized the mistake they had made in their calculations when they overlooked airlift possibilities. All supplies were flown in from West Germany along narrow, prescribed corridors alloted us by the Russians, from which our pilots rarely diverged, except in cases of bad weather or excusable deviation in view of the new tactics adopted by the Russians to impede the flow of food into Berlin. Russian Yak fighters started buzzing transport planes. The first airlift casuality was a collision between a transport and a Russian fighter. On occasion, the Russians warned us ahead of air maneuvers involving our corridors, but nothing deterred us from maintaining our regular schedules.

All these airlift performances added up to a magnificent total, but conditions still were grim in the Western sectors. By careful economy and allocation, we managed an average ration of 1,790 calories a day. We had to keep our fingers constantly on the pulse of the patient, and at the same time keep a watchful eye on his diet. Deliveries were so arranged that we wouldn't have to dig into our reserves, except in case of extreme necessity. Common prudence dictated this policy, and the economics of the situation endorsed it. Berliners couldn't be said to be living: they were subsisting doggedly until better times came.

As commandant of the American sector, and as the man whose name stood at the top of the first page of the Russian blacklist, I couldn't hope to escape special Russian attention.

Any time that Soviet Radio Berlin could think up something defamatory or insulting about me, the air was full of my misdeeds. I sometimes wonder how I managed to keep any friends at all in Berlin.

My house in Gelferstrasse was a regular Russian target. I used to get strange telephone calls late at night, designed to break my rest and keep my nerves jangling. Sometimes a strange voice out of the void would advise me to get out of Berlin, more often there was only silence when I picked up the receiver. My doorbell rang at the most extraordinary hours, but there was no one there when we answered. Originally, I had no guard outside our house, but I put one on later. All this unpleasantness was part of a terrorist campaign against me personally. I tried to keep this fact in mind when they woke me at three A.M. with an anonymous phone call.

Passing months showed the success of our resistance to the blockade, but we never were free from the possibility that the Russians would resort to military means to achieve what they could not obtain by the blockade. Soviet Radio Berlin constantly harped on the theme that the Western powers were on their way out, and if they weren't, they would be driven out. Every time this line came over the air, I was swamped with inquiries from anxious Germans.

With me in Berlin were Edith, my wife, and our four children. It was necessary that they stick it out, if for no other reason than to serve as a symbol of American determination not to be driven from Berlin. The Germans understandably would have been unnerved if top-ranking American families had suddenly started to pull out. As it was, the Russians announced periodically that Edith had become panic stricken and was leaving, but she never budged, although there were times when both of us wished fervently that she could take the children and get out of Berlin.

"You know we don't stand a chance if the Russians come in," I reminded her one day. "I'll be killed and you know what will happen to you."

Edith herself put it all in the proper cold light when she

replied, a little fearfully, "If anything happens, Frank, the Russians will throw me to the regiment."

We weren't being melodramatic; there was no guarantee that the Russians would not turn to force. Long before the blockade, I had slept with a pistol under my pillow, and the blockade only intensified my apprehensions of the ultimate intention of the Russians—if everything else failed. Force was a factor in which they had never lost faith.

The East-West split in the city government caused us many excursions and alarms, indicating the combustible nature of the situation. One of these incidents was the subject of a sharp disagreement I had with General Clay.

We received word that the Russians and the Communists were planning a big rally of supporters to march into the American and British sectors, their ostensible errand being to present a petition to the Allied Control Authority. Our undercover men in Communist organizations tipped us off and provided us with an order issued to the Soviet police to slip into our sector and make one hundred arrests during the excitement and confusion of the parade. We actually did arrest two of the ringleaders, armed with pistols, and carrying all the evidence we needed. Provided the Russians could assemble enough supporters, here was a direct threat to the American and British sectors.

Co-ordinating our plans with the British, we decided to block the bridges across Teltow Canal, which parallels the two sectors, and the two railroad bridges, using fire hoses and possibly tear gas. The British would follow the same plan, but would allow the leaders to cross before restraining the rest of the crowd, which would enable them to arrest at least a hundred key men. We would allow a delegation, not exceeding twenty, to proceed to the ACA.

I explained the plan to Major General Hays and to our Chief of Staff, both of whom approved. Then I was called in by Clay, and I also explained the plan to him. Clay rejected it, and instructed me to let the crowd into our sector and allow them to march to the ACA building, but not to enter it.

"It is my belief that the right of petition is basic," he explained. "It would be undemocratic to handle the matter in the way you suggest."

All I could do under the circumstances was to put my view before him in the most forceful manner possible, pointing out that, if we got that anticipated mob in our sector, we would have great difficulty holding it without using much more effective weapons than fire hoses and tear gas. The Russians had drummed up a crowd of seventy-five thousand for the dress rehearsal, and they had been harangued by no less a personage than a Russian colonel. But Clay was adamant.

Fortunately for us, the big parade fizzled out. Only a small number of troublemakers turned up for the demonstration, and the march to the ACA building failed to materialize. I had already canceled precautionary measures in the American sector but the British, being informed of what I had done under orders, stood fast—just in case.

The number of important visitors to Berlin seemed to increase after the blockade. In October, 1948, even John Foster Dulles, who everyone assumed would be the next Secretary of State if Dewey became President, flew into Berlin to look over the situation. Dulles was reported to be harboring a certain antipathy toward General Clay, and we all watched events with interest.

On Sunday, I was invited to lunch at Clay's home. When I arrived, I found Dulles in front of the fireplace with our host, Robert Murphy, James W. Riddleberger, and a State Department aide brought along by Dulles.

Despite the cheerful, leaping flames, the climate around the fireplace was anything but warm. Ice divided Dulles and Clay. We sat down to lunch, and I was given the foot of the table, facing Clay. Murphy is a man of great charm, but even under his influence the little conversation carried on at the table was stilted. The only subject on which Clay and Dulles appeared to agree was Rhine wine. On that theme they were in perfect accord.

Over the coffee, Clay suggested that perhaps the visitor would like to see Dr. Reuter, the unseated lord mayor. Dulles turned to his State Department adviser and asked if there were any political difficulties involved.

"I have the greatest respect for the opinions of General Clay and Mr. Murphy," the State Department man said. "If they think it is all right, I think so, too."

"I might just as well have left you in Paris," snapped Dulles, "if that's all the advice you are able to offer me."

Reuter arrived soon after lunch and we all sat down in a circle with Reuter, the German. Their chairs were only three feet apart, but their backgrounds and thinking were three leagues apart. The two talked for perhaps ten minutes.

"Will the Germans stand fast during the winter?" Dulles demanded, wasting no time on preliminaries. "Or will they give up, accept Russian aid, and get us out of Berlin rather than take more suffering?"

Reuter's reply was emphatic and had the unmistakable ring of sincerity. "The people of Berlin are accustomed to suffering," he reminded Dulles. "We are willing to suffer a great deal more to escape Russian domination."

Dulles seemed impressed. He then asked Reuter if he thought that the Russians would attempt to bring in large quantities of food and coal in order to embarrass the Western powers in Berlin.

Where would the Russians get more food or coal, unless they robbed the Germans in their own zone, Reuter asked reasonably. There were great shortages, he added, not only in the Russian zone of Germany but in Russia herself and in her satellite countries. "I think the Russians will be reluctant to splurge in Berlin," he added. "They are more afraid of the Americans really putting on a show than we are of the Russians doing the same thing."

This was about the extent of their conversation. At its conclusion, Dulles and his civilian aide retired to Clay's study and prepared a press release reaffirming the American intention to stay in Berlin. With complete accuracy, Dulles added that this was an extraordinary situation, since allies of only a few years ago were no longer allies. The talk with Reuter was not mentioned.

Dulles returned to the States. Clay followed him, to give a speech in New York at the Alfred E. Smith Foundation dinner. The newspapers were full of pictures of the event, but the best one showed the principal guests: Cardinal Spellman, Dewey, and Clay. An American in Berlin seized the picture and promptly wisecracked, "There you have the man who prays on Sunday, the man who talks on Sunday, and the man who works on Sunday," the last remark referring to Clay, who had been so busy in Berlin that he was compelled to ignore the day of rest.

If Dulles thought that Reuter was speaking only to make a favorable impression, Berliners were not long in dispelling this doubt. The *Magistrat* followed the City Assembly over into the Western sectors, because it was impossible to maintain order at meetings in the Russian sector. The deciding issue rose over the action of Schmidt, the Communist labor head, who was legally removed from office but refused to vacate his seat and continued to attend *Magistrat* meetings. Dr. Friedensburg, as acting lord mayor, asked Schmidt to leave but he refused, arrogantly taking the floor and preventing the transaction of normal business. Deprived of any police powers, the only thing that Friedensburg could do was to adjourn the meeting and move the *Magistrat* over to our sectors.

In accordance with the temporary constitution we had given the city two years previously, the City Assembly had to prepare a provisional constitution and, at the same time, provide us with a procedure for new elections. Since only the three Western powers now met at the Kommandatura, we acted individually and approved both the constitution and the election procedure. Judged by Western standards, the constitution wasn't perfect, but we argued that, if it was what the elected government wanted, we were willing to accept it.

The final date set for the elections was December 5. As we anticipated, the Russians refused to approve the constitution, the election procedure, or the date. They didn't exactly say no, they merely attached conditions that the city government couldn't possibly meet.

Although the Russian obstruction machine had shifted into high gear against us, the democratic parties in the city government went ahead with preparations. They had to surmount high obstacles in the preliminary stages of organizing a city-wide ballot. To block election preparations, a Soviet tribunal was convened and found the leading democratic leaders guilty of being "Fascists and warmongers." Ignoring this ludicrous charge, the city government decided to proceed with the elections and, in all fairness, to permit delegations from the Russian zone to sit in on sessions of the *Magistrat* and the Assembly, if they desired.

Five days before the elections, the Russians completed the split· in the Berlin administration. A puppet *Magistrat* was established in the Russian sector, after an *opéra bouffe* meeting in the Berlin Opera House.

Always seeking well-known names for their political machinations, the Russians selected Friedrich Ebert, Jr., to head the new body, and he was "unanimously elected" by a group of (SED) Communist party delegates and various fancy fellow-traveler groups organized to give the farce at the Opera House some show of authenticity.

Ebert, a fat, repulsive man, was the complete opportunist and a pliable Communist dupe. He was the son of the first president of the ill-fated Weimar Republic. When Ebert's brother, living in Bavaria, heard of his new role, he publicly disowned him in an outraged effort to vindicate the memory of their distinguished father.

This establishment of a separate administration had been anticipated, but the timing was unexpected. We thought that the Russians would wait to make such a move until after the December 5 elections in West Berlin, which would give them an excuse to blame us for splitting the city government. Their action, of course, was thoroughly illegal, and I didn't hesitate to say so. In a press communique issued the same day, I pointed out that the Opera House meeting was "an arrogant action—in flagrant violation of the existing constitution of Berlin and of all quadripartite agreements pertaining to the city."

Faced with this challenge, the Russian propaganda machine showed unbridled capacity for downright evil. The Communists refused to allow their candidates to appear on the ballot,

so that it could turn all its vituperative fury against the democratic candidates. The Communists had supported the Russian
blockade and, quite understandably, dared not face the Berlin
electorate.

Their campaign was a heady mixture of gilded promises and
dire threats. The Russians forbade the elections in their own
sector and urged the Germans in the Western sectors to boycott
the polls. Through the puppet mouth of Ebert, they were
offered food, coal, power, and light if they stayed away and
rejected "American imperialism." The source of all these boun-
ties was not explained, with the usual Russian ability to ignore
hampering details.

And if the Germans pigheadedly spurned such inducements,
there was always the big stick. A whispering campaign was
started to frighten voters away. It was suggested that the polling
lists, bearing their names, would fall into Russian hands after
the early evacuation of the city by the Western Allies and
then . . . So convinced were the Communists of our impending
departure that the day before the elections the Soviet mouthpiece, *Taegliche Rundschau,* carried this front-page banner
line: "The Western Powers Will Leave Berlin in January."

Reports were circulated that Communist gangs would march
into the Western sectors and attack voters. I let the Russians
and their Red stooges know that, if anyone marched into our
sector, he wouldn't run into a handful of frightened, unarmed
Germans but into the United States Army. I put it very bluntly:
Attempts to use force would be met by force. The democratic
parties did what they should have done before: they organized
their own strong-arm squads to take care of Communist rowdies
at pre-election rallies.

Berliners in the three Western sectors replied to Russian
threats and blandishments by going to the polls in greater numbers than anyone expected. No longer did the multiplicity of
party programs obscure the decision. The issue was as clear as a
newly washed windowpane.

My official report reads: "It was a choice between two funda-
mentally opposed political systems: Totalitarianism, supported
by a police state devoid of any basic civil rights for the individ-

ual, and Western World Democracy, where the traditional constitutional safeguards of individual rights and political liberty prevail."

With no Communist candidates, the election campaign of the three democratic parties was not conducted along strictly party lines but as a joint demonstration against totalitarianism. Voting reached a total of 83.6 per cent of the electorate, far larger than in any American presidential election, in spite of bad weather and lack of public transport. The biggest turnout was in the American sector, followed by the British and the French.

The results were:

SPD	(Social Democrats)	64.5 per cent	76 seats
CDU	(Christian Democrats)	19.4 per cent	26 seats
LDP	(Liberal Democrats)	16.1 per cent	17 seats

The Social Democrats gained at the expense of the Christian Democrats, whose reputation was declining because of lack of positive leadership under Dr. Friedensburg who was inclined to fence-sitting and frequently showed marked sympathy with Russian aims.

After the elections, the City Assembly elected Dr. Reuter as lord mayor, reaffirming the previous decision, which had been vetoed by the Russians. Reuter replaced Frau Schroeder, who reverted to her rank of deputy mayor. This courageous woman had been absent from her office for a long time, owing to illness, and Dr. Friedensburg had substituted for her. Both were re-elected to office.

With this splendid manifestation of Berlin's popular will fresh in our minds, my consternation can be imagined when I was called into a conference a few days later with a group of high-level experts, who were preparing a study of the Berlin situation for the State Department. They showed me a draft of their cable report, which was an academic study, including every conceivable possibility ranging from an immediate compromise between the Soviets and the U.S. government in Berlin to an enforced ending of the blockade.

I am afraid that I blew my top at the discovery that our officials on the spot would waste time even considering any

measures other than definitely anti-Russian, antipuppet measures.

"You're planning appeasement before the murderer has had
time to wipe the blood off his hands," I charged. "You are
ignoring this terrific democratic demonstration at the elections
and selling the people of Berlin down the river at the very
moment that they're fighting for a cause that is also ours."

I also told Riddleberger, who was simply obeying orders, and
the conferees that we should let the Russians know that we were
damn well fed up, and that they must stop using force against us
and against the people under our control. I advocated a number
of positive measures against the Russians, including a counterblockade and official condemnation of members of the puppet
government in their sector as criminals.

Taking a deep breath, I protested, "Furthermore, I think it
is an international disgrace for us to announce to the world that
we would not negotiate until the blockade was lifted and then
send Ambassador Bedell Smith in Moscow to see Stalin for the
purposes of negotiating. It is my firm conviction that if we don't
show we mean business the Russians will continue to use force
against us and we may reach a point where war is inevitable."

I was not popular at that conference, either.

Clay called me in later and supported my view concerning
the necessity for strong measures. Discouraging speeches had
been made in Washington, including one by Senator Tom
Connally, who had expressed a preference for appeasement and
"getting along with the Russians." Clay, however, could not go
along with me all the way on retaliatory measures, such as denying the Russians the use of railroads, canals, and barges in our
sector. He agreed that such a policy would hurt the Communists, but it also might hurt many innocent Germans. He authorized me to make a staff study on effective counterpunches.

On November 1, the three Western powers had good news
for blockaded Berlin. We increased food rations by approximately 20 per cent, placing particular emphasis on fats and
sugar. Growing children, who had suffered most and were badly
undernourished, received an increase of almost 300 calories in
their daily ration. The new average ration for the population

was nearly 2,000 calories, or approximately 220 more than before the blockade.

I never saw a people react more quickly and pleasantly to good tidings than did the Berliners that day. It was the best news they had heard since the Western Allies arrived in Berlin. The measure was very popular, not only because of its immediate results but because of the confidence it implanted regarding the coming winter. The increase added another hundred tons to our airlift requirements, but the adjustment was made so skillfully that we felt justified in granting it. At this time our reserves stood at thirty-nine days' supply, three days more than our original figure.

Another source of help for Berliners was the people of West Germany. The siege established bonds of sympathy between the metropolitan inhabitants and the rest of the country that had never existed before. The Bavarians, and the citizens of other non-Prussian provinces, had always disliked the Prussians. But now, all over West Germany, mass meetings were held to raise funds and collect food and clothing for the relief of Berlin. We soon had a new problem on our hands. It wasn't a case of food or clothing shortages, but of air transport to bring in these gifts. In the end, we had to prevail upon the city government to send representatives into West Germany to instruct the people what was most needed in Berlin and how to organize their donations for air transport.

Hardly had we brought cheer into the dark lives of the people with this extra food ration and the gifts from their own people than the weather devilishly turned against us. Air deliveries began to sag alarmingly. We had realized from the beginning that the airlift could never meet all our requirements during the winter months, but would enable us to stretch our resources, maintain a minimum subsistence standard, and give us time to think. If the Western powers had been hurried into making a bad decision at that time and the result had been starvation, it would have meant a great victory for the Communists and we should have lost ground all over Europe.

General Weather, the unconquerable Russian general, positively frowned on us, and we could almost hear the Russians guffawing through the Iron Curtain. The worst enemy of air operations is not cold, but fog, and we had plenty of that, too—thick, impenetrable fog. November and December were bad months. During November, fifteen of the thirty days were almost impossible for flying, and December wasn't much better. It wasn't until spring, when we installed the most modern radar equipment available, that we began to lick the weather.

Mounting steadily from the first July shipment of 261 tons, carried in Army duffel bags, daily coal shipments by September equaled daily consumption, and we didn't have to make inroads on our stocks. But with the advent of winter and increased demand, we faced a grave situation. Our coal reserves declined rapidly. It was necessary to have on hand at least fourteen days' supply to maintain utilities, but the frightening way in which our stocks were disappearing warned us that, unless we replenished them at once, they would be exhausted within a week or—at the most—ten days.

At that time, we had thirty-one days' supply of food on hand. Hoping for a break in the weather and a better flow of deliveries, we decided to have coal deliveries made at the expense of food. Gas and electricity were down to a new low. Trolley cars and trailers, meant to carry 124 persons seated and standing, had to pack in 175. Our decision caused food reserves to dwindle to twenty-seven days' supply, but served to hold coal stocks at a nineteen or twenty days' level.

Fortunately for Berliners, it was a mild winter, but even so there was considerable suffering among the 920,000 families entrusted to our care. Where positive suffering was absent, there was the continual, dreary darkness. Light and power were off except for two daily periods of two hours each. Families with electric stoves couldn't eat when they wanted to because of these staggered hours. Some housewives had to get up at three o'clock in the morning to cook their meals. Others trailed along during the day, the periods rotating to maintain an even supply. People couldn't read, because there was no light most of the time. If they visited their friends, they did so in the dark. Gas, used for cooking by the majority of Berliners, was shut off at nine o'clock each night. People with gas burners often forgot this, and when the gas went on in the morning were often gas victims. Exhausted by the grim existence that was the lot of them all, they were asphyxiated in their sleep.

In December, we made a special issue of twenty-five pounds—not tons—of coal to each household, increasing this amount to one hundred pounds for homes with children below school age, sick or blind persons. With healthy children of my own, I was never able to forget that the tubercular children in the hospitals didn't have blankets so the windows of their wards couldn't be opened for life-giving fresh air.

At the same time, we started to encourage extensive wood cutting. All over the city, bands of Germans went out thinning the woods, stripping the parks, and digging up half-buried roots for firewood. The original order sent to the *Magistrat* was to cut 350,000 cubic meters of wood, but the city fathers came back with a plan to cut only 120,000. Berlin is a city of beautiful parks and wooded spaces. Cutting down a tree is almost sacrilege to a German. I raised no objection to the city government's reduced plan. As far as I was concerned, this was a matter for the Germans themselves to decide. Personally, I thought it wiser to cut the trees and keep warm. Trees can always be grown again. For our part, we would bring in as much coal as the airlift would permit to ensure adequate heating, but it wouldn't be a great deal.

The Communists, who never before revealed any aesthetic leanings, started screaming against the Western powers for threatening to blight the Berlin landscape by cutting down her fine trees and against the city government for sanctioning such "barbarism." The city, the Russian radio shouted, will be completely denuded of trees. This will wreck the watershed and, they suddenly discovered, "the temperature of the city will be ten degrees hotter in the summer without trees."

Our only direct interest in the wood-cutting project involved the case of General Herbert and Dr. Friedensburg, the acting lord mayor. The facts seemed indicative of childish behavior to me, but the case showed how important it was for commandants to preserve their poise and a balanced viewpoint; otherwise a trifling incident could be magnified into international proportions. Herbert, who was chairman of the three-power Kommandatura that month, tried to tell the city government how it should operate and got into a squabble with Friedensburg. The British commandant claimed that after an interview, the Acting Lord Mayor released information to the press that was contrary to what had been said. Herbert thereupon called in Friedensburg and gave him a dressing down. The German made another public statement, and Herbert repeated the treatment.

The first time I heard of the incident was when my liaison officer told me that Friedensburg was going to write a letter to Herbert, accusing the commandant of trying to kill him politically and of threatening him in other ways. If this letter had been delivered and released to the press, it would have had repercussions in Paris, where the Council of Foreign Ministers was meeting to discuss the Berlin situation, and all the way to the United Nations in New York, in whose lap the Western powers had dumped the Berlin question.

Had the letter been published, the Russians would have had a legitimate reason for declaring that our protestations to the United Nations against their actions in Germany should not be taken too seriously in view of the fact that a Western commandant had tried to intimidate the acting head of the Berlin city government.

I first talked with Friedensburg and persuaded him not to write that letter. Then I talked with Herbert and pointed out the grave dangers of the situation. We both realized that the Acting Lord Mayor had a good mind, but that he was cunning and an opportunist. I am convinced that he would have enjoyed playing the exalted martyr, under attack by both the East and the West commandants.

Ever since the Russian walkout, the Kommandatura building in our sector had remained vacant. It took me until the end of December to persuade our two allies that we should remain in the building. The makeshift arrangement of meeting at each other's offices was entirely unsatisfactory, causing confusion and doubling our difficulties. The orginal reasons for needing a Kommandatura building had not lost their validity. Allied secretariats had to return to the building to have access to common files, rather than triplicate files. There were the obvious difficulties of operating at three headquarters instead of one. In November, I gave my two colleagues the choice of returning or closing the building for the winter owing to the scarcity of coal. They then agreed on tripartite meetings, and on tripatrite provision of coal for heating, based on the rotation of chairmanship.

Our decision to return was made at Ganeval's headquarters. A joint press release announcing the fact was decided upon after I had requested the change of one significant word, which indicated that the Russians could return to the Kommandatura any time they chose. I insisted that the verb be made conditional, indicating that they *might* be received back into the Kommandatura if they so desired. My opinion was that too much had happened since they walked out. A blockade had been clamped on Berlin, and the Russians, in my estimation, had sacrificed their right to come back. We had been forced to spend millions of dollars to fly food, coal, and supplies into Berlin. Up to that date, twenty-seven Americans and seven Britishers had died in the airlift. Internally, the Russians had completely and unilaterally split the city government. I thought they had plenty of explaining and adjusting to do before we should receive them back on an equal basis—if ever.

As it turned out, I was not present at our actual return to the Kommandatura. I had gone to Baden-Baden as the guest of General Koenig and couldn't get back in time because all planes were grounded at Frankfurt by bad weather. My nonappearance upset the Soviet-licensed press. All the puppet papers had stories written along the same line—the British and French commandants were stooges for the American commandant. One cartoon showed a giant exaggeration of my five feet ten, feet planked on the Kommandatura conference table, with miniatures of Ganeval and Herbert in my pocket.

Christmas week end was of great importance for Military Government in Berlin. Two groups of top VIP's arrived. Bob Hope, Jinx Falkenburg, and Jane Russell composed one group sent to cheer Americans in Berlin. The other included Vice-

President Alben Barkley, Secretary of the Army Kenneth C. Royall, Secretary of Air William S. Symington, General Jimmy Doolittle, Ambassador Bedell Smith, Elmer Davis, and a battery of other heavy artillery and their wives. As guests of General and Mrs. Clay, they all sat in the two front rows at the Titania Palast for the Bob Hope show.

After the performance came the speeches. Secretary Royall announced the issue of a ribbon for the Berlin airlift and decorated two sergeants. Vice-President Barkley made a homey sort of speech, which Hope promptly parodied. For at least thirty seconds, the comedian, with mock humility, delivered a rapid-fire monologue about the man who had made President Truman's election possible. We all expected him to say Barkley, who sat there beaming. Hope's punch line was "Dewey"! The Vice-President plainly enjoyed the joke.

The day after Christmas, Royall called on me at my office for a briefing on the Berlin situation. It was the strangest "briefing" I ever gave.

First, I asked Royall how much time he had. He said he had "enough time." I then started with the history of Berlin, beginning at the Elbe. Royall interrupted and said, "I know all about that."

I made a second start, talking about the Kommandatura. Again he cut me off by saying he was familiar with that, too.

I started a third time, along the lines of how the Russians had slapped on the blockade. "I have all that material back in my office," he said. "And I don't want to see any more charts, either. I've seen hundreds of them."

"Well, what the hell do you want?" I asked.

Royall seemed startled, then he grinned. "What I want to know are things that apply today," he said, "not ancient history." Then he began asking specific questions. "For instance," he said, "what would have happened if we had brought an armored convoy into Berlin when the blockade started last June?"

I wasn't troop commander and therefore was aware of the limitations of my knowledge on that subject. But I said that if he wanted a direct answer he could have it.

"We would have got our *derrières* shot off," I replied—except that I have never been known to use the word *derrière*.

"Then what would happen if we brought one in this month or at some future date?" he pursued.

"We'd have a better chance," I assured him. "But you must remember that the Russian decision will be based solely upon their estimation of our willingness to fight, weighed against their own ability to fight and to put on a better show than we do. Our chances will increase as the willingness of the American people to fight increases, and as our rearmament progresses."

The Army Secretary asked a number of questions about what steps the Russians could take in Berlin to injure us further.

"Short of marching in," I replied, "they can't do much more than they've done already. If the Russians had thought there was anything more they could do to us, they would have done it already."

I quoted him facts and figures, and went through my favorite topic—retaliation, counterblockade, and other aggressive measures, until the blockade was lifted.

Royall never indicated to me whether he approved or disapproved of my answers, but he certainly got them all straight from the shoulder. In a very short time, I gave him a lot of up-to-the-minute information on the Berlin situation. Later, I understood that he was instrumental in having me promoted to the rank of brigadier general. The Regular Army view, as it had been firmly outlined to me, was that a Reserve colonel couldn't expect promotion with so many Regular Army officers ahead of him.

CHAPTER XIII

FOG-BOUND November and December were the acid test of the airlift. If we could put these two normally bad flying months behind us without serious disaster to the people we were feeding, and get well into January, we should know that we had the blockade licked. As it was, although we had sacrificed food shipments to build up our coal stocks, by the end of the year our coal reserves had slumped to a dangerous low of sixty-five thousand tons.

When conditions seemed blackest, the weather miraculously improved, and thenceforth air deliveries increased rapidly. More planes began to arrive daily, our new radar equipment reduced the weather hazard, we perfected loading and handling techniques, and very soon reached eight thousand tons a day, building up both our reserves and our confidence in the future. Short of military action, which might lead to another war, there was nothing the Russians could do to make their wicked plot succeed.

The airlift became a two-way traffic operation that hit the Russians. A small amount of industrial activity was revived in our sectors, owing to our ability to spare a limited quantity of coal and power, and manufactured goods started flowing into Western Germany. We defiantly stamped all boxes and crates, "Made in Blockaded Berlin," which had a certain cheering effect when the freight reached its destination.

Not a factor essential to minimum living or to minimum industrial maintenance was overlooked by our technicians in organizing expanding air deliveries. In addition to food, coal, petroleum products, and raw materials, we brought in clothing, sanitary supplies, soap powder, cutlery, hot-water bottles, and even adding and calculating machines.

We had our difficulties. Take, for instance, salt, a household commodity whose presence on the kitchen shelf is so taken for granted that its vital importance to human existence is often overlooked. Domestically and industrially, West Berlin consumed thirty-eight tons of salt a day, or about five planeloads. Salt, we discovered, could not be carried in ordinary aircraft because it leaked from its containers, worked its way through the floor, and corroded the controls.

British Sunderland flying boats were the answer. They brought in salt from Hamburg to the seaplane base at Havel, the former Luftwaffe base near our sector. When bad weather halted flying-boat operation, we employed ordinary land craft, with outside panniers under the fuselage to carry the salt—a modern version of the ancient methods of the salt caravans of Asia.

Evidence, more convincing than statistics, that we had licked the blockade came from the Russians themselves. One of my Russian-speaking officers, wearing civilian clothes, took the subway toward Potsdam. Entering the train, he sat down beside two Russian officers, a colonel and a major. Pulling out a German newspaper, he pretended to be engrossed. The two Russians were chatting idly until an airlift plane headed for Tempelhof came down fairly low and the roar of its engine interrupted their conversation. That was at a time when supply planes were dropping out of the sky every five minutes.

"The Americans seem to be making out all right with the airlift," said the major to the colonel.

"Yes, they are," his companion agreed, "but this morning I was talking to Alexander Gregoreovitch—"

"Who?" the first officer interrupted.

"You know, the General," the second Russian reminded him cautiously. The Russians never used the last names of their generals in conversation or, if they did, they disguised them carefully. I suspect the general they were talking about was Kotikov.

"Alexander Gregoreovitch also says the Americans are doing

all right," he continued, "and he says that we'll have to give them the old wart treatment."

"What's the wart treatment?" his obviously unenlightened companion asked.

"Well, you know when you have a wart on your finger," the colonel explained patiently, "you put a string around it. Then you tie the string very tight, and keep on tightening it. Then, he says, you wait until the wart falls off."

But Alexander Gregoreovitch was wrong; we didn't get the old wart treatment. Everybody, including the Russians, knew that the airlift was a success and that the blockade had failed.

While the Kommandatura had no official contacts with the Russians during the blockade, we established individual relationships. If I had business with the Russians, I jumped into my car, drove over to the Soviet military headquarters and marched in to see Kotikov, or whomever else I had come to see.

This approach brought an extraordinary call one day. Colonel Kalinin, Kotikov's Chief of Staff, phoned and asked if I would send my chief liaison officer over to his office to pick up an American soldier, who had got into trouble. When I told Kalinin that he could turn the man over to the Provost Marshal in the usual manner, he demurred. That was impossible, he explained; he had some other matters of importance to discuss with my liaison officer.

I sent over my man and he picked up the soldier. There was nothing sensational about the case. An American had got drunk in a bar in the Russian sector and started kicking up a row. Kalinin, however, said that the real purpose of the interview was to make a request: In all Berlin matters, the Russians would like to deal directly with me.

"General Kotikov would rather deal with General Howley than through any other military or civil channel," Kalinin said. "While we find him a hard opponent, we like his frankness and businesslike way of handling things."

This was a backhanded compliment—but was another proof that they would rather deal with a tough opponent, who is frank and wastes no time, than with the long-winded diplomatic smoothies, who don't fool the Russians with their indirect methods. General Smirnov, Kotikov's predecessor, in one of his rare lonely-hearts confessions, had said, "Colonel Howley knows only one attack—straight to the jaw. We respect his honesty—but this method means that he often gets personally hurt."

What I am trying to prove is that the boys sitting in the Pentagon and the State Department who, at this late date, still favor appeasement rather than a tough, honest policy, simply don't know the Russians. And what's even more important, they won't earn the respect of the Russians by their smooth methods.

Tight lines were drawn between the Soviet sector and the three Western sectors, but they didn't prevent intermingling during the blockade. A check in December showed, along the seventy-seven-mile boundary of the three Western sectors, a ring of ninety-two control points manned by Soviet police—one at every street leading from our territory into theirs. Actually, of course, it was impossible for the Russians to seal hermetically the three Western sectors. About eighty thousand Germans, living in our sector and working in another, or doing business outside their own sector, went back and forth daily. Those carrying Western sector newspapers, or obvious parcels of food, were stopped and the contraband confiscated. At times, when the guards felt particularly energetic, even pocketbooks were turned inside out. Theoretically, the Germans were not permitted to bring anything into our sectors, but the Russians, so keen on searching people on the slightest pretext, shrank at the formidable task of searching eighty thousand every day.

However, this intermingling did not mean fraternization as far as the Americans were concerned. During the Christmas holidays, my Chief of Staff attended a party with French and British Chiefs of Staff. In good Yuletide spirit, they telephoned over to Soviet headquarters, talked with the Russian Chief of Staff, and indulged in the customary pleasantries.

I learned of this incident on the same day that my secretary placed on my desk a letter from the widow of one of my Military Government officers who had been killed in an airlift crash. I didn't feel in any mood to have any American mislead the Russians into thinking we didn't care about our own people or that we were willing to forget what they were doing to us and to the entire city of Berlin.

Without delay, I issued an order banning fraternization, making particular reference to inviting Russians into our sector to eat our food. It didn't make sense to me—at least emotionally —that we should fly in food at the cost of American lives, while the German population suffered the agonies of cold and hunger, and still continue to be friendly with the people who were responsible, even committing the social error of letting them eat the very food they were trying to keep from our mouths.

My order brought down considerable criticism on my head, but I refused to rescind it. There wasn't a great deal of fraternization in any case, and the little there was came from our side, not theirs. As one Russian general told me, in the earlier and happier days of our Berlin occupation, when I suggested that we exchange soldiers in order to know one another better, "Personally and frankly, it is against Red Army orders and regulations for us to mix with foreigners more than is absolutely necessary to accomplish our missions."

Once—and only once—I was compelled to invite Kotikov to a lunch conference during the blockade. Chicken was served and, somewhat ungraciously under those particular circumstances, he complained that it was tough.

"It ought to be," I pointed out reasonably, "it had to fly all the way from Frankfurt."

The General glared at me, started to say something, and then thought better of it. It was evident that he was not amused.

In any case, blockade or no blockade, social relations with the Russians had cooled considerably since the early days of the occupation. The warmth of hospitality had disappeared partially because of the literal manner in which the Russians accepted invitations. During our erstwhile cordial period, one of my aides—a stickler for doing the right thing socially, who now is back in Texas, running a bond company—suggested that I ought to give a cocktail party for the Russians.

I fell for the idea and accordingly the aide contacted Soviet Military Headquarters and tactfully suggested that Colonel

General Gorbatov should bring along "a few officers" for cocktails with Colonel Howley.

That afternoon, I had left the office early to be ready for the party and was in the bathtub when the aide burst in and babbled, "My God, Colonel, you'd better hurry. I said five o'clock. It's just on the hour now and they're here—and how!"

I grabbed a towel, dried myself hurriedly, and climbed into my clothes. Glancing out of the window, I saw a sight. There, in front of my house, were at least 250 Russian officers, all the way from Colonel General Gorbatov down to junior lieutenants. They had come in cars and in trucks and formed into columns in the street. Doing a left face, they marched in.

Fortunately, most of the Russian officers had never been to a cocktail party before and simply toyed with their drinks. This simplified the beverage question, which might well have been critical. We served only the usual cocktail sandwiches, not the mountains of rich food Russians load their tables with, and the few sophisticates dropped broad hints to the neophytes about strange American customs. The parade drifted away when they found there was nothing substantial to eat.

One of my calls on Kotikov involved a threat to our communications. On February 4, which happened to be my forty-sixth birthday, I was called in by Larry Wilkinson, General Clay's economic adviser. Lieutenant General Borsov, chief of the Soviet zone communications, had written that he had issued instructions to cut five communications cables leading from the American sector to the American zone, in West Germany. These cables were for civilian use, a portion of the forty made available to us.

Much to my surprised satisfaction, Clay reacted violently to this threat and instructed me to inform Kotikov that, if these lines were interfered with, appropriate retaliatory action would be taken. I told Wilkinson that I thought the question should be settled on a higher level than mine, but he replied, "The Old Man says this job calls for the Howley Technique."

I made an appointment with Kotikov for that afternoon and, with an interpreter, took off for the barricaded and heavily guarded Soviet Military Headquarters. I must have acquired quite a reputation around the Red Bastille, because I had only to mention my name before I was saluted into Kotikov's office. With the General were his deputy, Yelizarov, and his Chief of Staff.

Getting right down to business, I told Kotikov that we had better start by reading Borsov's letter and gave him a copy in Russian. He read it carefully. "This letter deals with an authority higher than ours," he said. "What do you expect me to do about it?"

"It may be on a higher level than ours now," I replied, "but it certainly will be on a level of direct concern to you and me if I am forced to take retaliatory action. I want you to let General Borsov—or Marshal Sokolovsky—know that we take this matter very seriously."

One of two sets of conditions applied, I pointed out. Either Borsov really believed that we didn't need these lines—in which case he was mistaken, for we did—or he did know that we needed them so badly that this was the first of a series of steps designed to cripple telephone and telegraph service between Berlin and the American zone.

"We will tolerate no interference with these lines," I told Kotikov. "If you do cut them, we will take any action that seems appropriate."

Half smiling, the Russian asked, "You say you are going to beat me up if I do this thing? What sort of retaliatory action do you intend to take?"

I told him that he could figure out as easily as I could what I might do, but as far as I was concerned, I already had enough trouble on my hands without going out of my way to look for more.

"Well, if you do anything," he appeared to meditate aloud, "I will take retaliatory action. Then you will take more retaliatory action, and then I'll take more and we'll go on indefinitely...."

"You get the point," I replied bluntly, "and I don't object to making an issue of this case. But I think that we should do our best to avoid trouble."

Kotikov promised that he would get in touch with his superiors.

That night, Kotikov called me and said that the whole matter was "entirely technical" and he was sorry I had been involved in the details. He gave me his assurance that the lines would not be cut and that Borsov's letter was "not intended as a basis for cutting the lines but simply for discussion." The British, whose lines also had been threatened, received a similar bland assurance.

Therefore, I considered this another case of "mission completed," thanks to the fact that I had employed the proper technique. The Russians knew perfectly well what I could have done in the way of retaliation. I could have cut their cables passing through our sector, depriving them of communications with the Russian zone. They then would have cut all ours, but we wouldn't have been badly hurt. We had installed adequate radio circuits to handle all military and telegraph needs, press requirements, and, a reasonable amount of German civilian traffic. The Russians would have been out of luck.

In my diary I find another interesting entry *in re* Kotikov vs. Howley, which further illustrates my technique. It reads:

> I have received another letter from General Kotikov in which he claims, and correctly so, that I have 700 tons of oil belonging to him. This was the result of an over-all blocking of oil stocks in the Western sectors, A German plant in the American sector was apparently purifying all crankcase oil for the Red Army.
>
> I intend to hold the oil and will not permit the German plant to do any more work for the Soviets. I intend to notify Kotikov of this and will say that records will be carefully kept and he will get full credit for these, and other stocks, when the blockade is lifted and/or when he returns to us stocks belonging to us, which he has confiscated.

Most of the visits I made to Soviet Military Headquarters during the blocade and most of the visits Russian representatives made to me were linked with the fact that I had something Kotikov wanted. When the Russians started being friendly, you knew they hoped to grab something. Though the Russians held a number of big cards, I had some small trumps.

In March, I was promoted to brigadier general and, the day after General Clay had pinned the star on my shoulder, Kotikov telephoned his congratulations using Colonel Kalinin, his Chief of Staff, as his interpreter. The Russians began to address me as "General of the Armored Cavalry." A little later, Kalinin phoned me again, rather mysteriously, and asked if he could call on me that afternoon. He explained that it was regarding a matter that couldn't be discussed over the phone.

When he arrived, Kalinin broke the ice by again expressing Kotikov's congratulations on my promotion and thanked me for taking care of a difficulty concerning one of the bridges across the Teltow Canal. General Kotikov's ulcers were bothering him, he chatted on, and he also was suffering from flu, which aggravated a bad heart condition.

I thanked him for the congratulations, expressed appropriate sorrow at General Kotikov's difficulties, and then asked, "But what do you really want that we couldn't discuss over the phone?"

"Well," the Russian Chief of Staff said slowly, "we are building a large monument in Pankow to our Russian dead, and some of the material is tied up in the American sector. You have twenty-five tons of bronze wreaths, plaques, and statues, and delivery has been stopped. We wondered if you would permit the factory to deliver this material to us. It was ordered a long time ago; and, since, we provided the factory with the metal, it really belongs to us."

I called up our Economics Department and asked what they knew about the order. They confirmed Kalinin's story, but added that the Russians hadn't paid for the material. The contract price was 186,000 marks, and, since the deal had been consumated in the Western sector, the firm concerned—the Nowak Company—wanted West marks. They were only too glad to get rid of the stuff and had no intention of taking any more Russian orders. The material had been held as a countermeasure against the Russian sector; nothing could leave our sector without my approval.

Putting down the phone, I turned to Kalinin and said sharply, "I will issue an order immediately so that you may have these plaques and statues this afternoon, or any time in the near future you wish. But I want you to tell General Kotikov that I am doing this as a mark of the high respect the Americans have for the Russian soldiers who fought so valiantly during the war. We admire the courage of the Russian soldier and for this reason—and no other—I am releasing this material.

"Please also tell General Kotikov," I continued, "that the United States Army is not at all pleased by the way it is being treated by the Red Army. The American people likewise are becoming increasingly incensed at the cruelty of the blockade. It is my personal opinion that, unless you put a stop to current policies toward us, there will be more Russian and American war memorials.

"I am sure that General Kotikov will understand that this is neither a threat nor a lecture. Personally, I hope that the blockade will be lifted and that Russia will show a different spirit, so that we may renew the friendship that existed during the last war."

Kalinin winced slightly, we exchanged a few personal remarks, and he left with the promise, "I will convey your message to General Kotikov."

I forthwith released the monument material, and the Russians took delivery. Two weeks later, they were back again. This time the visit concerned a mural produced in our sector. I investigated and found that Kotikov was indeed in a spot.

A giant head, glorifying Lenin, was an integral part of the same war memorial the Russians were building at Pankow. The rest of the work had been delivered, but the German responsible had the foresight to hold out for payment in the more valuable West marks. He was holding Lenin's head as security. The Russians offered only East marks, then one fourth the value of West marks.

This time I considered the matter beyond my competence, and I wasn't in the mood to do anything, anyway. "You can have Lenin's head as far as I'm concerned," I sent back word to Kotikov, "but you've got to make your own terms with the Germans responsible for the work."

"But we must have the head!" he wailed in return. "How can we unveil the monument next week without it?"

"Too bad," I said. The Russians grimly forked over the West marks.

Russians on official business were in and out of our sectors during the entire blockade. Although they tore up one agreement after another, we stuck to our pledged word and allowed them to occupy various premises in our sectors. Under Allied Control Authority agreements, these included the German Railway Administration Building and extensive railroad repair shops. In the early days of the occupation, the Russians were continually dismantling equipment and tearing up tracks in our sector for use in theirs. This went on until Clay wrote a letter, amounting almost to an order, that looting must end. They were free to operate the railroads, as we had internationally agreed, he said, but they must stop tearing up our tracks.

With the Russian foot jammed in the door of the American sector, we were constantly receiving reports of dismantling, even during the blockade. The principal objective, the railroad shops, was in Schoneberg. Night after night, I received these wild reports, and they proved baseless. Then, about three o'clock one morning, my Public Safety officer, Ray Ashworth, called me out of bed with some alarming news. Ashworth was a colonel during the war but a professional policeman in civilian life, always a calm and competent man.

"This time it looks as if there's something really big cooking," he said.

"Have you been inside the repair shops to see if they are moving things out?" I asked sleepily.

"No," he admitted, "but our people report that there is an entire train outside and a thousand or even more German workers inside. Something must be happening. The Germans say the Russians are going to dismantle the shops."

Three o'clock in the morning is no time to send troops or police into a place where they might get into a fight, I told

Ashworth. Keep investigating. Don't let any of your men inside the building until daylight, and then I'll be along.

Early in the morning, I went over to the repair shops. Ashworth is a giant of a man and he had another six-foot-three, 220-pound Goliath with him, M.P. Colonel Tom Lancer. Together we entered the shops. German police first tried to block our path, then the German director of the shops said we couldn't go in without Russian permission, but I reminded him that this was the American sector and as commandant I was going in.

A mass meeting was under way inside. A fat little German, with a rapt expression on his round face, stood on the platform, waving his arms and bringing his fist and palm together with loud slaps. He was making no reference to dismantling. All he was doing was giving the workers their weekly pep talk on higher production and urging them to stop sabotage, including a lot of brown-coal brickette stealing.

We were attending the weekly Communist propaganda session, to which the bored workers listened regularly. They rather enjoyed our sudden appearance; the Communist line has little variety.

No dismantling was taking place. I looked over the eight forges and other equipment and it appeared that the Russians actually were improving the plant, not wrecking it. The joke was on us, but the trip served to bring me in touch with the Soviet railroad director, Major General Petrov, a fair-skinned, blond youth, who looked very boyish and unsophisticated beside his political adviser, a short, balding gnome, all wrinkled and intellectual looking. Petrov's reputation was that he had a fearful temper, but he never revealed it to me.

"You were down at the repair shops yesterday," he said when I called on him the next day. "Did you find any dismantling?"

"No," I replied, and continued firmly, "and I don't want to find any in our sector. But I'm sick of getting these reports at the most ungodly hours. I have to investigate them, so I'd like to have an understanding with you."

"What is the understanding you wish?" Petrov asked.

"I want you to know," I told him, "Allied orders are that you will dismantle nothing in the American sector. If you try, I will use any force necessary to prevent it. I'm not looking for a fight but, if you want one, you can have it. You can run all the railroad cars you want through our sector, but you can't take out any equipment."

"What do you mean by equipment?" he asked petulantly. "Last night I sent out a typewriter to be repaired, and one of your policemen stopped the man, and I haven't got the machine back yet."

He went on to enumerate a number of things he would like to do, such as move some machinery from one of the smaller and little-used shops to the main shops and transfer signal equipment to a new point.

"No," I told him, "no equipment must be moved. You'll have to wait until the blockade is lifted if you want to make changes like that. We can adjust matters then."

I knew at the time that the Russians were building another spur railroad in their zone and they believed that the easiest way to get equipment was to cannibalize the American sector, even while the blockade was on.

Furthermore, I told Petrov, the Russians had the right to operate the railroads but not to use them against the U.S. Military Government for political purposes. Communists had hung banners in the railroad yards advertising their phony government and had tried to get petitions signed on the platforms of American sector stations.

The Russian leaned back in his chair to light one of his eight-inch cigarettes, with a long paper holder. "My dear General Howley," he began, when the operation was finished, "how can you possibly separate politics from economics?"

He was quoting a well-known Communist principle, but I had the answer. "Perhaps you can't in Soviet philosophy," I conceded. "I know that line comes straight from Marx to Lenin to Stalin to Petrov, but remember you're in the American sector now and we do separate the two."

He laughed and offered me one of his long-stemmed cigarettes. "I suppose your people report to you that we are dismantling because I take all my records home at night," he observed slyly. "Ever since you put guards on the building eight months ago, I've taken the records home each night. But I always bring them back again in the morning."

That may have been an attempt at persiflage, but it also was a revealing remark. I deduced that he wasn't too sure that we wouldn't throw the Russians out of the building one day and deny them the use of the railroads. Assuredly, we had every justification for putting them out of the sector entirely.

Several questions naturally arise at this point. While the Russians were trying to strangle us and the German people, why did we allow them to function in our three sectors? Why didn't we prevent them using the railroads running through our territory, when they denied us the use of the railroads between Berlin and the Elbe? Why didn't we deny them the use of the canals running through our sectors, along which they moved most of the food and coal for theirs? At times, I was strongly in favor of doing exactly this. But I didn't. It was my ace in the hole. We could always use the possibility as a threat and I considered this fact of tremendous value, because the Russians never were certain that we wouldn't act, as a last resort.

In view of their own tactics, the Russians always were astonished that we didn't resort to more violent measures. We certainly had them at our disposal. Time and again, I was approached by Germans who had belonged to wartime underground groups with sabotage plans against the Russians. Never was there any lack of offers; had we so desired, we could have had an underground army working for us. One proposal, developed in detail, was to wreck the Blue Express from Moscow at a point in the Russian zone just outside Berlin.

"Sokolovsky might be traveling on that train," the German who made the suggestion added significantly.

All these offers I firmly rejected. It wasn't the American way. We should have been stooping to the Russian level if we had armed lawless men and condoned murder and destruction. Our way was the open road, not the furtive path of the hired assassin.

The blockade raised other thorny problems. One of the quadripartite duties of the sector commandants in Berlin was supervising the custody of the seven principal German war criminals, held in Spandau Prison in the British sector, where they had been transferred from Nuremberg after the trials. Reports we received said the men were in bad shape physically. All of them had lost weight, and there were further indications of inhuman treatment by the Soviet prison director.

Unilaterally, and over the objections of the Soviet director, the three Western powers authorized certain dietary changes. Special foods were substituted for ordinary prison fare for those suffering from diabetes and anemia, and we also insisted on proper medical attention. Otherwise, some of the prisoners might have died.

It took nine weeks for Kotikov to get around to our action, and then each of the Western commandants received a letter from him alleging violation of quadripartite agreements concerning the seven, without specifying the particulars. I wrote back that the only inference I could draw from the letter was that the ameliorative changes had been made at the prison. The British commandant added dryly that conditions at Spandau now were more in keeping with penal standards in civilized countries, and Ganeval, with Gallic irony, observed that he was touched by Kotikov's concern for quadripartite agreements.

The Russian walkout at the Kommandatura complicated matters, but we still had control of the prisoners. In rotation, the Russians would take over chairmanship of the prison supervisory board in March; but, since we were at loggerheads over the blockade, it seemed highly unlikely that we could agree on the prison issue, regarding which the Russians had definite, and somewhat barbaric, views.

The three Western commandants met in February to discuss the matter. Members of the legal committee didn't hide their misgivings about what the Russians might do as chairmen the following month. The committee suggested that we try to improve conditions at once, failing which we could remove the men to a prison in the Western zone, or possibly return them to the countries who had captured them. In that case, Admiral Raeder would be handed over to the tender mercies of the Russians, a fate worse than Spandau.

Eventually, we decided to take no special action, but to allow the Russians to assume chairmanship, interfering if we heard of inhuman treatment under Soviet orders. There was no desire on our part to coddle the German war criminals, but we all knew that the Russians were determined to shorten their lives.

When we took over the prisoners at the beginning of December, after the final month of Russian chairmanship, Admiral Karl Doenitz's weight was down to 125 pounds from 148, Raeder had dropped to 115 from 138, and Baldur von Schirach to 129 pounds from 147. Our contention was that we had been ordered to keep these men prisoners, not to starve them to death. Furthermore, we expressed the opinion that, by walking out of the Kommandatura, the Russians no longer had the right to control the war criminal prisoners.

Another point we made—and one that still is worrying the Berlin city government—dealt with the ridiculous economics of the prison. These seven are the most closely guarded and the most expensively incarcerated prisoners in the world. Due to the quadripartite order whereby custody became our responsibility, an entire prison, capable normally of housing five to six hundred prisoners, was given over to seven men. To operate and guard Spandau requires sixty-five German employees, an internal guard of thirty, and an external military guard of seventy. Under the quadripartite system, whereby each power was in control of the prison for one month at a time, the prison director and the external guard of troops changed according to the rotation. This represented a total of 165 persons to do a job a platoon of twenty could handle easily.

The last time I saw the world's most closely guarded prisoners was in August, just before I left Berlin. The Americans had the chairmanship that month. I found the stellar characters of the Nazi regime looking like the world's greatest sad sacks. They wore ordinary German prison clothes, a shade more disreputable than old G.I. overalls, and laundered out of all recognition.

They had difficulty keeping their pants up. Instead of suspenders or belts, they were issued with a slender string, that wouldn't support a weight of 150 pounds, in case they tried to hang themselves. Raeder constantly complained, not of food or living conditions, but of the fact that he hadn't been sentenced to be hanged. Plastic glass shielded prison-cell windows, so the men couldn't break it and cut their wrists. There were no direct lights, only reflected illumination, in case they tried to electrocute themselves.

Inside the jail compound, the prisoners were allowed to cultivate a garden, producing carrots, turnips, beets, and other quick crop vegetables. The garden was merely a form of exercise and diversion, but it revealed that, even in defeat, the German leaders maintained social standards.

The upstart Rudolf Hess, second in power to Hitler, who flew alone to Scotland in a harebrained attempt to induce the British to surrender, was completely ostracized. Despite the degradation of Spandau, the other prisoners carried themselves with a certain superior bearing and openly showed their contempt for him.

I talked with Hess one day, as he was languidly turning over the sod with a spade held in one hand. The others were working at the far end of the plot.

"How are things coming along?" I asked.

"Oh, all right," he replied abstractedly. Other questions brought the same lifeless dismissal. Hess epitomized the complete negation of hope and spirit of the fallen Nazi.

During the spring, with the Russian grip at our throats loosening, we made two more important moves to wrench ourselves free and turn on our torturers. In addition to our counterpunches, the British and French finally agreed with us in imposing a counterblockade on the Soviet sector, forbidding the Russians the use of a large number of items of vital necessity in their occupation area but manufactured in the Western sectors. It was almost impossible to stop trade entirely between the Eastern and Western sectors because many industries, especially the textile, were located in one sector but depended upon plants in other sectors for processing and finishing.

I drew up two lists for the American sector, the first of which was a complete ban, the second conditional upon Military Government permission. General Clay, whose attitude toward the

Russians was hardening day by day, ordered me to clamp down on practically everything, and under my control action took the form of an almost complete blockade.

Originally, I had envisaged the counterblockade as a tripartite move, but only the French supported me. The British were inclined to do a certain amount of business with the Russians on the basis that this trade helped keep industry going, and that they would benefit more than the Soviets. Such an attitude probably was a residue of the departed General Herbert's muddled economic thinking. I totally disagreed with this premise, and told the British that I thought we were not justified in using the airlift to bring in coal to produce anything at all for the Russians, or for Germans under Russian control.

Major General G. K. Bourne had succeeded Herbert. I found him to be a man of great discernment, forthright in his opinions and direct in his actions. I sensed an immediate affinity with Bourne the first time we met, and I was not mistaken—he recreated British-American co-operation. Bourne, Ganeval, and I worked well together. Despite his eighteen months in Buchenwald, Ganeval maintained the utmost fairness and objectivity in dealing with the Germans. He was a firm friend and a dependable coworker.

Bourne was disinclined to change the traditional British economic policy immediately, but we agreed to pool information and meet two months later to review the situation, with General Ganeval, and compare the different systems and their effectiveness. We did, and agreed on a compromise plan against the Communists.

The second move involved currency. On March 20, we made the West mark the sole legal tender in West Berlin. This step did not necessarily outlaw the East mark, Russia's practically worthless money, but we ruled that it was no longer valid for payment of rent, taxes, food, utilities, and other necessities of life. When we introduced the West mark into Berlin on a limited scale the previous June, after the Russians had tried to seize control of the city politically and economically by means of their own currency, we left the door open for a joint currency, with East and West marks both acceptable.

Instead of getting a single currency, or common acceptance

of two currencies, the question went to the diplomats. It dragged through various committees at the United Nations, survived international discussion at Geneva, returned to the United Nations Security Council and, finally, on March 18, was dropped by the UN. That body had ruled that the Berlin currency problem was not technical, but political.

To Berliners, this confusion brought plain hardship, injuring residents, manufacturers, everybody. The East mark fell to a four-to-one ratio with the West mark; political, business, and even church leaders begged us to make the West mark the sole currency.

By taking advantage of the week end, when the banks were closed, which allowed the United Nations to make its announcement in New York and gave the three Western military governors time to break the news to Sokolovsky officially by letter, conversion went along smoothly on the following Monday. Except for some blasts by the Communist newspapers, Russian reaction was negligible. Once more, they were faced with a *fait accompli*, a method that they could understand.

Acceptable as the new currency was, it further emphasized the division of Berlin—a city torn between East and West. By the beginning of January, the break between the democratically elected city government, housed in the Western sectors, and the rump government of Communist stooges, administering the Russian sector under Russian direction, was complete. All branches of the administration were split. Berlin had two governments claiming to run the city, two *Magistrats*, and two Assemblies.

On January 15, when the new Western city government was seated in its new chamber in the Taberna Academica, members lost no time in confirming the election of Prof. Reuter as lord mayor and initiated efforts to straighten out the city budget and clear away the administrative debris left by Communist members, who had spent the past two years tying up government affairs. The *Magistrat's* "State of the City" message was presented to the City Assembly by Reuter, reaffirming the legality of the West Berlin *Magistrat* as the government for the whole of Greater Berlin, and setting forth a plan for the reorganization of the twelve borough administrations in the Western sectors.

Reuter's message also stressed the necessity for certain economic and financial measures, especially the introduction of the West mark as sole legal currency—which the Western powers did later—and expressed the hope that control of the police and the judiciary would be transferred completely to the city administration.

On this point, the Western powers were not in such unanimity. At the Kommandatura, for months the American point of view had been to return a higher degree of responsibility for self-government to Berlin. The French came back at us by reading a paper on the Germans, smacking of the attitude of 1918, not 1949. On the question of police organization especially, our viewpoint was that the return of complete police control to the city government would be one of the last acts under military occupation, but we did feel that a greater measure of control should be placed at once in the hands of the elected government. Since the split in the Communist-dominated police force in the Soviet sector, which drove Dr. Stumm into the Western sectors, the new West Berlin police he was organizing was becoming an efficient force.

The British and French views differed. The British wanted to run the police force in the strict military manner they ran their troops in Berlin. Filled with suspicion engendered by long, scarred memories, the French were reluctant to place such a powerful weapon in the hands of the city government. We insisted on eventual return of police control, although we recognized that, for the time being, it couldn't be as extensive or as unfettered as the powers the city government exercised in religious, educational, and civic affairs.

The matter had to be dropped from the Kommandatura agenda until General Robertson, the British commander, brought it up at the Allied Control Council and, surprisingly, proposed that the city government should be given greater powers of self-government. General Clay agreed sagely: "The most effective way I ever found to put Military Government out of operation is to reduce its numbers." General Koenig concurred, but there was no Russian comment because Sokolovsky was not present. Like the Kommandatura, the Control Council also had become tripartite.

In retrospect, the question of democratic self-government stirred me greatly. Perhaps more than anyone else in Berlin, I was convinced that the German people should get it, within stipulated limits if necessary. We had seen so many demonstrations of the German democratic will: the first Social Democrat–Communist party referendum; the elections of October 20, 1946, and December 5, 1948; the decision of the democratic members of the city government to meet in the Soviet sector until they were driven out by Communist hoodlums; and the great mass meeting outside the *Reichstag*.

All of these, to my mind, were important landmarks in the long, hard march toward democratic freedom. The early stages of the journey showed that the Germans lacked leaders capable of attracting and retaining popular support, and some of the Western sector commandants, including myself, had to fill the vacancy without overt interference. But, since the last elections and the inspiring *Reichstag* meeting, a fantastic but nevertheless logical situation had developed.

Popular strength had grown, and a great assembly stood behind the German leaders. Why was this the case? Because we had supported their faltering steps. Never in history had the Germans known their own minds so clearly, never had they stood so firm against one occupying power. It would be fair to say that, in the three Western sectors, the people were not so much behind their officials as behind the Western powers that had sustained them.

This sounds like an extraordinary statement to make about a conquered people and their conquerors, but it was brought about by the German fear of a greater internal enemy, fostered by the Russians—communism. They felt that their only protection came from the Western occupying authorities. Now, the people were backing their elected officials, not in small numbers but with majority strength. This fact in itself reduced the importance of Military Government and coincided with the American policy of restoring control to the Germans.

CHAPTER XIV

SPRING came back to blockaded Berlin, rustling her green skirts in the bright sunshine, and radiant with resurrected hope. No longer did we anxiously scan the skies, as we had in the dread winter months, trying to penetrate the thick veil of fog hanging over the city for food planes that failed to arrive. No longer did we dolefully contemplate our dwindling stocks, wondering if they ever would be replenished.

The airlift was running like clockwork. It had ceased to be a novelty; the swarm of planes overhead had become a noisy factor in humdrum metropolitan life. Supplies averaged eight thousand tons a day, sometimes hitting ten thousand. We had plenty of food, and to spare. Reserves were built to new highs. Rations were increased until they stood higher than in the Russian sector, contradicting specious Communist propaganda and, what was more important, we were able to add variety to the monotonous diet of West Berliners.

Then came the record days, when the Russians might just as well have given up, instead of trailing the skeleton of Western wickedness along the international corridors of Paris and New York, and postponing the inevitable end of the blockade. On April 11, 1949, the millionth ton of supplies was flown into Berlin. On April 16, the airlift made 1,383 flights, bringing into our three airfields 12,849 tons. Throughout the day, a plane landed in Berlin every 63 seconds.

I went to Tempelhof field that evening to greet the last of the planes—a C-54 with the day's record of flights and tonnage painted on its fuselage. Less than a year ago I had stood at the same airfield and watched the old "Gooney Birds" bring in our first two hundred tons of flour, agonized at the prospect of feeding 920,000 families by air. It hadn't seemed possible at the time, but we were doing it, and a succession of these record loads would see us holding out in Berlin until the Kremlin toppled into the Red Square.

We definitely had the upper hand in the feeding of Berlin. Germans living in our sector, who—due to Russian pressure or sheer fright when we had to fall back on dehydrated foods during an emergency in the early stages of the blockade—had gone over and registered for food in the Russian sector, began to return. Our rations were better, and they were convinced that the Western Allies wouldn't be driven out of Berlin.

I had no sympathy with these spineless German backsliders. Two and one quarter million people had stood by us the whole time, even when conditions were at their very worst. These few were the quitters. We had a heated discussion at the Kommandatura, when the question of permitting them to reregister for food in the Western sectors came up.

Proud of the stamina of the majority of West Berliners, I said, "To hell with these weaklings! Let them stay where they are. In fact, if you leave it to me, I'll make it easy for anyone who wants to go to move into the Soviet 'paradise.' "

The British and French didn't share my emphatic view. They contended that the fact the people were shifting their allegiance was a victory for us, and that such persons should be allowed to reregister in our sectors. I did not want to appear vindictive, especially since less than one hundred thousand Germans were concerned, and it was very possible that a proportion of those had been coerced by the Russians. Therefore, I compromised with my colleagues and agreed to give them another chance.

All Berlin knew that we now had the whip hand. In six weeks, more than half the backsliders—about sixty thousand—left the Made-in-Moscow paradise and registered for airborne food in our sectors.

From the beginning of the airlift, all planning had been done on a long-range scale. We had to anticipate requirements and deliveries months ahead. In the spring of 1949, we were so far advanced in our conception of future needs that, instead of casting a speculative eye upon the next few months, we had a year's program mapped out, carrying us until July, 1950.

The Americans looked even farther into the future. The War Department asked us to prepare an individual plan for the next three years' requirements, taking us through 1952. This request was made, I believe, largely because of the lessons in airborne supply we had learned in Berlin, which could be applied to military problems. The speed demanded by Washington in working out this plan—the details of which are still on the secret list—was such that we could not even consult our Western Allies. It is a compliment to the skill of A. W. Moran, my deputy for airlift operations, and his staff, that our first estimates rushed to Washington were practically the same as those worked out afterward on a tripartite basis.

If the blockade had continued until July, 1950, our daily deliveries would have been 8,600 tons, more than twice the amount I had calculated in my original "Basic Assumption." Plans provided for an increase in the food ration for the winter of 1949–1950; the stockpiling of 210,000 tons of coal for domestic heating, in addition to normal supplies for power and light; and more freight space for the importing of raw materials and the exporting of finished products.

All these plans were closely co-ordinated with augmented airfield facilities. Tempelhof, in our sector, and Gatow, in the British sector, had reached maximum efficiency, but Tegel, in the French sector, had room for expansion. There we planned a new, larger runway for the increasing numbers of C-54's that were replacing older, smaller, and slower aircraft.

On their side, the British brought in new equipment. Their eighteen new tanker planes were capable of carrying fifty thousand tons of kerosene, which was to be allocated to German homes for heating, thus saving us the one hundred thousand tons of coal set aside for that purpose.

A committee of Western-powers experts worked for three weeks on these details, based upon the past year's experience, and then forwarded the report to the commandants. At the Kommandatura, opinions on the recommendations differed very slightly, and reflected the desire to increase and improve airlift supplies in Berlin, rather than any contentious national viewpoint. Both the British and the French favored increasing tonnages, but I was forced to object on the grounds that this question had already gone to the American higher command and that we had obtained as large a commitment as it was possible to get. It must be pointed out, in this connection, that the United States was providing the bulk of air transport.

The British suggested that we set aside special planes for passengers. During the first weeks of the blockade, they had flown several thousand persons out of Berlin, including Western-zone residents trapped by the blockade, Germans with permission to go abroad, students bound for Western Germany, and the sick. This service was continued throughout the blockade, but the British now wanted to fly 250 approved Germans in and out of the city every day. I thought this figure excessive and suggested that it be cut to 50 persons, one planeload.

Another difference of opinion concerned coal. The British favored issuing five hundred pounds of coal per family for the entire winter, but I stuck to my figure of not more than four hundred pounds, since these families would be getting other fuel.

On the whole, however, our differences were minor. The official report on our requirements, which we sent up to the Allied commanders for approval, reflected the great amount of co-operation among the three Western powers, at every level. The report also showed, in an incontrovertible manner, that the danger from a Russian blockade was a thing of the past. We no longer feared it.

But the diplomats made these long-range plans unnecessary. The Berlin question had been in the international diplomatic mill for many months. After countless rumors, the Russians lifted the blockade.

Talks between the U.S. delegate, Phillip C. Jessup, and the Soviet delegate, Jacob Malik, during the General Assembly of the United Nations at Lake Success, led to an agreement on May 4 by which the four powers—the United States, Russia, Britain, and France—resolved to end the blockade and the counterblockade on May 12. Why the Russians should suggest that date is another mystery. It was just an arbitrary date, but the Russians always stall, even when they're beaten. Perhaps they hoped to save face by delay, as if they didn't have enough faces to make Janus dizzy. However, the Lake Success agreement showed that the Kremlin had had enough and recognized defeat.

With customary unconcern for the men on the spot, Washington neglected to inform us directly in Berlin of what was happening. I knew nothing about the negotiations, and I am sure that Clay was in the same unenviable position. We didn't even know that the American and Russian delegates at Lake Success were discussing the matter, although we did hear faint rumors that something in our department was developing. Robert Murphy visited Berlin during the discussions and never dropped a hint. He must have had orders from Washington to keep it dark. It was a disconcerting position for Clay and me, responsible for American Military Government in Germany and Berlin.

I first learned that the blockade had been lifted from a State Department release to the newspapers. The release read:

> Agreement has been reached between the three Western Powers and the Soviets regarding raising the Berlin blockade and the holding of a meeting of the Council of Foreign Ministers. All communications, transportation and trade restrictions imposed by both sides since March 1, 1948, and between Berlin and the Eastern Zones will be removed on May 12. Eleven days subsequent to the removal of these restrictions, a meeting of the Council of Foreign Ministers will be convened in Paris to consider questions relating to Germany and problems arising out of the Berlin situation, including the question of currency in Berlin.

The way I interpreted the statement was that it dealt only with the blockade and the counterblockade, and that no attempt had been made to solve the political differences splitting Berlin.

I had received no orders on the subject, and therefore went

to our military headquarters and called on everybody up to Clay himself, seeking instructions. Larry Wilkinson, our Economics chief, came to my aid and explained how the lifting of the counterblockade was to be handled in the American zone, so that I could apply this formula to the Berlin sector. Beyond this, he had no pertinent information to give me.

My instructions were far from clear cut but, as far as I could gather, I wasn't to see too many ghosts of broken promises in the closet and should assume that the Russians had made the deal in good faith. I was informed that we would have no contact with the Russians, unless serious difficulties arose, and that German agencies would work out the technicalities of adjustment.

At my invitation, the three Western commandants met and drafted the following order, BK/O (49) 92 in the long list issued since the Kommandatura was created:

> To the Lord Mayor, City of Berlin: Effective 0001 hours on May 12, 1949, all counter-blockade restrictions in effect on communications, transportation and trade since March 1, 1948, by the United States, French and British Military Governments, or by the Allied Kommandatura, Berlin, will be cancelled.
>
> You are instructed to issue the necessary orders to the Chief of Police and officials of the Magistrat to implement this order.

Discussing the agreement and the effect of lifting the counterblockade, I didn't see eye to eye with my British and French colleagues. The French thought that the Russians immediately would rush in and take delivery of machinery and other products from such factories as Siemens, which had been piling up since the counterblockade. Both the French and the British leaned toward the idea of calling a meeting with the Russians.

I contended that the delegates at Lake Success hadn't called for a conference in Berlin; they had called for lifting the blockade and the counterblockade. We should carry out this arrangement wholeheartedly, I maintained, but also should keep a watchful eye on developments and report any violation by the Russians, whose past record of nonfulfillment of promises was so notorious that they could be expected to wriggle out of this agreement in the same way. This we all agreed to do and saw to it that, as far as was possible under Moscow's conception of a bargain, they kept their part. The Russians were both dilatory and reluctant, and had to be prodded frequently.

During the blockade, the Berlin airlift cost the United States thirty-two million dollars a month, but as soon as surface transportation was resumed and food and supplies started coming in through normal channels, this staggering sum diminished. However, although the pressure was off, we didn't halt the airlift immediately. Air deliveries continued through May, June, and July, 1949, at the rate of between seven and eight thousand tons per day. At the beginning of August, with several months' stock of fuel and major commodities built up, air operations slacked off. The fleets of food planes vanished from the Berlin skies and the arrival of a lone C-54 became almost an occasion.

On the morning of May 12, the City Assembly held a special meeting to celebrate the lifting of the blockade. The three Western military governors—Clay, Robertson, and Koenig's deputy Moiret—were the principal guests and General Clay made a farewell speech to the Assembly. He left for the States three days later.

One of the steps taken in Washington by the three Western powers, after the United Nations meeting, was to draft a Statute of Occupation for Western Germany, providing broad, new powers for the new Western German Federal Republic, which came into existence at Bonn after the Western German elections of August 14. Two days after the blockade was lifted, the three Western Berlin commandants agreed on a "Little Occupation Statute" for Berlin. Its official title was, "Statement of Principles Governing the Relationship Between the Allied Kommandatura and Greater Berlin." This statute returned similar broad powers to the city government, with restrictive rights confined to such fields as finance, economics, and public safety.

Within a week of the end of the blockade, when rail transport was back to normal, Berlin was plunged into another crisis. Eleven thousand railroad workers went out on strike, and the Russians were back at the old stand, peddling lies and terror, and ready for another act of duplicity.

The railroad workers had been the hardest hit by the introduction of the West mark, and still were the largest single group paid in East marks. Although the majority lived and worked in the Western sectors, they were employed by the Soviet-controlled Railroad Administration, which refused to abide by the laws of the territory in which it was operating and continued to pay the men in depreciated East marks. After numerous efforts to induce the Russians to negotiate, the UGO, the independent trade union to which most of the workers belonged, called a strike for May 21, and the entire city's rail system, including the subways, was at a standstill.

The strikers had other legitimate grievances. Attempting to smash the UGO, which had defied the Communist-directed union, the FDGB, the Russians inaugurated a policy of firing lifelong workers who joined the new union, and forbidding UGO meetings. The strikers made three demands: for pay, for protection against dismissal, and for freedom of speech and assembly.

In addition to its primary objective—tying up transport—the strike had important secondary results. Telegrams came from the AF of L, the CIO, the British Trade Union Congress, and the Internationl Transport Workers' Federation supporting the UGO move. With this international backing, the number of strikers shot up to fifteen thousand and UGO increased its original three thousand rail-worker membership to eight thousand.

The railroad strike developed into Berlin's worst labor extremity. In accordance with the Lake Success agreement, the Council of Foreign Ministers was meeting in Paris to discuss the Berlin situation. The strikers grasped the delicate international situation and agreed to maintain skeleton crews to operate supply trains, resumed after the blockade was lifted. When the yards were jammed, the strikers further offered to increase their crews, but the Russians refused to permit them to do so.

The American and British attitude toward the strike was the

same: "Hands off!" As far as we were concerned, this was a dispute between the workers and the Soviet-controlled Railway Administration. Then the Russians brought in thousands of strikebreakers, supported by black-coated railroad police armed with rifles, pistols, and clubs. The scabs promptly clashed with strikers and their sympathizers. At Neukoelln station, in the American sector, the Communist police fired into a crowd and inflicted many casualties. There were numerous bloody encounters of this type in the British sector.

I called a meeting of the commandants and told them that, under such circumstances, the strike was our business. We must step in to maintain law and order in our sectors. I had received visits from Frau Schroeder, who had recovered from her long illness and was acting as lord mayor while Prof. Reuter was on a trip to the United States, and from Dr. Stumm, head of the West sectors German police. They both demanded that the Soviet police be evicted and the West German police put in charge of all stations. To my astonishment, the British commandant ignored the facts and declared that all was calm in the British sector. Therefore, he said, the Soviet police should be allowed to function until violence occurred. Only then would he authorize the city government to move in its police. The French supported him.

I was outvoted, but this fact didn't prevent me from raising strong objections to such injustice. "If this rough stuff continues," I told them, "labor people all over the world will ask us for an explanation. If we allow such intolerable conditions to prevail, I'm damn sure American labor leaders will want to know just what sort of democracy I'm supposed to be teaching the Germans."

The next night exposed the futility of this supine policy. At the Berlin Zoo station, seven hundred Soviet police fired into a crowd of two thousand strikers and sympathizers. A number were killed. This was too much even for the British, so they permitted the West German police to take over not only the particular station where the shooting occurred, but three others, including the Tiergarten.

The problem went up to the military governors, now that

the issue had become an East-West struggle rather than a strike, and all Berlin commandants were authorized to move out the Soviet police. We obeyed promptly. The West German police were put in charge, as they should have been long before, and there was no more violence.

Each time that the Western commandants had put a plan for settling the strike before the Russians, they had been met with Kotikov's statement that the strike didn't exist—because he refused to recognize the UGO. I finally called in the UGO strike leaders and got from them a back-to-work promise based on two points: 60 per cent of their pay in West marks, and the assurance that they wouldn't be victimized by the Russians if they went back to work. This assurance was imperative. All over the Soviet sector were posters promising to hang any striker the Russians could lay their hands on. This agreement became known as the "Howley Proposal," and was accepted by everyone, including the Russians.

To obtain Russian approval, I called on General Kvashnin, the Soviet transport chief. I had dealt previously with his deputy, Major General Petrov, but the gravity of this situation sent me directly to the top. With my deputy, Colonel Babcock, and an interpreter, I sought him out at his shabby headquarters in the Russian sector, climbing rickety stairs to his office. I was surprised to find the sinister Maximov, the political adviser who had engineered the Kommandatura breakup, sitting at Kvashnin's elbow. His presence should have warned me, but we discussed the situation; and, in the end, I obtained Kvashnin's assurance that the terms of the "Howley Agreement" were acceptable, although I couldn't get his promise to recognize UGO.

Back at my own office, I spent the hours until midnight talking with strike leaders, finally convincing them that the Russian offer was good. I also promised them that, if they returned to work, they would receive an additional 15 per cent of their pay in West marks, through the city government, although actually it would come from us. Therefore, the strikers would get 75 per cent of their wages in West marks. I had already got British and French concurrence to this offer.

The offer was submitted to the men for vote. Then the Russians pulled a fast one. Waiting until it was impossible for the other papers to get the news, the Soviet-licensed *Taegliche Rundschau* came out with a story denying the agreement I had negotiated with Kvashnin. Against the background of a loud radio chorus of Western abuse, the strikers were informed that no such negotiations had taken place. This, the voice of Moscow in Berlin screeched, was just another Western trick to settle the strike, because "General Howley can guarantee nothing!" Eighty per cent of the strikers wisely voted not to go back to work.

Whether the Communists in Berlin had outsmarted themselves, or whether Kvashnin had received new orders from the Kremlin to prolong the strike while the Paris conference was in session, I can't say officially. But personally I am convinced that Kvashnin was sincere with me and that his word was set aside by his superiors. The Russians are the world's greatest opportunists, and the strike provided them with an excuse for refusing to implement their promise to lift the blockade.

Dominating the strike was the mounting fear of reprisals if the men did return to work. The Germans had no faith in the Russian word; they took another vote, and 86 per cent of the strikers voted to stay out. Their decision was a great blow to me, for I had spent considerable time and effort trying to reach a settlement. We called a meeting of the four commandants, but got the brush-off from Kotikov. There was, he parroted, no strike. The strikers were simply a gang of saboteurs who were preventing operation of the railroads.

Nearly a month had elapsed since the strike was called. Both personal mediation and tripartite negotiations had failed. Terrified by Russian threats, the workers were beginning to panic, and apparently wouldn't go back to work under any circumstances. After the Russian double cross, I was inclined to wash my hands of the whole business and leave it where it was originally—a matter between the employees, the railroad workers, and the employer, the Soviet-controlled railroads.

Then Major General Bourne, the British commandant, had a good idea at a commandants' meeting. "I think the Russians have made a mistake and are afraid to admit it," he said. "Let's make another try. Right out in the open, let's send a letter to General Kvashnin, signed by the three of us, and ask again what those terms were, and if he really reversed your agreement."

I had no objection to this proposal, and the letter was written. It was a week before Kvashnin answered. Then he wrote a letter to each commandant, confirming every point of the agreement, promising to pay at least 60 per cent of wages in West marks, and guaranteeing immunity to strikers after they returned to work. He made only one exception, adding that "saboteurs and others" who had committed "criminal acts" would be punished. On the basis of this letter, though it lacked clarity, we asked the strikers to return to work.

The saboteur proviso alone was enough to throw a new scare into the strikers. On June 22, the UGO strike committee decided not to accept Kvashnin's terms. They said frankly that his letter was insufficient guarantee of their safety.

So, once again, we were back where we started. Washington and London cables started to buzz. Unilaterally or tripartitely, any way that was possible, we were instructed to end the strike. The success of the Paris talks hinged on peace in Berlin, we were reminded. How could we obey? One suggestion was that we send the strikers a letter, almost constituting an order, asking them to return to work at once, and backing the letter with an order to the *Magistrat* to cut off unemployment pay if the men refused.

Without exception, we all felt that to capitulate to the Russians and throw down the independent trade union would be a grave mistake, for the future as well as for the present. But we had no choice. The three sector commandants conferred with the deputy military governors, and a plan was evolved to end the impasse and get the men back to work by June 28. We called in the strike leaders and told them that we were not issuing an order but that they must return to work; we couldn't allow fifteen thousand men to jeopardize the city. With winter ahead, we were falling behind in coal shipments, which should have been coming in for future domestic heating.

We explained our proposals to them and they went back to work on our promise that they would receive 100 per cent of their pay in West marks, of which the Russians would pay 60 per cent; that the Western powers would support UGO; and that strikers fearing serious reprisals from the Russians would be helped to find other jobs. The strike was settled—in spite of the Russians.

When I left Berlin in September, things were normal again. The Russians were behaving exactly as Russians always behave. The Soviet radio was popping its tubes with glee over my resignation as commandant. For some reason, I was suddenly "Howley, the Rough Rider from Texas," and the Russian radio, to the accompaniment of cowboy music, was deriding me for refusing to be drawn into the web again in the Kommandatura.

I didn't relish the idea of conceding that the Kommandatura was back in business on the old, official basis. All Kotikov wanted was the chance to start over again after the blockade fizzled. If I conceded that the Kommandatura was functioning officially once more, it would be giving tacit recognition to the illegal government the Russians had set up in East Berlin. The result was that we now met more or less informally, expressing "points of view" instead of signing agreements.

I rather think that Kotikov will remember our farewell. The Kommandatura had just concluded its meeting and, as the departing chairman, I was host at the inevitable buffet in the next room.

Kotikov had used up a good portion of the meeting complaining about various things, including my "rudeness," but now he was unusually affable. A waiter brought a tray of drinks as we stood talking. Kotikov communed with his ulcers and announced that he wanted a "weak" drink.

"Champagne?" someone asked.

Kotikov puffed out his cheeks and shook his head. "Makes me belch," he said.

"Have a Martini," I said shrewdly.

"What is a Martini?" Kotikov asked.

I pointed to the lethal drink on the tray. Innocently, Kotikov picked it up. I took champagne. Kotikov raised his glass.

"To a successful journey to the United States," he proposed, fairly bursting with glee at the prospect of my leaving. We all drank. To my astonishment, Kotikov gulped the entire contents of his glass—Martini, olive, and all. A look of wonder crossed his face. I proposed a toast. Another Martini clanked down to the Russian's ulcers. There were two more toasts and two more rapid Martinis for Kotikov.

I looked at him curiously. His disarmingly cherubic face was twisted. Obviously his stomach was on fire.

I nodded toward another Martini.

"*Nyet!*" he gasped.

Happily, I steered the suffering Kotikov over to the table. I ran my hand through the gray hair he had given me. At last, we were even.

I returned to the United States on board the United States Army transport *Maurice Rose,* taking advantage of the ocean voyage to get in a little of the rest denied me during my four years in Berlin. When I stepped off the boat in New York, I was asked the same questions that are being asked today, with even deeper concern: The Berlin airlift cost us close to half a billion dollars; was it worth the price? Was Berlin a noble experiment, to be written off as a costly blunder, or was it an invaluable testing ground?

To answer these questions, we must consider the complete political map of Germany, of which Berlin is the microcosm and Germany the macrocosm. The struggle between East and West, which split the city, has expanded until it has divided the whole country. Beyond the Iron Curtain is the Russian-sponsored Eastern Democratic Republic of eighteen million people, with a Communist government headed by Premier Otto Grotewohl, who was instrumental in creating the SED, the Socialist Unity (Communist) party. In the West is the Western Federal Republic, supported by the three Western powers, a state of forty-seven million people, with a Conservative government headed by Chancellor Konrad Adenauer, leader of the Christian Democrat Union, former mayor of Cologne and three times prisoner of Hitler's Gestapo.

These two states were born of the East-West mortal struggle

for power, which has raged in Europe since the end of World War II. Paradoxically, both Russia and the Western democracies are wooing their former enemy as a potential ally, and concessions made to the German longing for independence are based on the all-important fact that, even in defeat, Germany remains the key to the European problem, and the world group able to dominate a revived and strong Germany will hold the balance of power in Europe.

Therefore, Berlin was worth the price, for a number of reasons. The city was an invaluable testing ground, where the American people learned the real intent and meaning of communism. From the viewpoint of a noble experiment, Berlin was a first-rate illustration of our desire to co-operate wholeheartedly with Soviet Russia in a peaceful world, and of our inability to fulfill this desire.

Here, as in other parts of the world, we were unable to obtain agreements with the Russians on basic principles. On that score alone, Berlin was a costly blunder. Through a policy of appeasement, which is understandable now but nevertheless was wrong, we led Russia to the verge of war with the Western powers. By our generosity and self-effacement, we encouraged the Communists to think in terms of a victorious war against us, unwittingly misleading them as to our strength and determination.

As a proving ground, Berlin was without peer. There, before three and a quarter million intelligent persons, living in a great modern city, the ideologies of East and West came into conflict. The spotlight of world attention was focused on communism and democracy in action, and as far as communism was concerned, no holds were barred. The Russians employed the blockade in the hope of driving the Americans out of Berlin, causing our allies to desert us and making us lose face in Europe. Their propaganda charge to Europe was that the United States was close to economic collapse and the American people were sufficiently decadent to sacrifice principle for immediate dollar gain. Had the United States pulled out of Berlin under Russian pressure there would have been no room for us on the European Continent, and no Marshall Plan would have repaired the error, for who wants generosity from a coward?

The manner in which the Western powers forced Moscow to lift the siege prevented war. The Germans refused to be stampeded, and took heart from our stand. Our food stocks gave us time to think, and the airlift showed that we were willing to fight for our rights. Great, peaceful air missions could be converted very easily into bombing missions. This the Russians realized, and they felt themselves unprepared for the type of war that a nation like ours could wage against them. They admitted defeat.

Europe, and especially France, learned a lesson from Berlin. "Yes, it is very easy for you to be positive and strong in your opposition to the Russians," a French general said to me, "but bear in mind that if Russians armies overrun France, as everyone assumes they will, by the time you Americans come to liberate us two years later, I will be dead, my family will be dead, and the entire *bourgeoisie* of France will have been exterminated."

That is the reason why it was so important for General Omar Bradley, chairman of our Joint Chiefs of Staff, to make the announcement that we could and would fight to hold any enemy east of the Rhine. The Bradley statement ended any doubts among the democratic European powers as to where their place was in the line-up; they joined forces with the United States to check the advancing tide of communism. Berlin had pointed the way.

As far as the Germans were concerned, smashing the blockade gave the people new hope. For years, over the radio and through the Soviet press, they had been told that communism was their only chance of salvation. Russia was contrasted with the United States in violent political attacks on our system. Had we fled from Berlin, the Germans would have surrendered to the Reds; there would have been no pinnacle of Western democracy and freedom to which they could raise their eyes. By staying and placing them in the position of allies, we inspired determination to continue on the slow, difficult road to democracy.

Berlin also taught us lessons. First of all, the Berlin experience shattered the illusion that the Russians were our allies any longer, and convinced us that Soviet Russia and her Communist party stooges the world over are our enemies and represent death to everything we stand for. I admit that this attitude is a sharp change from the admiration we felt for Russia during the war. The still smoldering embers of this admiration were fanned into our policy of appeasement after V-E Day.

I asked one very high American official why we had followed such a policy. "By the fall of 1945," he replied, "I knew that our appraisal of Russia was wrong, and that Russia was our enemy—not our friend. Yet we would not have been justified in breaking our early engagements, or in accepting this appraisal as a fact so soon after Russia had suffered twenty million casualties fighting the same enemy we had fought."

Perhaps the same emotion charged the air at the Council of Foreign Ministers meeting in Paris after the Berlin victory. Moscow's bluff had been called. Airlift plans had been projected three years in advance. We were in a wonderful position for bargaining. Instead, the foreign ministers exuded forgiveness and sunshine, eager to let the Russians know that the United States had swallowed the biggest insult in history. There was no condemnation of Moscow's action; no half-a-billion-dollar airlift bill; no compensation demands for the seventy Allied airmen killed supplying Berlin.

The most we did in Paris was to make a mealy-mouthed inquiry regarding one of the three means of entry into Berlin—and then offer to sacrifice our claim to canal and railroad rights in exchange for assured highway rights. In other words, we were willing to surrender two thirds of the things we had fought for during the blockade.

Berlin taught us other lessons. The U.S. Army handled Military Government in Germany, taking on a job for which the men were not trained, and did surprisingly well. Yet, until civilian experts were recruited to strengthen their ranks, Military Government was woefully inadequate both in the economic and the political branches. I am happy to learn that today our armed forces are attempting to overcome these handicaps and, in the future, I am convinced that no major decision will be made on a purely military basis. Fifty lives saved today, by a strictly military decision, may cost a million lives tomorrow through ignorance of political implications.

In the future, our armed forces must prepare for three distinct phases of warfare: first, the traditional combat job; second, industrial mobilization; and, third, Military Government, to bridge the critical interval between actual defeat of enemy forces and the point when peacetime agencies take over.

Efforts are being made in all our armed-forces schools to inculcate senior officers with a practical understanding of industrial, economic, and political problems. This broadening program should be extended to the State Department, where the first phase of diplomacy should be the ability of career officers realistically to observe and understand potential enemies, as well as friends of the United States.

A field in which the present State Department officials are entirely untrained is propaganda. It is pointless for the United States to donate millions of dollars' worth of goods to help a country if, through our silence, we permit a few thousand dollars' worth of words, well-placed by the Communists, to twist the meaning of our generosity. The "Voice of America" is a step in the right direction, but it is only a beginning, and if we are not constantly on the defensive abroad, we must have competent propagandists selling our concept of democracy.

There are two ways of "getting along with the Russians" and preventing them from doing what they please in the world. The first, in which we have made considerable progress, is the defensive policy of containing communism. It has, however, all the weaknesses of Maginot Line thinking. We are following this policy at the cost of more than fifteen billion dollars a year in armaments alone. To continue, we must be prepared to defend our position piecemeal all over the world. We must maintain big armies and pour out aid to all of Russia's neighbors. We must never allow Russia even a fifty-fifty chance of successfully using force against us. So far, the Atlantic Pact, European aid, and other measures have discouraged any such Russian attempt.

This was a risky and expensive method, but reasonably safe until we knew that the Russians had the atom bomb. Now, the question naturally arises, can Russia, at some time in the future, offset our industrial, physical, and moral superiority by a sneak punch with atom bombs? One thing is certain. Russia will attack us without hesitation when she judges that the time and the conditions are right.

Will the democratic nations of the world permit Russia—who has repeatedly announced her intention to destroy us, our government, and our way of life—to accumulate this new means of annihilating us?

The USSR today has millions of men under arms. The people are being deprived of the advantages of peace in order to mobilize industry for war. By forced labor, they are worked night and day to increase the country's war potential, and a high percentage of scientific energy is being directed to the production of atomic bombs.

Certain proof of the Russian intention to employ the bomb is provided by Andrei Y. Vishinsky, the Russian foreign minister and vociferous Soviet spokesman. To the peace-minded United Nations, and through them to the American people, he says the things we want to hear, which are the direct opposite of what Russia really intends to do. He clothes his words in peace to hide Moscow's plans for war.

"If any power resorts to the use of the atom bomb in war, Soviet Russia is able to take care of herself," he says, and adds with his usual glibness—the glibness that covered so many broken promises in Berlin—"but we are utilizing atomic energy only for the requirements of peace and for the service of mankind." These are the things we Americans, in our peace-loving hearts, like to hear. But, beware! This is the 1950 Soviet lullaby, meant to close our eyes to the big and fearful surprise the Russians are preparing for us.